The East,
the West,
and Sex

ALSO BY RICHARD BERNSTEIN

Out of the Blue: A Narrative of September 11, 2001

*Ultimate Journey: Retracing the Path of an Ancient Buddhist Monk
Who Crossed Asia in Search of Enlightenment*

The Coming Conflict with China
(with Ross H. Munro)

*Dictatorship of Virtue:
Multiculturalism and the Battle for America's Future*

Fragile Glory: A Portrait of France and the French

*From the Center of the Earth:
The Search for the Truth about China*

The East, the West, and Sex

A History of Erotic Encounters

RICHARD BERNSTEIN

ALFRED A. KNOPF NEW YORK 2009

THIS IS A BORZOI BOOK
PUBLISHED BY ALFRED A. KNOPF

Grateful acknowledgment is made to the following for permission to
reprint previously published material:
Continuum: Excerpt from *Interracial Intimacy in Japan: Western Men
and Japanese Women, 1543–1900* by Gary P. Leupp, copyright © 2003
by Gary P. Leupp. Reprinted by permission of Continuum
International Publishing Group.
McIntosh & Otis, Inc.: Excerpts from *Flaubert in Egypt: A Sensibility on
Tour,* translated and edited by Francis Steegmuller, copyright © 1972
by Francis Steegmuller. All rights reserved. Reprinted by
permission of McIntosh & Otis, Inc.
Yale University Press: Excerpt from *Harems of the Mind* by Ruth Yeazell,
copyright © 2000 by Yale University. Reprinted by permission of
Yale University Press.

Library of Congress Cataloging-in-Publication Data
Bernstein, Richard, [date]
The East, the West, and sex : a history of erotic encounters /
Richard Bernstein. — 1st ed.
p. cm.
Includes bibliographical references and index.
ISBN 978-0-375-41409-1 (alk. paper)
1. Erotica—Asia. 2. Erotica—Developing countries. 3. National
characteristics, Asian. 4. Orientalism. I. Title.
HQ460.B47 2009
306.77095'090511—dc22   2008055079

Manufactured in the United States of America
First Edition

To Zhongmei

Tho' I walks with fifty 'ousemaids outer Chelsea to the Strand,
An' they talks a lot o' lovin', but wot do they understand?
    Beefy face an' grubby 'and—
    Law! wot do they understand?
    I've a neater, sweeter maiden in a cleaner, greener land!
    On the road to Mandalay . . .

—Rudyard Kipling, "Mandalay"

CONTENTS

The East,
the West,
and Sex

CHAPTER ONE

Bohemians at Home and Abroad

SOMETIME IN 2006, a foreign English teacher in Shanghai posted a message on the Internet in which he bragged about how easy it was for him to have sex with young Chinese women, mostly his former students. "I was with Star on Saturday," the teacher wrote. "I was with Yingying on Sunday. In between, I contacted Cherry via MSN. I telephoned Rina, and I used SMS to flirt with Tulip. I sent Susan an e-mail to flirt with her, and I professed my love to Wendy on her blog."

The writer of this kiss-and-tell memoir called himself China-Bounder on a blog he maintained, "Sex in Shanghai: Western Scoundrel in Shanghai Tells All." He appeared to be British, though that was not certain. In any case, he gave no name or other clearly identifying detail about himself, which was perhaps not very brave, though maybe a life-saving precaution, given the murderously furious response he elicited from Chinese men.

A psychology professor, Zhang Jiehai, of the Shanghai Academy of Social Sciences, led the charge, posting a long article titled "Internet Hunt for an Immoral Foreigner," in which he urged the entire Chinese nation to track down this person who had insulted and humiliated China and throw him out of the country. "Several days ago, a friend told me about a blog run by an English man in Shanghai," Zhang wrote. "I read it and I was shocked, angered, and disgusted." After a lengthy, quotation-rich summary of the blogger's comments, Zhang concluded with a call to Chinese men to take action. "Please think about how this foreign piece of trash has dallied with your sisters and made fun of your impotence," he wrote. "Do you want to say that this is no big deal? Do you still want to treat the foreigners as important? Do you still quiver when you see foreigners? Please straighten out your backbones."

The foreign blogger's account was scattered with clues that might help track him down, Zhang said. ChinaBounder described hotel rooms that he had used for his trysts with his ex-student girlfriends, for example, and perhaps these rooms could be found and the hotel's guest register checked. His name might be Brian, Zhang said (though in 2008 the *Guardian* reported on a man named David Marriott claiming to be ChinaBounder). He disclosed details about his sex partners—for example, that the woman he called Tingting was a married doctor—and these bits and pieces of information could be put together to identify the foreigner. "Let our compatriots act together on this Internet hunt to find this foreign trash until we kick him out of China," Zhang wrote.

It should be noted here that, while it is illegal in China to lure women into prostitution, there is no law against consensual sexual relations between adults, even when one of those adults is a boastful foreigner and the other an innocent Chinese woman. ChinaBounder did not seem to have broken the law; nor did there appear to have been any effort by China's police to find him or charge him with any crime. But the publication of his exploits nonetheless produced an explosion of sexual nationalism among Chinese men, who wrote to online forums to express their feelings, their fury directed as much at the ex-students who had presumably slept with ChinaBounder as at ChinaBounder himself. While he was viewed as immoral and vicious, the female students were seen to have debased not only themselves but their country as well in submitting to the advances of what one commentator called "this white ape."

"These women are all bitches," one man wrote in a typical online comment. "They gave up their dignity for money [though in fact there was nothing in ChinaBounder's blog to indicate that he gave money to any of his partners; they all seem to have submitted willingly to his advances]. It would be better to sleep with a dog than with this foreign pig. This humiliates the hearts of Chinese men, as well as of the Chinese people. I feel ashamed for those women's parents and friends. They are worse than prostitutes."

ChinaBounder, for his part, responded in kind, posting an entry on his blog calling Professor Zhang a "lunatic," "a mouth-frother," a "knee-jerk nationalist," though, whatever else one might say about this seedy exchange, at least Professor Zhang did not hide behind a mask of anonymity. In any case, ChinaBounder's blog, thanks to the attention Zhang called to it, was soon blocked by China's Internet censors, and he himself began writing from another venue—Thailand—where, continuing his saga of the conquest of Chinese womanhood, he told a story of seducing a member of a Chinese trade delegation he encountered in his hotel lobby, who told him to "pretend I am a prostitute."

Never mind. We'll get back, a bit regretfully, to ChinaBounder and his blog shortly. But first, a question: Imagine this situation in reverse—a Chinese teacher has come to the United States or Britain and brags online about how many American or British women he has slept with, how easy it was to get them to engage in noncommittal recreational sex, and how much more sexually attractive he was than "lesser" local men. Would anybody even notice, or care? Maybe some people, a few guardians of sexual morality, would look askance, but for the most part the matter, if it got any attention at all, would be regarded as the idiosyncratic braggadocio of one particular Asian man. No esteemed professor from an august research institute would be calling on his wounded countrymen to track the bastard down; there would be no howls of nationalist outrage and no declarations that an entire proud country had been humiliated. So what were the underlying issues that produced such a storm of anguished protest and recrimination in China?

Quite a few things can be said about the episode of the anonymous English teacher. For one thing, his ecstatic communication was an especially vulgar expression of an attitude that has been peculiar to Western men in Asia for centuries. ChinaBounder was allowed liberties with local women that he would not have been permitted to enjoy back home, or at least the circumstances would have been a good deal more difficult. That, I understand, is an arguable statement. Plenty of men have multiple sexual partners in the United States and the United Kingdom, as they do in China for that matter. Yet the mere fact that ChinaBounder posted his blog demonstrates that he had found something extraordinary in China, possibilities for erotic play far different from what he could expect back home. And what he found extraordinary was not just the ease and multiplicity of the encounters he described but their utter casualness; what China allowed was indicated in his self-identification as a bounder, a cad, a figure of self-satisfied unscrupulousness, the implication being that what came about for him so effortlessly with young Chinese women would be a lot harder to attain with more sophisticated, less easily manipulated women back home. It doesn't seem likely in this sense that a Chinese teacher of Chinese in Liverpool or London or New York would find several girls in his class willing to go to bed with him, or that he could flirt with them in so untrammeled a fashion, or that he could talk to them about their physical properties in the way ChinaBounder talked to his Shanghai girlfriends.

"My dear Tingting," he wrote to his married lover (in a passage of his blog angrily cited by Professor Zhang as a demonstration of China-Bounder's viciousness), "you have a wonderful, glorious, beautiful body. I have found it hard to stop thinking about your beautiful skin, your lovely, smooth soft breasts, your sexy, smooth delicate stomach, your sweet and graceful legs and arms . . . oh and, of course between your legs, how beautiful you are, how sexy, how perfect!"

Adding insult to injury, ChinaBounder had a few derogatory comments about Chinese men, who, he wrote, are "dull, dull, dull," traditionalist, hidebound, unimaginative, and less attractive than their Caucasian counterparts. Chinese women, even virgins, he contended, are impressed by the size of his penis, compared with the ones they have seen on Chinese men. Tingting even admitted to him that her Chinese husband was unable to satisfy her, a problem that she did not experience with Brian. This notion of the superior potency of Caucasian men is pretty common in China. Or at least Brian is hardly the only one to have made reference to it.

This is not to say that I think ChinaBounder's experience would be so easy to duplicate, or even that he was telling the whole story as he recounted his effortless and almost innumerable conquests. The likelihood is that a lot more former students rejected his advances than accepted them and that China as a whole is not quite the sexual adventurer's happy hunting ground that he described. Still, there is something to what he said, something about an advantage that Western men have in the competition for the favors of young women there, something sensed by Zhang and his cohort in their complaint about the Chinese worship, as Zhang put it, of things foreign. "Here's the problem," Zhang wrote in an e-mail message to me. "This is not a single case. In China there are innumerable such China bounders." Indeed, around the same time that ChinaBounder caused a stir, there were several widely circulated and fervent discussions about other foreign men boasting of their sexual conquests in China. One of them concerned a forty-two-year-old American named Robert Kugler, who posted pictures of seventy-nine Chinese women with whom he claimed to have had sexual relations—such that, according to Professor Zhang, "Robert Kugler" constituted the most searched-for phrase on the Google and Yahoo! search engines in China during that time.

In 2007, on a visit to Beijing, I interviewed several professional Chinese women, all of whom had, or had had, foreign boyfriends, and these smart, sophisticated, and self-possessed women readily agreed that foreign men do have an aura about them, that they are commonly deemed desirable by many Chinese women, including them. Why? I asked.

"Size matters!" was the cheerful and instant reply of one of them, the very comely owner of a dress shop, only half joking, because the belief that Western men have bigger penises than Asian men does persist. In fact, the young woman in question was in the process of breaking up with her foreign boyfriend, and she was leaving Beijing to join a Chinese lover who lived in the provinces, so evidently size didn't matter above all else.

This matter of foreign-Chinese romance is complicated. In Shanghai, the derogatory term for a foreign man, used by unabashedly cynical Chinese women, is "airplane ticket." In Thailand it is "walking ATM." Western men may think that they have some special charm for Asian women when, in truth, what they may really represent is nothing more than a chance for material gain—or perhaps the fantasy of a richer life someplace else. But it's not only that, especially now that China's economic boom has generated a class of wealthy Chinese men just as able as their Western counterparts to produce a lavishly decorated apartment, a car, Gucci handbags, and trips abroad for their wives and girlfriends. One of the first observations I made in my own years living in Asia—one that led, decades later, to the idea for this book—came in the early 1970s, when I was a language student on Taiwan. It was obvious to me then that young American men of the somewhat nerdy and bookish sort (like me), the kind of guy who had trouble getting a date to the senior prom when he was in high school, were often able to attract very pretty and desirable Taiwanese girlfriends.

What were the reasons? Part of it was no doubt the exciting possibility of life in America, which, especially in those days (much less so today, since Taiwan has become a democracy with American-level living standards), seemed free and rich by comparison with life on Taiwan. But the evidence was strong that simply being a foreigner conferred an unearned distinction on young Western men. It was in itself a romantic adornment, a value added in the eyes of more than a few urban educated young Taiwanese women.

On that 2007 Beijing visit, I asked my well-educated and professionally successful female interviewees if they felt that foreigners benefited from the advantage I had first observed on Taiwan, and the answer was emphatically yes. The Western male advantage rested, in their view, on identifiable characteristics. What it came down to was less money itself and more a certain refined style of living associated with the West, along with a sense that to have relations with a Western man is somehow more sophisticated, exciting, daring, adventuresome, and worldly than to be in a more conventional relationship with a Chinese man. And these feelings are more than reciprocated by single (and sometimes married) Western men, for whom a Chinese girlfriend or two is a big part of the adventure of living in Asia.

"Western men have learned the techniques of being gentlemen," one woman, a professional businesswoman, told me. She used the Chinese term *junzi,* which was Confucius's term to describe a man of cultivated manners and good breeding. "Asian men have lost that," she said, and she cited in particular the enduring impact of the long Maoist years, when good manners were seen as bourgeois and reactionary and peasant-proletarian coarseness was prized. "Western men haven't. Asian men are rude and coarse. They drink. They gamble. When they get some money, they have little wives" (meaning concubines).

"Even when a Chinese man gets money, he uses it in a way to get power over his wife," this woman said. "He'll buy her things because of the prestige of the label, Gucci or Fendi, not because he thinks his wife will like it. Just the other day, I was with some rich friends, and the husband said, 'That handbag isn't good for you; I'm going to buy such and such a handbag because it's the only one in China.' He didn't ask her opinion about it or if she would like it but just ordered her to wear it because he can then show everybody that he has the money to buy his wife that handbag."

The other Chinese women I interviewed on this topic, including two editors with an online news service and the dress-shop owner, had similar opinions about the better manners and habits of Western men—though it must be remembered that the sample of the Western male population that Chinese women are likely to encounter is highly skewed toward the upper social and educational reaches of the spectrum. Among the reasons the women gave for their own attraction to Western men was, they said, that Western men had better hygienic habits—that they took more showers and better care of their teeth. This, like much else on this topic, relates directly to China's relatively low standard of living until very recent years.

"Chinese men don't feel that men need to be clean," one of the editors said. "In our university, you couldn't go into the boys' dormitory because . . ." She made a gesture of repulsion.

"Ten years ago, it wasn't that easy to keep clean," the editor's colleague said. "In the dormitory at our university, one hundred people shared one bathroom. Most people had to use the public toilet and bath, which was pretty disgusting.

"It's a reason that's easy to forget—why I first liked Western men," she continued. "It wasn't me; it was my nose."

They gave other reasons as well. Western men are less traditional than Chinese men and more likely to be supportive of their careers. Western men don't have quite the institutionalized habit of finding second and third and even fourth wives, which is endemic among Chinese men, some women told me. Other women spoke to me about the lack of options available to Asian women when marriage with an Asian man goes sour. A more powerful stigma attaches to divorce in China than it does in the West—or at least it is more difficult, some women have told me, for a divorced woman in China to remarry than it is for a woman in the West. Meanwhile, the consolations that Asian men find so readily in second and third wives are not available to Asian women. The woman who told me about the greater gentlemanliness of Western men also said that such men, especially those of a high level of education and cultivation, were less likely to be violent at home.

"Even if a Western man has a big, really bad argument with his wife, he won't beat her," she said. "But in China it's very common for a husband to beat his wife. It's accepted as normal behavior. And there's no point in calling the police because the police won't do anything. They'll just say it's a family matter; handle it yourself."

Unfortunately, the truth is that plenty of Western men beat their wives, though at least in Europe and the United States such behavior seems to arouse more social opprobrium than it does in China and some other Asian countries. Moreover, none of the answers that these Chinese women gave to the question of why a Western man seems like a good catch to Chinese women would quite explain the sexual success of ChinaBounder, whose clear goal in life was to have as many shallow relationships with women as he could, rather than one deep and enduring one. ChinaBounder may illustrate only that, in China's mood of explosive material acquisition, some women see Western men in the way they might see the ersatz Italianate villas springing up all over the country— as accoutrements to the rich life, the rich life being defined very much in nouveau riche terms as one loaded with imitation European possessions. "China's nouveau riche prefer things, well, nouveau," *The New York Times* has reported. "To be seen with a Western man is chic," yet another woman, a university-educated researcher for a foreign news organization, told me. "To be seen with a Chinese man is ordinary."

To be sure, the overwhelming majority of Chinese, men and women, fall in love with and marry each other, even as many, probably most, Western men who live in China with Western wives do not chase after Chinese women. Few Chinese have social contacts with foreigners at all. Moreover, there are plenty of Chinese men who are perfectly well mannered, intelligent, and enlightened in their attitude toward women, who do not pursue concubines, are devoted fathers, and are entirely disinclined from domestic violence.

This question of the presumed attractiveness of Western men is on the minds of members of only a very thin urbanized layer of Chinese society, those who nurse cappuccinos at Starbucks in Beijing or frequent the hip late-night bars on Huaihai Road in Shanghai, but that is the layer that Brian was talking about in his blog. It is what might be called the bourgeois-bohemian segment of Chinese urban life, borrowing the phrase invented by the commentator David Brooks to distinguish a certain pleasure-loving and self-consciously stylish culture in American society. For these Chinese women, the West in general represents an exciting alternative to the more restricted and inhibited conventions of Chinese society. It goes with wearing jeans and listening to the latest pop music; it's modern, fashionable, and a touch risqué. Drawing on his rich experience of pillow talk, ChinaBounder wrote in his blog that for Chinese women, dating foreign men is "a chance for a different level of personal freedom," which, he adds, gives the foreign men in question "an avenue of exploitation." And, true enough, the Western men in China are bohemians abroad, interested in having a good time without the social and moral restrictions of home, happy to be the beneficiaries of the unearned added value that their status as Westerners gives them. They appeal to the women not only because they may have better hygiene on average than Chinese men but also because, when relationships become serious, they are more comfortable than Chinese men—again, on average—with the idea of equality, more apt to help with housework, and less persuaded that a woman's place is serving her mother-in-law.

In this sense, it is understandable why ChinaBounder had some success finding willing Chinese women and why that success aroused so powerful a sense of wounded national dignity. China is a country that is both in thrall to foreign ways and resentful of that very thralldom. It's a country with a sort of collective thin skin, especially when it finds some element of humiliation in its relations with the West. The angry response to ChinaBounder is analogous to what seems to many foreigners the unreasonable fury aroused by Western support for the Dalai Lama, who is seen in China not as a wise, peaceful victim of Chinese bullying but as a conniving politician striving to split the motherland, in part by exploiting the West's animosity toward China.

In 2008, a well-known Chinese artist attracted some attention when he protested the animated movie *Kung Fu Panda*—an enormously successful production that played in theaters all over China—on the grounds that it "exploited" a Chinese national symbol. The panda-movie protest didn't gain a great deal of traction in China. Still, it illustrated the same sensitivity that was involved in the case of ChinaBounder, a sense of exploitation that stems from China's relative backwardness of recent centuries and the experience of colonialist invasion and domination, which, while long over, still powerfully influences Chinese attitudes about themselves and the rest of the world. The patina of prestige that attaches to foreign men in Asia is a cultural leftover from the century during which European men were the masters of most Eastern societies.

Though every sort of combination does take place, we are speaking of general trends here, and the general trend of recent years has been that the overwhelming percentage of Chinese-foreign pairings involves foreign men and Chinese women rather than foreign women and Chinese men. Several explanations for this are commonly given: Asian men believe Western women to be more aggressive than Asian women; there are fewer Western women than Western men living and working in Asia; Western women fear that Asian husbands will expect them to be submissive and obedient. There would appear to be a complicated mixture of image and experience at play here. But almost everything in this picture relates to the experience of colonial power, which has always enhanced the prestige and glamour, and therefore the aura of masculinity of Western men while reducing that of Asians.

China, unlike India or Indochina, was never entirely colonized, but foreign armies inflicted several humiliatingly easy defeats on it, starting with the Opium War of 1839–42, when China was forced to open its territory to traders and missionaries whom it would have preferred to exclude. Starting in the mid-nineteenth century, foreign concessions were set up in major cities—Canton (now transliterated as Guangzhou), Shanghai, Qingdao, and others—that, along with Hong Kong and Macau, were in effect mini-colonies along the Chinese coast. And as one of the online news-service editors told me, even today, all these many years later, the sexual conquest of Chinese women by foreign men is felt as salt in the historical wound.

"We were very poor for two hundred years, and Western men are the symbol of something very strong and rich," she said. "The Europeans took a lot of things from us, our wealth and our strength, and if they are also taking our most beautiful girls, they are also taking our pride."

Around the same time as the incident with ChinaBounder, some Chinese Web sites and forums posted anonymously and secretly taken photographs of Chinese women with their foreign boyfriends, walking on the street in Shanghai or sitting at cafés or embracing on the Bund, the broad esplanade that runs between the former European quarter's banks and hotels on the one side and the Huangpu River on the other. There was even a special series showing Chinese movie and television actors, all of them female, with foreign boyfriends. How extraordinary this is! Imagine somebody in New York taking pictures of white women with Chinese or other foreign men and posting them anonymously and without permission on the Internet for all to see. It is hard to imagine such a thing happening, not because we're more ethical about such matters in the West but simply because there is no particular interest in the topic. But to take and post such pictures seems somehow natural in the more tormented psychohistorical atmosphere of China.

The posted photographs were not meant to convey how sweet, how romantic, how touching it is that European and American men have come to China and found true love with charming local women. The message was that what was depicted, the foreign man and the rather trendy Chinese woman, often nicely coiffed, wearing close-fitting jeans, casually soigné, was something shameful, that a Chinese woman giving herself to a foreign man is humiliating in a country that remembers— and is encouraged by its government to remember—the humiliations of the past, the wars and invasions, the unequal treaties, the coastal mini-colonies, the financial indemnities, and the poverty and submissiveness of China. I am a foreigner when I travel in China, and I am married to a Chinese woman, and neither my wife nor I have detected any hostility or anger during the many trips we have taken together there, though my wife has confided to me that some Chinese male friends have expressed polite chagrin at her decision to marry outside her native group. "They say, 'Richard's very nice, but what's wrong with us?' " she's told me.

But those photographs in Shanghai, the volume of commentary on Web sites, and the furious response to ChinaBounder in 2006 reveal that the subject of sexual relations between foreigners and Chinese is a fraught one, and not all the material presented to public opinion comes from clandestine photos. There are plenty of foreign blogs besides our English teacher's that depict a social world whose very icon is the Western man posing with his Chinese girlfriend, and these arouse their own share of aggrieved commentary by Chinese men, as in the reaction of one such man to an online photograph posted in Shenzhen, the booming special economic zone in Guangdong Province near Hong Kong. It showed a Western man, maybe thirty years old or so, his bare midriff emblazoned with a tattoo, his head shaven, his belt buckle forming the word PIMP, with his arm around a comely, laughing young Chinese woman wearing jeans and a sleeveless black blouse. The photograph was one of a couple of dozen posted on the Web site of something called Shenzhen Party, an online diary of life for foreigners in Shenzhen. All of the photos showed Western men and their Chinese girlfriends, many of the couples in gleefully rakish, frat party poses. No Western women were pictured, and their absence from the scene is a demonstration of the focus maintained by a certain fun-loving male set on local women. They aren't in China to go out on decorous dates with the girl next door.

"Anger!" the Chinese blogger wrote. And angry he was. "Are Chinese girls this shameless in front of foreign men?

"Is it for the money?" he continued, seeking an explanation for the willingness of Chinese womanhood to be part of this immoral, foreign hedonism. "Well, Chinese white-collar types don't lack for money. In any case, the girls who go with foreigners do it for free. Is it for the sex? But aren't Chinese men also able to go on all night, to do it with two girls at the same time? I don't know what to say. This kind of thing is the disgrace of Chinese men and women."

Professor Zhang wrote a scholarly paper about such tormented reactions as that one, "White Paper on the Psychological Problems of Chinese Men." In it he found a troubling phenomenon of "self-abasement" among Chinese. "It is caused by the under-development of

China during the past hundred years," he wrote, continuing, "We have to admit that the modern world is led by white people and that the contribution to contemporary culture made by China is almost nonexistent. In addition, it is a fact that men are playing the leading role in the functioning of modern society, so the inability of men is related to the backwardness of their country. Although China's economy boomed in recent years, the confidence of Chinese in social contacts with foreigners has not grown, and the Chinese people are often over-concerned with criticism and praise."

There was a fictional illustration of Zhang's point. ChinaBounder's girlfriend Tingting seemed like a real-life version of the main character in the novel *Shanghai Baby* by Zhou Weihui, a novel that made something of a sensation abroad, becoming the inspiration for a movie reportedly being shot as of this writing. The novel tells the story of a girl whose Chinese boyfriend is impotent but whose foreign boyfriend is virility itself, as if private sexual relations embodied the historic weakness of China over the past couple of centuries, especially in its dealings with the Western colonial powers and Japan. Not surprisingly, the book, which sold well in Europe and North and South America, was banned in China, though given the Internet and the rich flow of information from abroad, many Chinese know about it.

This, anyway, is the context for ChinaBounder and why he stirred up something of the troubled inner soul of China at the dawn of the twenty-first century, a time when China is simultaneously the muscle-man on the beach and the skinny boy having sand kicked in his face. And though what ChinaBounder seemed mostly to be conveying in his blog was simply what a wonderful place Shanghai is for the single Western man, he was also, it would seem, well aware of how insulting a description of his life would be to local men. You don't talk about satisfying women whom other men can't satisfy without a certain degree of hubris, and in the case of ChinaBounder, that hubris joined with a racial and cultural element that was bound to give offense.

In other ways, in fact, ChinaBounder expressed contempt for China. He questioned whether Xinjiang, the mostly Muslim autonomous province in the far west of the country, really ought to be part of China. And he raised similar questions about Taiwan, a hazardous point of view in China, which brooks no dissent on its position that

Taiwan is a renegade province, which it will go to war to reincorporate if ever it tries formally to become independent. In addition, China-Bounder found China to be a country exhibiting a masochistic love of suffering, a country that makes something of a fetish of its history of exploitation at the hands of others, that brandishes its pain and even uses it as a tool to whip other countries into a guilty obedience to its wishes. The Chinese, the English teacher seemed to be saying, practice a foreign policy of blame and insult, portraying themselves, through the use of selective memory, as perpetual victims, especially of Western and Japanese imperialism.

What redeems China, in the teacher's account, is its marvelous sexual possibilities, the fact that the Western man is a sort of superior being there, with a big penis and an unlimited supply of willing and desirable women. As ChinaBounder put it, "We don't come here because we are rotten; it is rather that the inner rot that lies in the core of most men can grow and flourish here." So, yes, ChinaBounder could see that his life in China was, as he called it, "decadent." But never mind. For foreign men like him, he joyously declared, China is "a paradise."

How China has changed—and remained the same. When I lived in China in the early 1980s, it was no paradise, sexual or otherwise. There was so little possibility of romantic adventure with Chinese women that I was resigned to not even try seeking it, though I was young and single at the time and would have been perfectly happy to have an amorous relationship or two. It isn't that some Chinese women wouldn't have been available to go out with foreign men had they been in control of their own lives. It's that almost any private and unsupervised interaction between foreigners and Chinese was unofficially banned, especially if that interaction involved love or sex.

I was the *Time* magazine correspondent in China from late 1979 to the end of 1982, the period just after the United States had established full diplomatic relations with China and the country was on the verge of what was to become a revolutionary opening to the outside world, complete in time with a turn to unrestricted capitalism. But in the early 1980s, just four or five years after the death of its great leader, Mao Zedong, China was still impoverished, colorless, and repressed. Big

Brother was always watching. I did meet Chinese women from time to time, though under the most restrictive of circumstances. There was one in particular. She was living in Beijing clandestinely because she didn't have the residency permit that was, and still is, required for any Chinese person to live in the country's capital, but she was protected by her otherwise disapproving father, an important Communist official. I had a close relationship with her. She told me a great deal about herself and her life, including her sexual life (or, more correctly, her lack of sexual experience, even at the age of thirty). But we did not have romantic relations, and it would have been very hard for us to have them if we had wanted to because there was no place to go.

There was another woman as well with whom I kept a limited sort of company for a while. We met in 1980, during a brief couple of months when the Chinese authorities allowed Saturday night dances to take place in a basement nightclub located, of all places, in the National Minorities Institute on Changan Jie, Beijing's Main Street. Foreigners got in by showing their passports. Chinese had to show their Beijing household registration cards, and security officials at the entrance noted their name and "unit," their workplace or school affiliation. Mostly only the children of people with important posts in the Communist Party or the Chinese government dared to risk this entry procedure, which would have been too intimidating to ordinary, politically unconnected young people.

My friend, whom I called Little Wang,* had the necessary connections, and one night she was at the Minorities Institute in the company of a group of friends, all of them children of government or party officials and all of them rather savvy in the ways of China. They weren't exactly gilded youth, but they had advantages, which, a generation or so later, would translate into such privileges as the right to develop real estate near Beijing's Third Ring Road, on which they would drive their Porsche Cayenne SUVs, each of which cost, with import duties, about $160,000. But at the time I first met these young people, they were just a bit different from most—more confident, more knowing, and a touch more cynical. They told me how to read license plates so as to

---

*A common casual form of address in China is a person's last name with the prefix *xiao,* meaning "little," used mostly for young people, and a different prefix, *lao,* or "old," for people older or in a position of authority.

identify unmarked Public Security Bureau cars and where to find the restricted stores where foreign movies and books were sold to Chinese with the proper security clearances. They read *Reference News,* a digest of foreign news stories that was made available to officials but not to ordinary people.

After meeting Little Wang initially with her friends that first Saturday night, I saw her at the same place the next Saturday night, when she seemed to have come by herself. On that second occasion, I drove her home (only foreigners were allowed to have private cars in China in those days), and I saw her several times after that, usually to go to the same Saturday night dance—until the authorities closed it down—and once to go to a restaurant. She was pretty, even in her standard-issue blue Mao suit and pigtails, and I felt a lot of affection for her though even if she had been willing (and I never knew if she was or not), again, there would have been no place to go. The dances at the Minorities Institute took place to recorded music amid soft colored lights, an intimate setting for the very anti-intimate China of those days. Once while on the dance floor I kissed her on the cheek.

"Better not do that," she told me.

"Sorry," I replied, "I couldn't help myself."

"It's okay," Little Wang said, "but we're being watched."

"We are? Who's watching us?"

"Look at the men standing by the wall," she said, a bit of exasperation in her voice. How could anybody be so naïve to think that at an event like this we wouldn't be chaperoned by the Security Bureau's guardians of public morality? I scrutinized the room and noted a couple of men in dark blue Mao suits standing along the wall on the edge of the dance floor, watching.

China was like that, though there were some signs of loosening, or at least the totalitarian supervision of private life and private thought of the extreme Maoist years was diminishing somewhat. My first trip to China was in 1972, when I was a student, and then the Chinese went beyond the mere regulation of sexual activity. Like Stalin's biologist Trofim Lysenko, who supposedly proved that characteristics acquired through environmental changes could become hereditary, the Chinese were proving that sexual desire could be altered by political indoctrination. People were supposed to be attracted to the purity of their prospective partner's political thought.

The group I was part of had a guide, a friendly and bright man whom we called Little Huang, and on one very long train ride we tried relentlessly to get him to admit that he might be attracted to a woman simply because she was pretty or at least that some women were prettier than others. He steadfastly denied it, insisting that all he cared about in a potential life partner was what he called her worldview, and I never knew if his stated position represented a belief he had been indoctrinated with or he was simply lying.

It wasn't that bad by the time I began working in China at the end of the '70s. People didn't have to fall in love with somebody because of the depth of his or her love for Chairman Mao, but for foreigners things remained pretty arid. The principle supposedly guiding sexual life was something the Chinese called socialist morality. It was a vague concept mostly undefined in Chinese law, but everybody knew that the loose ways of foreigners were a major danger to it, and over the course of the 1980s and early 1990s, China's propaganda machine issued repeated warnings against the "spiritual pollution" that often came with increased foreign contact. I had one colleague, the correspondent for ABC News, who was visited in his hotel room by a female colleague from Hong Kong one evening in 1980 or 1981. At a certain point, the two of them, who were just sitting and talking, noted figures flitting over the roof that was visible from the window. A short time later, there was a knock on the door. Stern security officials, who had apparently been spying on the couple, demanded to see the woman's identification—luckily for her, she was not a citizen of the People's Republic of China—and warned the two of them that in China a man and a woman who were not married to each other were not allowed to be together in a hotel room late at night.

And then there was the celebrated case of Li Shuang and Emmanuel Bellefroid. Li was a moderately dissenting painter who was not a member of the official Artists Association. Bellefroid was a Sinologist employed as a cultural attaché and translator at the French embassy in Beijing and a man who maintained close contacts with China's early pro-democracy activists.

The two of them were living together in the compound reserved for foreigners, enclosed by a wall at whose gates Chinese army guards were posted twenty-four hours a day, so Li Shuang could hardly come and go without being observed. Clearly the Chinese government and security apparatus didn't like Bellefroid because of his open sympathy with the country's political dissidents. On one occasion, he used the diplomatic pouch to smuggle to Hong Kong a dissident text that was subsequently widely disseminated in the foreign press—to the vehemently expressed displeasure of the Chinese authorities. It wasn't only sexual relations that the Communist Party didn't want Chinese citizens to have with foreigners; it was any sort of relations that, in their view, tarnished China's image. Bellefroid had diplomatic immunity, but by living with a Chinese woman, he gave the authorities a perfect excuse to punish him for his transgressions—by punishing her. One day when arriving at the compound, Li Shuang was arrested. She was imprisoned for two years for her "immorality" in living with a foreigner, though after she was released from prison, and as a result of quiet diplomacy exercised by France, she was allowed to leave China and join Bellefroid in Paris.

For thirty years or so following the Communists' seizure of power in China, intimate—and not even all that intimate—relations between foreigners and Chinese were forbidden. True, this was also a time of a generalized sexual puritanism in China, when any quest for sexual pleasure was officially viewed as a bourgeois affectation. To seek erotic enjoyment was counterrevolutionary because it put the emphasis on private pleasure rather than the triumph of the proletariat. It was common in those days for Chinese couples to be assigned, with total bureaucratic indifference to their personal concerns, to separate and distant locations, so they were able to see each other for just a couple of weeks a year, the priority being duty to the country rather than the satisfactions of private life. In his novel *Waiting*, Ha Jin described the myriad rules and regulations governing relations between the sexes in the army, so that, for example, it was forbidden for a man and a woman not married to each other even to walk together off the base. In China's cities, the party activists on the ubiquitous neighborhood committees closely monitored the comings and goings of ordinary people, ever watchful of "immoral" behavior like premarital sex or adultery even when it didn't involve a foreigner.

By the late 1980s, as China got used to more and more foreigners in its midst, many of the practices that had limited contact between foreigners and Chinese were discontinued. The sullen security officer in his green greatcoat who rudely blocked local Chinese from entering hotels where foreigners stayed disappeared. I remember feeling something close to elation the first time I was able to invite a Chinese friend into the lobby of a hotel—the then-new Jianguo Hotel—so that we could have coffee together. It was 1988. Still, when it came to romance and sex, the course of true love did not run smoothly. Around that time, the foreign press reported several instances in which heavy fines were imposed on foreign businessmen after they had been caught in bed with Chinese girlfriends. The situation was grave enough for the U.S. Embassy to put out a warning of legal risks stemming from "relationships with Chinese nationals of the opposite sex." Some confusion arose when an official of the Ministry of Health announced that "casual sex," along with homosexuality, was indeed a criminal offense in China, only to be followed by a spokesman for the Ministry of Justice announcing that neither extramarital sex nor homosexuality was against the law. As I said earlier, China did, and does, have laws against prostitution, which, by definition, has to involve a payment of some sort, and these laws seem to have been invoked in the cases of the foreign businessmen who were fined for having sex with Chinese women, even though in at least some cases foreigners were fined for sleeping with their Chinese fiancées, who were decidedly not prostitutes. But clearly, especially in those still-early days of China's opening to the outside world, the need to quash spiritual pollution made zealots of some.

This tight regulation of sexual life, and the even tighter ban on intimate relations between Chinese and foreigners, could be explained by the Communist mania for social control in general. But in the Chinese context, the reasons for it went deeper than that, to the wounded national feeling given expression by Professor Zhang in his reaction to ChinaBounder—that sense, evoked by one of the women I interviewed, that foreigners had always exploited China and that their latter-day enjoyment of Chinese women was another sort of exploitation. In the Opium War, the first of several foreign-imposed humiliations of China (which led the Qing dynasty rulers to cede Hong Kong to Britain, among other things), rumors that British soldiers were molesting local women were among the things provoking local antiforeign fury. Those rumors led to a spontaneous massing of peasant troops near a place called San-yuan-li, outside Canton, where the Chinese scored a rare victory over the British. San-yuan-li has ever since been played up as the site of a glorious popular victory, especially by China's Communists, who have ensured that every schoolchild knows of it.

Yet the sexual contact between foreigners and Chinese reaches back to long before the Opium War. The eighteenth-century memoir of a British seaman named William Hickey describes an outing to Lob Lob Creek, near Canton in about 1770, where Hickey and a friend acquired "two very pretty girls" from a Chinese pimp who brought the women to them by boat. But by the nineteenth century, xenophobic hatred of the foreigner had reached a peak, fueled at least in part by the local propaganda's insistence on labeling all foreigners as lewd, immoral, and debauched. The mood, the historian Frederic Wakeman wrote, was one of "xenophobia and sexual hysteria."

The reform movement that sprang up in Beijing and the Chinese coastal cities in the late nineteenth century and sought ways to revitalize the decaying imperial way of life made sex and sexuality a national concern, probably for the first time in China's long history. Some of this concern was entirely progressive. Reform-minded intellectuals were persuaded that traditional Confucian ideas about sex, including the subordinate position of women and the obedience they owed men, were among the things that had made China weak. When the reformer Kang Youwei in 1898 petitioned the emperor to abolish the ancient practice of foot binding, he did so on the grounds that the practice weakened what he called the Chinese race and therefore impeded the increase of military strength. Some Chinese social reformers saw an analogy between China's unequal treatment of its women and China's unequal status among the nations of the world—that weak, humiliated China was, metaphorically, a woman forced into submission by the stronger foreigner, who was a man.

The general idea making its way among the Chinese elite was that stronger people would emerge from unions of stronger and more equal partners. For the first time, the idea that marriage ought to be the exclusive, voluntary arrangement of a man and a woman took hold, replacing the typical polygamous model, in which the wife bore children, was obsequious to her mother-in-law, and kept quiet about her husband's concubines. In the 1930s, there even grew up a substantial literature, including any number of periodicals, that gave sexual advice to modern couples, with instruction on such matters as how to behave on the wedding night and how to enhance one's partner's pleasure. "Only a display of gentleness and consideration will convince the kind and pure bride that the husband is warm, loving, and full of affection," intoned one such manual, *Secrets of the Bedchamber,* published in 1938. "A few warm and tender words will fill her heart with joy and arouse her sexual instinct."

This is all very modern and enlightened, though how much it really influenced Chinese sexual behavior, including, as we'll see in a minute, the practice of good old Confucian and patriarchal concubinage, is unclear. But bringing sex out into the open also made it a state concern in a way it had never been before, precisely because it was seen as a critical element in both the national decline and the possibility of national regeneration. Sex, in other words, even before the Communist revolution, came to be a matter for state intervention and regulation. The eugenics movement was strong in China in those years. Some radical reformers talked of the need to slaughter "inferior" children for the sake of improving "the race." Venereal disease, which was rampant in China, was of great concern, and to an extent it was blamed on foreigners. Indeed, here is where imperial power and sexual nationalism became intertwined.

The truth is that some venereal disease, notably syphilis, poetically called "the poison of the plum" because of the shape of the initial chancre sore, was introduced into China during the early contacts with European traders, so it was a sort of foreign pollution. By the Republican period, China, according to studies carried out by Western doctors, had a syphilis-infection rate three times that of the United States. As one scholar has put it, this "allowed the ultimate blame to be fastened upon an entity called 'the West.' " He continued, "China had been colonized by the dual force of foreign capital and fatal disease. Imperialists

'violated' the country's territorial integrity, and germs 'encroached' . . .
upon the urethra."

Of course the actual practices of foreigners in the areas of the treaty
ports that they administered did nothing to alter this image. For nearly
a century, the toleration of prostitution and the prevalence of gang-
sterism in the International Settlement and the French concession in
Shanghai, under mostly British and entirely French control respectively, made Shanghai perhaps the leading sex-for-sale capital of the
world. It was the place that, certainly for the first half of the twentieth
century, epitomized the idea that in the gorgeous, sinful East, everything was possible, and that idea was based on a reality—not everything was possible perhaps, but a great deal was. *Shanghai: City for Sale*
is the title of one book, written by Ernest Hauser and published in
1940, suggesting that everything was bought and sold in Shanghai,
especially illicit pleasure. It was a city renowned for its singsong girls, as
courtesans were commonly known. The tabloid press, most notably a
newspaper called *Jingbao* (*Crystal*), which was published every three
days for two decades starting in 1919, chronicled the comings and
goings, the affairs, and the quarrels of the city's best-known courtesans,
along with the names of the brothels where they could be found and
their phone numbers. At a lower level were the more numerous and less
fortunate "pheasants," common streetwalkers, so called for their gaudy
clothes and their custom of flitting from place to place, who were notorious for the aggressiveness of their solicitations, their desperation, and
their debased status. Surveys conducted around 1935 estimated that
there were one hundred thousand prostitutes at work in Shanghai, or
about one for every thirteen women. In the French concession alone,
where just under forty thousand women were registered to live in the
1920s, one in three of them was a prostitute. Not all the prostitutes
were Chinese. Among the most celebrated prostitutes of Shanghai were
White Russian women, induced by circumstance into the sex trade
after fleeing the Russian Revolution. At the very lowest level were the
girls working in "flower-smoke rooms," opium dens where, for a fee, a
pipe could be procured, along with the right to fondle the women, who
lured customers at the entrance to these tawdry establishments while
singing lascivious songs.

The foreigners who controlled Shanghai made efforts to reduce the scope of the sex trade, and certainly a host of mostly Christian charities attempted to help women for whom the sex trade was the difference between destitution and survival. Still, for the decades of foreign control of the treaty port of Shanghai, the sex trade flourished unrestricted there as it did in few other places in the world.

It's not hard to understand, given this background, that when the Communists seized power, in 1949, sex in general was seen as a legitimate sphere of state control and sex with foreigners was seen as echoing imperial-era humiliations. China's division into two parts, moreover, brought into being for the first time, but decidedly not the last, a division into two erotic zones: a pro-Western and pro-American zone, where, erotically speaking, everything remained possible, and another, anti-American zone of absolute erotic prohibition. Taiwan, to which the Nationalist Chinese retreated in 1949 and which the United States, until 1979, officially recognized as the legitimate government of all of China, was a sexual paradise for Americans, including the troops who were based on the island and, in the 1960s and 1970s, those who went there on "rest and recreation" from Vietnam. By contrast, the People's Republic of China closed itself off to foreign men. Later Vietnam, too, became divided, not only into two warring camps separated by different political and economic systems but also into two separate erotic cultures. One, South Vietnam, was where Western men could get laid each day by three different women, and the other, North Vietnam, was where they couldn't get laid at all.

Nonetheless, by the 1990s, China had become more or less like any other country, as sexual relations in general were liberated from party control, and it was in this sense that, viewed over the long term, China had remained the same. With Mao Zedong safely preserved under glass in his Memorial Hall in Beijing, China moved out from under the sexual repression he had demanded of ordinary people (while exempting himself), and by the 1990s China was, erotically speaking, a far different country from the one I had observed in the early 1980s. It seems to be part of the natural history of Communism that first it proclaims sexual equality and sexual freedom, then it imposes a regime of sexual repression, and after a certain interval the forces of the untrammeled libido return.

Not that old China had ever completely disappeared for Chinese men of power and influence; it had disappeared entirely only for foreigners. Even during the Maoist years, while a regime of sexual abstinence was being imposed on the vast majority of the population, Mao himself fully and unabashedly enjoyed the sexual perquisites that were traditional for Chinese rulers. We know this from the memoirs of his personal physician, Li Zhisui, whose contact with the chairman was extremely close during the entire period of Mao's rule. For almost his entire time in power, Mao was provided with sexual partners by his security guards, who were well aware not only that he had a penchant for female companions but also that he preferred the young, innocent ones to more sophisticated, older ones. "Asceticism was the public watchword of the Cultural Revolution," Li has written, "but the more ascetic and moralistic the party's preachings, the further the Chairman himself descended into hedonism. He was waited on constantly by a harem of young girls. It was at this time, the height of the Cultural Revolution, that Mao was sometimes in bed with three, four, even five women simultaneously." When he was home in Zhongnanhai, the lacquer-columned compound west of the old Forbidden City that was reserved for the highest Communist officials, Mao enjoyed the services of a bevy of pretty young women, and during parties he would retire with several of them at a time to his room, which was near the swimming pool. A large opulent room, number 118, in the Great Hall of the People, the immense government reception building on Beijing's Tiananmen Square, was set aside for Mao's use, and again according to his physician, "some of the young female attendants there and from other rooms in the Great Hall of the People also served his pleasure."

In 1957, Mao was criticized by Peng Dehuai, an army marshal who had commanded Chinese troops during the Korean War and who would be purged in 1959 for his act of lèse-majesté with regard to Mao. One of the elements in Peng's bill of indictment was that Mao behaved like an emperor, building villas and swimming pools for himself and maintaining a harem of three thousand concubines. Perhaps the number was exaggerated, but certainly Mao's harem, even if smaller than a typical emperor's, took on the characteristics of harems of yore, with bitter quarrels among its residents and Mao's female favorites enjoying influence and prestige inside Zhongnanhai. In the last years of his life, Mao's speech became so slurred that none of the other party leaders could understand him. And so, in scenes that must have seemed straight out of the imperial past, party leaders depended on the unique lip-reading skills of a certain Zhang Yufeng, a longtime train attendant and mistress of Mao's, who relayed to them the chairman's instructions, which she alone could decipher. Mao was a believer in Daoist sexual lore, and he used to give a Daoist sex manual, *The Plain Girl's Secret Way,* to his sex partners. Mao's doctor didn't say so, but it is unlikely that such a book would have been available to the public in the years of Mao's reign. Mao and the Daoists believed that men needed to ensure their longevity, to replenish their male energy, or *yang,* with a constant supply of *yin shui,* the vaginal secretions of young women, preferably virgins.

It is unlikely, given the nearly feudal nature of the Chinese Communist hierarchy and its total immunity from public scrutiny and accountability, that Mao was alone in his enjoyment of a kind of harem—a harem, it should be noted, that existed although Mao was married the entire time he held power, his wife, Jiang Qing, being among the so-called Gang of Four who were purged after Mao's death. Still, officially speaking, sex outside marriage was strictly proscribed in China's revolutionary decades, and it was precisely the hallowed tradition of sex outside marriage that made a comeback when China turned officially from socialism to capitalism. By the late 1980s, the neighborhood committees that used to supervise people's private lives had faded away. Prostitution had become common, the laws against it inconsistently applied. A lone male traveling in China today need only look around the lobby of his hotel, and he will most likely see women of the night discreetly waiting for him to approach them (they used to offer their services aggressively, but the better hotels put an end to that practice). Touts standing in wait outside the major hotels yank open the doors of departing taxis carrying foreign men to throw visiting cards at them. The cards advertise outcall massage services, usually with a picture of a languid, semi-nude beauty and a phone number. There are numerous bars and clubs in the big cities where people can mingle, including gay bars and clubs—a very big difference from the Maoist past, when homosexuality was repressed with especial brutality.

I once asked my research assistant in China, who had recently graduated from a university in Beijing, where young people went for privacy, since so many of them, unable to have quarters of their own, lived with their parents or shared dormitory rooms with several others.

"Around the universities there are lots of small, inexpensive hotels," my informant told me. "That's where they go."

That's also, it seems, where ChinaBounder took Star and Yingying, Cherry, Rina, Tulip, Tingting, Susan, and Wendy. When I lived in China, no local woman could possibly have visited the home or hotel room of a foreigner. The security guard at the hotel entrance would have swiftly turned her in.

In other words, China is restoring itself erotically, becoming, as it was in the past, a place where sex for sale is readily available and more blatantly publicized than it is in the West. Prostitutes, of course, can be found in all countries, but it is one of the characteristics of the East, including China, that prostitution is more integrated into ordinary life, less sleazy, less dangerous, and less entrenched in the underground than it is in most places in the West. There are online sex guides for traveling Westerners, and they are filled with commentary on the ease of purchasing sexual pleasure in China—even, according to one forum, in what otherwise appear to be ordinary barbershops.

Other, equally traditional practices had been restored in China by the 1990s as well, especially the practice of keeping concubines, whereby men of wealth and power expect as a perquisite of their status to enjoy the favors of at least one mistress, often many more than one. In the early days, emperors not only had their *nei-gong,* or inner palace, as the place where their concubines and their guardian eunuchs dwelled during his lifetime, but in some celebrated cases they were also accorded tomb dancers, young women who spent their lives performing inside the tomb of a deceased emperor so that he might have the pleasure of female company in the afterlife as well.

Fortunately, the tomb-dancer part of the Chinese tradition did not make a comeback in China, but certainly by the 1990s and the early years of this century concubinage had once again become widely practiced. There were official disclosures of this. According to one scholarly estimate, published on the Web site of the *People's Daily* in 2007, some 95 percent of officials found to be corrupt in an area of Guangdong Province had mistresses. Another article at around the same time said that two thousand officials in Henan Province, in central China, had been found to have violated China's strict one-child policy, most of them by having second, third, and even fourth children by their second, third, or fourth *xiao-nai,* or "little wives."

To deal with what the top officials of the Communist Party see as the unfortunate resurgence of an undesirable social custom, new regulations were passed that defined new forms of corruption, so that for the first time gifts given not to an official himself or to a member of his family but to his mistress were designated as bribes. Passed by the State Council, China's highest administrative body, these regulations required that civil servants found to have lovers be warned against the practice; those "whose acts are more serious should be degraded or dismissed from his or her positions," the regulation specified, and "one whose acts are very serious should be expelled."

And that brings us back to ChinaBounder the blogger, who illustrates a return to traditional practices in far deeper ways than he perhaps realized. It is the main thesis of this book that for centuries the East, broadly defined to include most of the world's territory from North and East Africa to South, Southeast, and East Asia, represented a domain of special erotic fascination and fulfillment for Western men. This East contained many cultures, languages, and peoples, and was certainly never a single zone of civilization, except that much of it was colonized, or partly colonized, by Western countries, and most of it belonged to a sexual culture very different from that of the Christian West. The contact between West and East in this sense was variegated and complex, involving conquest and ideas, exchanges of wealth and of beliefs, but one continuing element in this contact was sexual. The encounter and confrontation of the West with this broadly defined East, taking place over three centuries and more, involved a meeting of two very different sets of erotic practices and values whose benefits, like that of colonialism itself, flowed largely in one direction, giving Western men opportunities that would have been far more difficult, often impossible, for them to have at home.

This mingling of East and West illustrated something about not only the societies in which Western men took their pleasure but also the societies they came from, in which those pleasures were forbidden. On one side was Christian monogamy in which sex was shrouded in religious meaning and prohibition, regarded as sinful when enjoyed

outside of marriage, and even sinful within marriage when unconnected to procreation. On the other side was an Eastern culture
wherein sex was strictly regulated, especially when it came to women,
but where it was disassociated from both sin and love. The world, in
other words, divided itself into two large zones. There was the Western
erotic zone of guilt and repression and the Eastern zone of the harem,
of multiple sexual partners, in which it was assumed, for good or ill,
that it is entirely natural and healthy for a man to enjoy the favors of
many women and that there needed to be a class of women to satisfy
what were seen in the West as illegitimate and insalubrious desires, better repressed than indulged.

The East therefore presented Western men with a spectacle of difference at the very core of life, the deep zone of instinctual pleasure,
and for many men this opened up a vista of exhilarating, sin-free, and
irresistible possibilities. To be sure, there were also men for whom the
stories and images of Eastern sexuality evoked a powerful revulsion,
revealing an East that was a den of iniquity, a moral horror, a Sodom
that cried out for moral and religious instruction. The East, as the
writer Ian Buruma has put this, attracted both missionaries and libertines, the one determined to stamp out its pagan licentiousness and
the other to take advantage of it, though the latter seem to have been
more numerous than the former. I am speaking here of an almost
exclusively male Western phenomenon for the simple reason that it
was mostly Western men who went East, and the sexual culture they
found there was created by men for the pleasure of men. Thousands of
Westerners—administrators of the East India Company in British
India, French rubber planters in Cambodia, American infantrymen on
leave from combat duty in Vietnam—discovered that they could set
themselves up with harems of their own, like the sultans and emperors
of yore, though in lands that were not their own.

That's what ChinaBounder did in creating his life in what he
regarded as his Chinese paradise, and that's why his boastful account of
his conquests rubbed the wrong way. The paradox is that even as China
was returning to its former self as an Eastern culture, it had simultaneously adopted as its own many of the sexual values of the West. And
so, even as it was once again offering the pleasures it had denied to

Western men for more than thirty years, it was feeling ashamed and humiliated for doing so.

Like Western men of seventy-five and one hundred years ago in India and Shanghai and Tanganyika (present-day Tanzania), China-Bounder had a harem in Shanghai, and many Chinese didn't like it (even though many Chinese men were setting up harems of their own). To be sure, in a real harem of the sort enjoyed by, say, Kublai Khan or the great Qing dynasty emperor Qianlong, the female inhabitants had far less choice in what they did or where they were than China-Bounder's former students did. In a real harem, moreover, women were the exclusive erotic property of the sole man privileged to have relations with them—unless, as was often the case, he didn't want them anymore and gave them as gifts to his ministers and generals or to some foreign potentate with whom he wanted to keep the peace.

Still, these technical differences aside, being a foreigner and a teacher enabled ChinaBounder to act like a little emperor, with his own *nei-gong,* even if his *nei-gong* consisted mostly of rent-by-the-hour Shanghai hotel rooms. What was astonishing was that by the early years of this century an indiscreet foreigner was providing testimony to the fact that even a lowly English teacher from a race that was once regarded as unpleasantly brick colored and evil smelling and that, during the Maoist years, was barred from sexual pleasures with local women could have a harem too.

CHAPTER TWO

The Whole World as the White Man's Brothel

ON MAY 19, 1887, an anonymous writer for the *Pall Mall Gazette*, a London newspaper whose editor was deeply concerned about what he felt was a decline in British morality, informed his countrymen of the great shame of the British Empire. There were some five hundred thousand soldiers and policemen, colonial officials and clerks, most of them men and most of them unmarried, who transacted the business of the empire, the writer said. And a great many of this cohort had sadly fallen to the "level of the immoral heathen" because they formed "immoral relations with natives." In doing so, the writer continued, British officialdom had come to regard "English morality as a local English institution, to be left behind along with Crosse & Blackwell pickles or Keen's mustard, the corresponding substitutes abroad being better adapted to local conditions."

Leaving aside his moral judgments—and his assumptions about the relative worth of "the immoral heathen" and the practitioners of "English morality"—this writer's facts about relations with "natives" in the empire where the sun never set were accurate. Word did get around even in those distant days, and the word was that the administrators and soldiers of British colonialism took a large number of the women they colonized to bed with them. This is not to say that sexual relations between the British and the inhabitants of India, Ceylon (modern-day Sri Lanka), Tanganyika, and Malaya were always as common as the letter writer described them. Especially in the late part of the nineteenth century and into the twentieth, British soldiers and officials tended more than before to bring their wives with them to colonial posts, and their sexual relations with local women, girls, men, and boys were correspondingly less frequent, though such relations never ceased altogether. The article in the *Pall Mall Gazette* was an element in what was called the purity movement, a late-nineteenth-century campaign redolent of Victorian anxiety and avidly supported by the newspaper, which succeeded in imposing some sexual discipline on the British abroad. There were people in Britain throughout the history of colonialism, beginning perhaps with the philosopher Edmund Burke, who abhorred the sexual implications of colonial power and who, in addition, suspected that the fundamental violation of "English morality" was colonialism itself. But this was not the attitude of the purity movement, which was entirely pro-empire. The *Pall Mall Gazette* was giving expression to a narrow and racist worry pressed by an odd coalition of feminists, churchmen, Quakers, and various individuals from Robert Baden-Powell (creator of the Boy Scouts) to Horatio Herbert Kitchener (a commander in chief of India), all of whom worried that such customs as temporary concubinage and the patronage of local whorehouses eroded the desired separation of the British and the colonized peoples, and this in turn diminished the glory and prestige of the empire.

For much of the history of that empire, certainly since the ventures of the East India Company in the seventeenth century, many, perhaps most, of the soldiers and civil servants who were dispatched to Africa and Asia to run the business of the Crown and the East India Company were undisturbed by any such notions. They did leave behind the sexual ethics they had grown up with, and for their pleasure and convenience, and to assuage their loneliness and their longings, they did adapt to local conditions. Most likely they did miss Crosse and Blackwell pickles more than they missed the erotic prohibitions of the home country. Rudyard Kipling, who wrote suggestively, if obliquely, of the nocturnal sensuousness of Lahore (now in Pakistan), where he spent a few youthful years as a newspaper reporter, may have spoken generally of the white man's burden. Ronald Hyam, a leading scholar of British colonialism at Cambridge University, has written that one of the processes of colonialism was "turning the whole world into the white man's brothel."

There were many elements to this, not least that sexual adventure for the British in India—as for Europeans elsewhere in Asia—was part of the great colonialist adventure, an element in the exhilaration of it all, the sense of possibility that somehow seemed greater in the East than it did back home, which was where children were educated, morality prevailed, and life was hemmed in by irksome, if civilizing constraints. The East was a place where those constraints could be more easily neglected, where men got a temporary reprieve from the demands of what the *Pall Mall Gazette* called "British morality" but was really deeply inscribed in Western values and expectations. Kipling, he of the white man's burden, was also emblematic in this as the figure whose stories and poems gave expression to the great romance of India, which was the kind of place where a single white man could become a god to superstitious natives—as Daniel Dravot does in "The Man Who Would Be King," not failing to remind anyone who would listen to him that Kafiristan, where his adventure takes place, is "a mountainous country, and the women of those parts are very beautiful." Kipling's poem *Mandalay*—

> *By the old Moulmein Pagoda, lookin' eastward to the sea,*
> *There's a Burma girl a-settin', and I know she thinks o' me;*
> *For the wind is in the palm-trees, and the temple-bells they say:*
> *"Come you back, you British soldier; come you back to Mandalay!"*

—is all you need to understand the heart-racing allure that the East had for tens of thousands of adventurous Europeans, eager to hear the temple bell at dawn (which "comes up like thunder") and see the nut-brown girl who's waitin'. Or there was Lawrence Durrell's *Alexandria Quartet,* with his depictions of the gorgeous, corrupting heat of Egypt compared with the gray, cheerless, frigid territory of self-denial that was the home country, England.

To a great extent, the exploitation of native women by colonial soldiers, traders, and officials was nothing more than the working out of two constant principles in human relations. The first is that the sexual urge is a very powerful and preoccupying one. The second is that obtaining sexual pleasure is often an emolument of wealth and power as well as a goal of the adventuring spirit. In the case of the British empire, the widespread availability of native women was the simple result of British wealth and military supremacy. The British also established the relationships between empire and masculinity or, to put this inversely, between being a native and being feminine. It was the same relationship that was enacted in the post-colonial situation evoked by ChinaBounder, who was unabashed in his sense that the West is male; the East, including, in his view, the lesser men who inhabit it, female. Just as the colonizing country was deemed superior to the colonized in military strength, wealth, and power, so was the Western sexual adventurer in Asia the superior man, the kind of man to whom any sensible native woman would pledge fidelity and devotion. The idea that the East presented Western men with erotic possibilities impossible at home gave rise to numerous Western cultural expressions, from Montesquieu's *Persian Letters* to the Broadway musical *South Pacific*. Perhaps the most famous and emblematic work, which strikes the motif of the superior Western man most directly, is the story of the Japanese courtesan Cio-Cio-San and the American naval officer Pinkerton in Giacomo Puccini's opera *Madama Butterfly*.

The opera's story is well-known: Pinkerton, stationed in the port of Nagasaki in the late nineteenth century, arranges with a local broker to be married to Cio-Cio-San, who is a poor fifteen-year-old Japanese girl. Pinkerton's intention is to pluck the local flowers while he is in Nagasaki and then leave, which is what he does. But when he is about to return to America, he tells Cio-Cio-San, who has forsaken her family to marry him and believes she has become an American in doing so, that he will return to her in a year. Cio-Cio pines for him for three years, living in Pinkerton's "paper house," with its view of Nagasaki Harbor, ignoring the entreaties of those around her that she give up on him even as she contemptuously rejects another suitor, the wealthy and aristocratic Prince Yamadori, who has fallen for her. When Pinkerton does finally arrive back in Nagasaki, he is accompanied by his new American wife; he learns that Cio-Cio gave birth to his son while he was away, so he sends word to her that he and his "real" bride wish to take the child away. Cio-Cio, struck with grief, cuts her throat, leaving her son, an American flag stuck in his hand, for Pinkerton and his wife.

It is a sad and bitter story, and a complex one in its way, and we'll get back to it. For the moment, it stands as an emblem of a mostly unequal erotic encounter between the civilizations that took place in various guises for hundreds of years. The East was a place where money was made and imperial ambitions pursued. It was also a place where sexual fulfillment outside marriage was easy, inexpensive, and permissible, especially in comparison with the situation at home, where sexual fulfillment came with responsibility or, if it was bought and paid for, was expensive, illicit, and condemned as sinful by both legal and moral authorities.

Chiefly, Westerners went to Asia in pursuit of personal wealth and national glory. They also went to convert the heathen to Christianity. Yet one of the most ordinary and important of the further motivations was plain and simple curiosity. The West was driven by the desire to know the East, while the East had very little interest in knowing the West. Anthropology, archaeology, comparative linguistics, and other disciplines were Western, not Eastern, inclinations. The Chinese, the Indians, and the Malays showed no interest in, say, finding the source of the Danube, while to Englishmen of the nineteenth century, finding the source of the Nile was an obsession, the cause of fantastic expenditures and epic rivalries, comparable to the rivalry over being the first to send a man to the South Pole or, for that matter, to the moon. Indeed, as we will see, the exploration of the Nile and the exploration of Eastern sexuality were conjoined in the life of one extraordinary figure, Richard Francis Burton of England.

The sexual advantage of the Western man in the East is an aspect of Western dynamism, the questing spirit of Europeans, compared with the relative passivity of Asians in these matters. And there is a parallel in matters of sex, another great, generally unacknowledged force that lured Westerners to the East. There was for centuries, for example, a palpable obsession in Europe with the harem of the sultan of the Ottoman Empire, an obsession that produced an entire library of books and treatises, mostly in English and French, in which various travelers claimed to have penetrated into the harem's forbidden world.

This writing was mostly speculative. Few if any of the writers on the Ottoman harem could experience it the way the sultan did. Indeed, with a couple of exceptions, none of them ever saw it. Still, the East was under the gaze of the watchful West even before Westerners lived there in large numbers and experienced it on an everyday basis, and to be the object of someone else's curiosity carries with it an erotic element. The analogy is irresistible: the East was the woman whose forms and behaviors the West gazed upon for centuries. Then, with the full flush of colonialism and Western travel to the East, experience replaced speculation. As early as the sixteenth century, Portuguese seamen cohabited with local women in Goa, Malacca, Sumatra, and Japan. The British pursued the pleasures of the flesh in India from the seventeenth century to the twentieth; the French did so in Indochina and North Africa from the 1870s to the 1930s. After World War II, Americans by the hundreds of thousands inherited not only the mantle of empire from the British and the French but a kind of sexual imperialism as well, making it more crass, more vulgar, more commercial than it had ever been before, turning whole districts in Tokyo, Seoul, Saigon, and Bangkok into sexual emporiums, theme parks whose only customers were young, and not so young, men and whose sole attractions were young, sometimes very young, Asian women (and, of course, men and boys).

During all those centuries, sex defined a not-so-hidden broader aspect of the shared history of West and East. It reflected Western material superiority. It was made possible by Western conquest, which was translated into personal power and advantage. But there was an Eastern element as well, and that was a decidedly non-Victorian sexual culture that was receptive to Western desire. If the Western man became an erotic potentate in the East, he did so by grafting himself onto an Eastern erotic culture that had always been more frank and less morally fastidious about sexual needs than the Western Christian erotic culture, which valued exclusivity with a single lifetime partner and associated sex for pleasure with sin. This is a complicated matter because in most of the countries of the East, sex was viewed in much the same way that the Victorians viewed it, as something to be controlled by strict moral principles and parental regulation. Indeed, never was sex treated as casually in the East as it was, say, in Sweden or Cambridge, Massachusetts, in the late twentieth century. There were no Crosse and Blackwell pickles in the non-Western portions of the globe, but there was in most of them a culture of the harem that stood in sharp contrast to the sexual culture of Christendom. In the East it was taken for granted that there would always be a certain reserve of women, often the supreme models of beauty, cultivation, and charm, whose assigned role in life was to provide sexual pleasure for men. The further assumption of the harem culture was that men of power and wealth would enjoy the attentions of these women outside marriage. The existence of the culture of the harem was not the major inducement for Western men to undergo the hazards and the difficulties of serving their countries in Asia. The attainment of wealth and power and the conversion of the heathen remained the explicit, immediate motivations. But sexual pleasure made up a usually unspoken part of the history of East and West.

A British diplomat and writer, Paul Rycaut, whose *Present State of the Ottoman Empire* was first published in 1668, was among the first to foster the Western fascination with the Eastern harem. It was Rycaut who crystallized in a single sentence the two hemispheres' ideal attitudes toward love and sexual pleasure. "The western knight," he said, "consumes himself with combats, watching, and penance to acquire the love of one fair Damsel; here [in Turkey] an army of Virgins make it the only study and business of their life to obtain the single nod of invitation to the Bed of their great Master."

In fact, it's a bit strange that Rycaut, as late as 1668, took the knight and his damsel to be the models of Western love, since his era was a long way from the era of European feudalism, when, at least in the ideal, the values of courage, honor, fidelity, and chastity reigned supreme. Still, while the European aristocracy of Rycaut's day hardly behaved according to the chivalrous code, chivalry remained an ideal toward which men were expected to strive. The Catholic Church had for centuries made a unity of love and religious devotion, declaring marriage a sacrament and holding that sex for pleasure, rather than for procreation, was sinful, even within the sacrosanct confines of marriage. The analogy of the perfect love of a man and a woman was the marriage of Christ and the church, which by definition was a nonsexual love, a Platonic ideal, a spiritual attainment rather than a physical pleasure. Again, there was plenty of rebellion against this ideal. Even in medieval times, a cult of bawdiness and seduction existed alongside the official cult of fidelity and chastity.

Both kinds of attitudes have existed in Europe since the Middle Ages. The saint and the rake have occupied the same cultural territory, representing the view of love as a sacrament that can be fully experienced only as a spiritual matter, separated from sex, and the opposite of this: love as something that can be achieved only by defying the church and rejecting its pleasure-denying principles. But as the historian Johan Huizinga wrote, each of them in its way—the highly spiritualized variety whose inspiration was the love of Christ and the rebellious opposite that idealized pleasure—made love the essential ingredient of a peculiarly European sort of idyll. "Civilization always needs to wrap up the idea of love in veils of fancy, to exalt and refine it, and thereby to forget cruel reality," Huizinga said. And there were many realities to forget, including the inescapable brutality of life, the fickleness of human nature, the power of lust, the likelihood of boredom and disillusionment, the selfishness and egotism of people, and the inevitability of physical decay. So the charm of knightly courtesy and the bawdy song each represented "an attempt to substitute for reality the dream of a happier life." Both represent the powerful inclination to find through love or sex something of the transcendent or, as Huizinga called it, the sublime.

The history of Western sexuality is complicated in this regard because every attempt to impose a single, constant value on it fails. Religion permeated the European consciousness in both the Middle Ages and the Renaissance, and the Catholic Church and, later, Protestant churches fought mightily to separate love from physical need and impose monogamy as a legal and moral requirement. One rebellion against that was what came in later centuries to be called courtly love, the stuff of the songs of twelfth-century troubadours, whose subject was the faithfully faithless knight, the knight who directed the chivalrous emotion not toward his wife—because marriage was rarely a matter of true love—but toward some other woman, the lady in the tower, and the more impossible his illicit love, the higher his spiritual attainment in loving anyway. The great epics of the Middle Ages in this sense are full of infidelity—indeed, they are driven by infidelity. Sir Lancelot's passionate affair with Guinevere, the wife of King Arthur, is the event that brings about the dissolution of Camelot. In the epic poem *Tristan and Isolde,* Tristan is sent by his uncle King Mark to escort the king's intended, the Irish princess Isolde, across the Irish Sea to Cornwall, where their marriage is to take place. But because of an accident with a love potion they both drink on the voyage, Tristan and Isolde fall passionately in love with each other, even as they know that their respective vows to the king—Tristan to obey him, Isolde to marry

him—cannot be broken. Courtly love, as in the epic, was usually about
infidelity among the upper classes, tragic triangles in which the greatest
love is the one that can take place only outside social and ecclesiastical
convention. Of course infidelity, which has been more of an upper-
class luxury than a lower-class indulgence, has always been with us.
What distinguished medieval- and Renaissance-era infidelity is that,
like love hallowed by monogamous marriage, it was a sort of hallowed
and monogamous adultery. It was a tacit but never-acknowledged
recognition that true passion can never take place within marriage
because passion, to remain alive in the body and in the mind, must
either never find physical consummation or produce the briefest of satisfactions. "The spontaneous ardor of a love crowned and not thwarted
is essentially of short duration," the existentialist philosopher Denis de
Rougemont wrote. "It is a flare-up doomed not to survive the efful-
gence of its fulfillment."

And so sex played an ambiguous role in the extramarital monogamy
that was courtly love. Tristan and Isolde enjoyed the consummation of
their passion. They seem to have slept together on the very way to
Isolde's wedding; they did so again in the forest after their escape from
King Mark's court, though there is some ambiguity about this on
account of a sword placed between them. On the other hand, the great
chronicler of medieval love, Andreas Capellanus, recorded that the
pure, spiritual, and everlasting love of a knight for the lady who is not
his wife must remain unconsummated. The chivalric code, he said,
allows "the kiss and the embrace and the modest contact with the nude
lover, omitting the final solace, for that is not permitted for those who
wish to love purely"—while the less creditable "mixed love," which
"lasts but a short time," does culminate "in the final act of Venus."

But if love in the West was a complex and inconsistent matter, it
was in important ways consistently different from love in the East,
where it was precisely the final solace that was most expected, and for
those who had the necessary wealth or power, the harem provided the
venue for this entirely natural outcome. Of course there were many
Easts: a Muslim East, closer to the West in matters of sexual morality,
as well as Hindu, Buddhist, Confucian, Shinto, and animist Easts, and
others besides. And all societies, Eastern and Western, seek ways to
rebel against strictures that religion and morality place upon the satis-

faction of physical desire. All of them see unrestrained physical desire as a calamity. But it is difficult to find in any of the Easts a sustained debate of the sort that was common in the West—about whether love is physical or spiritual, moral or sinful, whether the sublime is to be found in observing the strictures of the church or in flouting them. This agonizing choice was a peculiarity of the Christian culture, with its beliefs in the holiness of procreation and original sin. And so in the West the rebellion against self-denial, which is virtually by definition contrary to nature and its most powerful impulses, took the form of illicit affairs, of anti-clerical irreverence, or of the adulterous but highly formalized and spiritualized adoration of the perfect woman. In the East, the rebellion against the repression of desire took the form of the harem, in which a certain set of women was set aside to satisfy male desire, thereby keeping other women, including other men's wives, safe from depredation. It was a patriarchal system of highly questionable benefit to women, and a system that exercised total control over female sexuality, whether that of the strumpet or the virgin, but as an approach to the handling of male physical desire, the Eastern way was vastly more realistic, less blinded by sentimental illusion about biological forces and the nature of men than the Western way. Certainly the East never confused sex with spirituality because the Christian notion of love and sex, with its expectation of lifelong sanctified devotion to a single person, never took hold. Nor was there the chivalrous ideal, in which the knight's love for an unattainable woman was an occasion for him to vaunt his virtue. Love and sex in the East were male prerogatives, and males unabashedly and unapologetically indulged them without the cultish fuss made over them in Christendom.

This is where Rycaut's comment is apt. In the West, the perfect woman was the object of virtuous and spiritual devotion, and the more unattainable she was, the more perfect. In the East, the perfect woman was an exquisite beauty selected for service in the harem, her calling not to remain pure and virginal but to serve the needs of procreation and male desire.

When Western men went to Asia, they became the masters in the boardroom, as it were, and in the bedroom. From the standpoint of the currently fashionable political morality, that appears very bad, an illustration of the unfairness of colonialist rule, a tremendous advantage for the male over the female, a manifestation of female inequality and male domination. But let's not be judgmental about this, at least not yet. Let's try to see the erotic history of the West and the East as part of the great human pageant, one in which the women, the girls, and the boys involved were not necessarily passive, powerless creatures swept unwillingly down the river of their experience. This is a rich subject with many layers of mutual use and mutual advantage. There is poignancy in it and even love. And there is as well a theme of liberation on both sides, liberation from extreme patriarchal conservatism in the East and from extreme sexual ignorance and repression in the West. Leaving morality aside for at least a preliminary moment, concentrating instead on what actually occurred rather than on how we should feel about it, we can note one remarkable part of this history, which is that Asia was seen as a place of erotic possibility in the West even before Western men began their experience there as soldiers, administrators, and power holders.

In A.D. 70, after Jerusalem fell to the Roman general Titus, the emperor Vespasian had special coins struck to celebrate the hard-earned victory. The coins show a Roman soldier, muscular and manly, his foot resting on a helmet, his hand holding a spear as he stands on one side of a palm tree. On the other side is a woman seated under the tree, her head down in a gesture of mourning and submission.

The woman represented her people and the conquered and despoiled country Judaea, and she has long been seen by historians as an emblem of the Jewish tragedy at the hands of the Romans, including

A Roman coin, ca. A.D. 70, shows Titus, the conqueror of Jerusalem, standing over a female figure representing Judaea weeping.

American Numismatic Society

the destruction of the Second Temple, which was never to be rebuilt. But it is possible to see another sort of symbolism in Vespasian's coin. It is Judaea in mourning, but it is also Judaea depicted as a woman while the swaggering, implicitly sexual Roman soldier stands over her, his stance blatantly suggestive of impending violation.

Long before there was an East India Company, centuries before Englishmen left their pickles and sexual customs behind them, they and other Westerners had seen Asia sensually. It could be said that since Antony and Cleopatra, the sexual conquest of the East by the West has been a persistent theme of the Western imagination and, indeed, of the Western experience. Indeed, the theme extends all the way back to Menelaus of Sparta and Helen of Troy, the deprived husband of ancient Greece and his wife, the woman whose face launched a thousand ships. Homer's *Iliad* introduces the notion of the Eastern woman as a prize of Western conquest, though of course it is too early, in the eighth century B.C., when Homer lived and wrote, to speak of East and West as they later came to be defined. The central theme of the *Iliad* is the rage of Achilles, which is provoked by an incident involving the competition of two powerful Western men over an Eastern slave, Briseis, who was taken by Achilles for his role in the sack of Lyrnessus, a city in Asia Minor. Briseis is perhaps the earliest illustration of the sexual implications of the Western conquest of Asia. When Agamemnon, the supreme commander of the Achaean (Greek) army, steals her away, Achilles avenges his loss by dropping out of the battle, to the tragic misfortune of the Greeks.

Nearly a millennium went by between the *Iliad* and the striking of Vespasian's coin, and it was during that long stretch of time that the notions of East and West as we know them today began to take shape, in such events as the conquest of Egypt by the Romans and, later, of Judaea by Titus. If already in Homer there is a kind of dramatic foreshadowing of the role of Asia as a domain of erotic delights for men of the West, the theme stands out with disquieting clarity in Vespasian's coin. There, Asia has been turned into something soft, tearful, and feminine while the Western conqueror is threatening masculinity personified.

In the long history of East and West, from the Romans in Judaea to American GIs in Vietnam, erotic pleasure has been far more than an incidental, surprise by-product of conquest, or the search for private wealth, glory, power, adventure, or exploration, or the expansion of empire. The expectation of pleasure was there at the beginning in two ways. The story of Antony and Cleopatra represents the dusky Asian woman as a sort of ultimate seductress, the siren on the shore, the exotic foreigner whom the Western traveler falls for almost to the point of self-enslavement. The abduction of Briseis and Vespasian's coin show the ancient practice of plunder and rape as spoils of conquest, and since it was with few exceptions the West that defeated the East, it was usually the East that was ravished and the West that was pleasured. So it is that in later centuries, when Western men arrived in large numbers in the Middle East, North Africa, India, and East and Southeast Asia, they already entertained fantasies of an erotic pageant very different from anything available at home.

The eroticized image of the East had long been produced by literature and legend; then, starting in the early Renaissance, the image was reinforced and intensified by the tales of travelers who visited the domains of Oriental rulers. The East, even when it was not depicted in explicitly sexual terms, was painted as a place of wonders and sometimes horrors, a domain like the oceans on medieval maps, where magical creatures—monsters, serpents, and beings that combined human and beastly features—dwelled. The East was a place where crocodiles wept as they ate men, where there was a fountain whose waters ensured eternal freedom from sickness, and where the bereaved ate their dead parents so that they would have no other sepulcher than the bowels of their children. The East was another planet, and it played the role that other planets would play in the science fiction fantasies of later centuries. Today we have travelers' tales of space creatures abducting earthlings and using them for sexual experiments. Something like that is found in some of the tales of journeys to the magical East, where it is not sexual experimentation but tales of pleasure palaces, polygamy, sexual slavery, and wanton women that focused the collective mind.

Most famous, of course, was the journey of Marco Polo, so full of fabulous descriptions of the court and country of the great khan of China that many of his contemporaries believed him to have made it all up. But in addition to Polo there were others, whose accounts corroborated the magical and erotic qualities of the East and who created an enduring Western fascination with Eastern sexuality.

In the thirteenth century, Friar William of Rubrouck, or Rubruck, a Franciscan missionary of Flemish origin who was born about 1215 in northern France, undertook a journey from Constantinople to the Mongolian capital of Karakorum on the orders of Louis IX of France. William had accompanied Louis on the Crusade of 1248, so his credentials as a good Christian and an honorable man were impeccable, as was his and Louis' goal of converting the Tartars, as the Mongols were called, to the one true faith. In this he did not succeed, though his encounter with the Mongols lasted for two years.

William was a careful and scrupulous observer. He was the first person to establish that the Caspian is an inland sea. His descriptions of the Mongol yurt, the jewelry of the women, the Mongols' marriage and funerary customs, and their worship of what he duly called "false Gods" are precisely detailed and entirely believable. And so, it would seem, is his description of a polygamous Mongol sexual culture very foreign to that of Europe. "And when he hath several wives," he wrote of the Tartar horseman, "she with whom he hath slept that night sits beside him in the day, and it becometh all the others who come to her dwelling that day to drink, and court is held there that day, and the gifts which are brought that day are placed in the treasury of that lady." He also introduced a concept that would give rise to intense fascination among Europeans in later centuries, the notion of the slave whose purpose is to satisfy the sexual pleasures of her master. "They punish homicide with capital punishment, and also cohabiting with a woman not one's own," he wrote. "By not one's own, I mean not his wife or bondwoman, for with one's slaves one may do as one pleases."

It should be noted that the Tartars were not some small, distant people who served to satisfy an arcane curiosity. They were the fearsome horsemen who had laid waste to half of eastern Europe in the conquests of the first third of the thirteenth century, the people whose prowess made kings tremble and children fear the dark. "For they are inhuman and beastly," said John of Pian de Carpine, who had journeyed to the Mongol court, also at the behest of the very religious Louis IX, in 1246, seven years before William, "rather monsters than men, thirsting for and drinking blood, tearing and devouring the flesh of dogs and men, dressed in oxhides, armed with plates of iron, short and stout, thickset, strong, invincible, indefatigable, their backs unprotected, their breasts covered with armor. . . . They have one-edged swords and daggers, are wonderful archers, spare neither age, nor sex, nor condition. . . . And so they came with the swiftness of lightning to the confines of Christendom, ravaging and slaughtering, striking every one with terror and incomparable horror."

The European wish was not that the Tartars would be conquered and colonized but that they would stay away, or, as Louis forlornly hoped, convert to Christianity. There is no portrayal in the writings of these travelers to the court of Kublai Khan of something superior and masculine about the West and submissive and feminine in the East. Nor, for that matter, were the Ottoman Turks, a later object of intense sexual curiosity in Europe, seen in the way that weeping Judaea was depicted on that Roman coin. These are some of the exceptions to the standard pattern emerging in the long convulsive history of East and West, in which the defeated, colonized, or at least compliant East furnished sexual possibilities for Western men. Still, even in those early accounts of the court of the great khan and the later accounts of harem life concealed within the walls of Constantinople's Topkapi Palace, there is a powerful erotic theme, an association of the East with a strange, perhaps immoral but mostly alluring sensuality. At least from late medieval times, sex in the East had a fabulous quality to it, like the strange animals and the weird funerary rites that, it was believed, could also be found there. The French sailor François Pyrard, who spent five years as a captive in the Maldives in the early seventeenth century, learned the local language, and wrote a three-volume account of his travels in the East, which was published in Paris in 1611, did not fail to observe the character of the women he encountered. "In truth, the women of all India are naturally much addicted to every kind of ordinary lewdness," he said, expressing a common belief of Western men, that the warmer climate of South Asia assured that South Asian women would be sexually warmer than their European counterparts. "But those of the Maldives in particular are so tainted with this vice that they have no other talk or occupation, and hold it a boast and a virtue one with another to have some bravo or gallant, upon whom they lavish all such favours and tokens of love as a man could wish of a woman."

The Voyage and Travels of Sir John Mandeville, which was widely read in the late fourteenth century, was the most important of the fanciful accounts of the East believed to be a reliable eyewitness testimony. Mandeville himself was almost surely an invention, possibly but by no means certainly of a physician named Jean de Bourgogne or possibly of a historian named Jean d'Outremeuse. Or he may have been a man named Mandeville from Black Notley in Essex. In any case, he wrote in Anglo-Norman, a language closer to French than to English and used in England after the invasion of William the Conqueror in 1066. He may have traveled, or he may have made the whole thing up, relying for his details on other books, going back to Pliny and Herodotus, who were among the first to portray the East as a place inhabited by monsters and dragons.

But if Mandeville hadn't actually gone to the places he described in his narrative, he certainly fooled a lot of readers of contemporary Europe, for whom his book served as a primary source. Mandeville's *Travels* was in the library of Leonardo da Vinci. Christopher Columbus read it for information on China before he set off for the East via the Atlantic Ocean. Rabelais read Mandeville when he researched the journey of Pantagruel to India. *The Travels* was translated into all the European languages, and all the Europeans who read it were introduced to an Asian world of wealth and wonders.

Whoever the author was, he introduced himself as an English knight who traveled over a period of thirty years in the early to mid-fourteenth century, serving for a time the sultan of Egypt and later what he called the great khan of Cathay. He recounts innumerable details, like these about the Tartars:

> The men of that country begin everything they have to do in the new moon, and reverence it much; they also worship the sun, and kneel often to it. They usually ride without spurs, but they have in their hand a whip or crop or some other thing to goad their horses with. They hold it a great sin to put a knife in the fire, to take meat out of a cauldron or pot with a knife, to hit a

horse with a bridle, to break one bone with another bone, or to throw milk or any other liquid that is drunk on the earth. The greatest sin a man can do, they say, is to piss in their houses where they live; if anyone pisses there and they know about it, they kill him. The place where a man has pissed must be purified or no man is so bold as to enter it.

Like other travelers, Mandeville had his eyes open for the women of the countries he visited, remarking on their beauty and the whiteness of their skin in some places, describing the rites and practices of polygamy in others. "There is another fair and good isle," he wrote, "full of people, where the custom is that when a woman is newly married, she shall not sleep the first night with her husband, but with another young man, who shall have ado with her that night and take her maidenhead, taking in the morning a certain sum of money for his trouble." Mandeville inquired into the reasons for this strange custom. "They told me that in ancient times some men had died in that land in deflowering maidens, for the latter had snakes within them, which stung the husbands on their penises inside the women's bodies; and thus many men were slain, and so they follow that custom there to make other men test out the route before they themselves set out on that adventure."

What a story, so suggestive of the hazards of the pursuit of pleasure. Snakes hidden in the vaginas of young virgins! Could this have been some symbolic representation of venereal disease, a punishment for lust? We don't know. Mandeville found on another "isle" the practice later known as suttee, by which women are burned on the funeral pyres of their husbands. "It is their opinion there that they are purged by the fire, so that no corruption shall ever after come by them, and, purged of all vice and all deformity, they will pass to their husbands in the next world." And then there was yet "another isle in the sea" where "they marry their own daughters, and their sisters, and their female relatives, and live ten or twelve or more together in one house. Each man's wife shall be common to the others who live there; each of them takes other wives, one on one night, one on another. When any of the wives bears a child, it will be given to him who first lay with her who is the mother;

and so there is no one who knows whether the child be his or another's."

The great khan that Mandeville presumably served (assuming he was ever in China) was Toghen Temür, a descendant of the great Kublai Khan, who conquered China and founded the Yuan dynasty in the thirteenth century. Toghen Temür, known in Chinese as the emperor Huizong, presided over the declining years of the Mongol Empire. Indeed, the Mongols were expelled by the new and very vigorous Ming dynasty in 1368, when Toghen Temür fled to Mongolia itself. Still, even in this period of division and weakness, the great khan established the East for Mandeville as the land of the harem, an idea that was to fascinate Europe for the next several centuries. "The lord leads a marvelous life," he said. "For he has fifty maidens who serve him each day at his meals and his bed, and do what he wills. And when he sits at his meals, they bring him meat, always five dishes at once; and while bringing them they sing a lovely song. They cut up his meat in front of him and put it in his mouth as if he were a child; for he cuts none and touches none with his hands, which he keeps always on the table in front of him."

It was Marco Polo, who journeyed to China fifty years before Mandeville, who was present in Beijing, the Mongol capital, during the great days of the Yuan dynasty, when Kublai himself ruled over China and most of Central Asia. "He has four wives of the first rank," Polo wrote, and "none of them have fewer than three hundred young female attendants of great beauty, together with a multitude of youths as pages, and other eunuchs, as well as ladies of the bedchamber; so that the number of persons belonging to each of their respective courts amounts to ten thousand." Besides his wives, Polo continued, Kublai "has many concubines provided for his use, from a province of Tartary named Ungut, the inhabitants of which are distinguished for beauty of features and fairness of complexion."

It is not hard to imagine the impression that such a description—a king with hundreds of beauties available for his pleasure—would make in Catholic Europe of the early fourteenth century, when the *Travels of Marco Polo* was published and quickly became one of the most famous books in history. It's not surprising, indeed, that Polo was viewed as a great fabulist, a spinner of tales, but the tales had an enduring impact. And Polo provided details. His *Travels* stipulated, for example, how the emperor's concubines were chosen in a kind of official survey of feminine beauty that was undertaken on his behalf every other year. Kublai's commissioners gathered the prettiest girls of Ungut and appointed "qualified persons to inspect them, who, upon careful inspection of each of them separately, that is to say, of the hair, the countenance, the eyebrows, the mouth, the lips, and other features, as well as the symmetry of these with each other, estimate their value at sixteen, seventeen, eighteen, or twenty, or more carats, according to the greater or lesser degree of beauty. The number required by the Great Khan, at the rates, perhaps, of twenty or twenty-one carats, to which their commission was limited, is then selected from the rest, and they are conveyed to his court."

This selection is followed by another, Polo told us, wherein each of the concubines is turned over to "certain elderly ladies of the palace, whose duty it is to observe them attentively during the course of the night, in order to ascertain that they have not any concealed imperfections, that they sleep tranquilly, do not snore, have sweet breath, and are free from unpleasant scent in any part of the body." Those candidates who pass this filter "are divided into parties of five, each taking turn for three days and three nights, in his majesty's interior apartment, where they are to perform every service that is required of them, and he does with them as he likes."

While one group of five administered to Kublai's erotic needs, another group waited outside the bedchamber to bring food or drink or anything else the emperor may have desired, so that waiting upon the emperor was done exclusively by these women especially selected for their beauty and smell. Those who fell below the imperial standard were given some other task in the palace, like dressmaking or cookery, and when some male member of the imperial household desired to take a wife, he was given one of these, the emperor's discards.

In conventional histories, Marco Polo's *Travels* is said to have awakened an awareness of a wealthy and civilized domain in the East, and that awareness, in turn, stimulated the explorations of the Renaissance. Isn't it likely that Polo stimulated as well a certain vision of the East that would awaken the desire of European men to become little emperors themselves, with the sensual advantages such a position accrued? The Venice that Polo returned to at the very end of the thirteenth century was not lacking in royal sumptuousness, but it was a society in which, officially at least, sex was a sin. But Polo's matter-of-fact description of Kublai Khan's harem carried with it no moral judgment, no censure. Whereas in the West, sex was an illicit pleasure or at best a pleasure sanctioned for the exclusive purpose of procreation, and pleasure itself was deemed corrosive of godliness, in the East, he seemed to be saying, sex was the natural and unquestioned accompaniment of power. One can also imagine that the very idea of being serviced night after night by five of the greatest beauties of the realm had a kind of dreamlike quality, an aspect of the same earthly paradise that Brian the English teacher found in twenty-first-century Shanghai. Most important, perhaps, figures like Mandeville and Polo established the image of the East as a place where young women were set aside exclusively for the pleasure of men.

There were, of course, always women in Western society whose purpose was to serve men, whether they were mistresses or prostitutes, high-class courtesans or streetwalkers. The difference is not that sex was available in the East and not in the West. To those with power or the ability to pay, sex outside marriage has always been available to men the world over, in the fourteenth century as well as in the twenty-first. It was Polo's stripping of the emperor's concubines of anything sinful or illicit that was the difference. The historian Simon Schama, writing about Dutch prostitution in the seventeenth century, talked of the brothel, which is a kind of democratized, commercialized harem, as the opposite of home, a wicked world parallel to the good world of normal domesticity. "The procuresses were the antimothers: their wrinkles those of evil rather than piety, their prayers to Satan rather than God. And the girls themselves made up a kind of antifamily lodged in an antihome where they unlearned all the lessons which the bona fide home was organized to instill."

What Polo established was the opposite idea, the Eastern harem as a natural extension of home, the whore made part of the family, wherein each woman served according to her abilities, the most beautiful serving sexually, the less so cooking dinner or sewing clothes. In the seventeenth-century Holland described by Schama, the servant girl was a kind of subversive inside the home, a likely seducer of the master of the household, who had to be watched. Polo's description implies a harmonious arrangement innocent of the intrigue, the competition for the emperor's favor, and the plotting of consorts on behalf of one's sons that are recounted in other descriptions of the Eastern harem. In his idealized account, there were none of the dangers of the sort Schama described to be wary of. In the West, utopia involved a world of spirit without flesh; in the East, it was a place where the flesh rotated every three days.

Europe remained fascinated with the harem for centuries. Various travelers tried to ferret out what were deemed to be its secrets, though nobody ever really told more about it than Polo, who, in any case, revealed the major one—namely, that harems existed, that at the heart of power in the East lay a dreamily sensuous establishment where men took their pleasure untroubled by religious or other moral scruples.

Yangsook

IF YOU ARE A MAN whose taste in women runs to the slim and delicate, you couldn't do much better than Yangsook, a thirty-seven-year-old Korean woman now living in New York. She is pretty, demure, talented, and intelligent. During years in her native South Korea, she had a successful career as a cartoon animator. If your children watch *SpongeBob SquarePants* or other offerings on the Cartoon Network, they have seen her animations.

Yangsook moved to New York in 2006 after a failed marriage back home that is mostly a tale of thwarted aspirations and disappointed love. But her story also provides an illustration of the reason some Asian women find it to their advantage to enter into relations with an American or European man. However, don't flatter yourself, Mr. America. It isn't that women like Yangsook are running to you because of your superior charm or manliness; it's that they are running away, both from somebody else and from a persistent tradition, an old-fashioned attitude, that modern women like her find deeply unsatisfactory.

In Yangsook's case, what was unsatisfactory involved what might have seemed a perfect situation. She comes from a middle-class family in Seoul, and a few years before she came to the United States, she married a Korean man of about her age who had been to a university in the United States. It wasn't a marriage of tremendous passion, though Yangsook was ready to give her all to it. For five years, while her future husband was a student in America, they had kept in touch by e-mail and phone. Then, suddenly, the young man came home for a brief vacation, and Yangsook learned two things from him: his father, a businessman whom she greatly admired, was sick with a fatal blood disease, and her boyfriend wanted to marry her.

She was somewhat surprised by the suddenness of his proposal, coming after five years. But she accepted it. For one thing, she loved him. "He was good," she told me. "He was gentle. And also I was getting older." In addition, she would be marrying into a wealthy and prominent family, and that pleased her parents. So, wearing a white dress, she got married in church.

But Yangsook's marriage was, she soon learned, far from the romantic ideal. It turns out that her husband, though bright and good and American educated to boot, had very old-fashioned ideas about the place and role of a wife. He had decided, in an act of traditional filial loyalty, to marry Yangsook because he felt it his duty to produce a daughter-in-law for his revered father before he died, and time was of the essence. In another act of filial loyalty, he decided to begin studying medicine in Korea, in a city somewhat distant from his parents' home, so that he could acquire the skills to treat his father. While he was away at school, he made it clear to Yangsook that he expected her to live with his parents and help care for his sick father.

It was not the first time Yangsook had been expected to sacrifice her own interests for the sake of a Korean man. For years, she had worked to earn money to achieve her dream of going to art school. She knew that she had some talent, and indeed she had taught herself to draw well enough to get a job as a world-class animator, but she wanted formal training. She had an older brother, however, who had an opportunity to study in America. Yangsook had to forsake her dream because there wasn't enough money in her family to send both children to school. Rather, her parents asked her to give her brother some of the money she had earned so that he could take it to America with him. She never went to art school.

Now Yangsook speaks with resignation about the traditional roles assigned to men and women in Korea. She believes that things have changed in the past decade or so. Educated Korean men in their twenties are much more like their American counterparts than men twenty years older—willing to help with housework, see their wives have careers, and be involved in child care. And perhaps things have changed for women too, in the sense that a young Korean woman, urban and educated like Yangsook, wouldn't accept without protest the role that Yangsook accepted. When her new husband determined that she should stay in his parents' house to help her in-laws, she agreed. "I felt it was my duty," she said. For three years, until her father-in-law passed away, she lived in her in-laws' grand house, rarely even seeing her husband. During that time, she played the obedient daughter-in-law, except that she insisted on continuing to work at an animation studio, refusing the family's requests that she stay at home full-time. Her in-laws couldn't understand why she wanted to work. After all, she didn't have to. The issue was a sign of the cultural gap not only between her and her husband's family but also between many educated middle-class Korean women and the demands of a society with two entirely contradictory messages: that women are equal to men and that they are required, nonetheless, to accept the duties of traditional family life.

Another sign of cultural difference appeared when Yangsook's mother-in-law began criticizing her for failing to have any children before the death of the family's patriarch. Yangsook replied sensibly enough, "How do you expect me to get pregnant when I see my husband so seldom?" But the blame in matters like this is always placed on the wife, never on the adored family prince. Neighbors whispered about Yangsook's failure to produce children. She felt unjustly treated and sad.

Then, even when her father-in-law's death freed her of the obligation of caring for him, her husband still wanted her to stay at his mother's house. He was continuing his studies, living in a dormitory room that was too small for them. Why this preference? Yangsook never knew. Was her husband in love with another woman? Did he have a mistress? Evidently he was sexually uninterested in his wife, but in a society where sex remains a covert and awkward subject, this was not a matter that a young couple could talk about openly and frankly.

Yangsook decided to ask for a divorce, which she was able to get, despite the opposition of her husband and his family, after a three-year struggle. And she applied for admission to a beauticians school in New York. Bruised by competition from both computer-made animations and animators in China and India, the animation business was shrinking in Korea, and Yangsook didn't know how long she would have a job there. She also felt that Korean society didn't offer hopeful prospects for a woman in her mid-thirties trying to make a new start.

"There aren't very many men in Korea who are willing to marry a divorced woman," she said. She believes that while things are changing, the rules in Korea are still stacked against women, though the situation is a bit complicated. Korea, the only Asian country with a Christian majority, is one of the world's most conservative in matters of sex. In 2007, forty-seven people went to prison for violating the country's laws against adultery, most of them men sued for infidelity by their wives. The same year, a famous soap opera actress, Ok So-ri, caused a sensation when she admitted to an affair with a friend of her equally famous husband, also a soap opera actor. But while the husband sued for divorce, Ok herself went to court to challenge the constitutionality of the adultery regulation, which, though generally seen as protecting women, she saw as an unjust intrusion on the rights of women to govern their own sex lives. Ok lost badly, though. The courts upheld the anti-adultery law in 2008, and late that year, she was convicted of the upheld offense and given a six-month suspended sentence. In October 2008, Korea's most popular actress, Choi Jin Sil, killed herself, in part, it seems, because after getting divorced in 2002, movie and TV directors would no longer hire her. To Yangsook the prejudice against divorced women was oppressive and inescapable.

So, Yangsook moved to New York and enrolled in a skin-care and massage-therapy institute. The truth is that she is a little lonely in New York, where she lives modestly and alone. She has some savings from her days working as an animator, but she has to be careful with money, and New York is expensive. Her English is not fluent, but it is serviceable and getting better every day. It's good enough for her to form friendships in America and to carry on a courtship, if she were to meet somebody she liked, which she hasn't so far.

She's a lovely woman, and perhaps one of these days some lucky man is going to win her heart. But at the moment that idea seems to Yangsook like a distant possibility. Though she's studying to be a beautician, she has rediscovered her original ambition. "Since I came to New York, I've gone to a lot of museums and galleries," she said. "It's fantastic. It made me dream again about becoming an artist." It's not a dream that would be encouraged by Korean tradition. Her parents, who want her back home, are against it. At thirty-seven, she's deemed too old to be going to school. But in her spare time, she is studying for the Test of English as a Foreign Language, which she has to pass in order to be admitted to an American art school.

When asked about her aspirations in her private life, she said that she is still sad about the failure of her marriage in Korea and not sure when she'll be open to a serious relationship with somebody else.

She might change her mind about this. It would depend on the character of any would-be suitor, his power to persuade her that another marriage wouldn't be a harmful mistake. And she has an open mind, is willing to give a chance to any man she loves, whatever his nationality. But at the moment, Yangsook said, she is doubtful that whomever she marries will be a Korean.

CHAPTER THREE

That Cad Ludovico

IT WAS IN THE VERY EARLY YEARS of the sixteenth century, with the travel adventures of Ludovico de Varthema, an Italian in the service of the king of Portugal, that a few of the motifs that would later reappear throughout the erotic history of the East and the West were introduced into Western literature, stimulating the already active Western imagination. Ludovico went from what is now Saudi Arabia to the Indonesian archipelago, stopping early on in Aden, on the south coast of the Arabian Peninsula. There he became embroiled in a romantic interlude with the queen of the realm, which serves as a kind of template, a narrative archetype for subsequent encounters.

Much occurs in Ludovico's tale, including an inversion of the most fundamental of human relationships, that of the love between a man and a woman. Or, to put this differently, Ludovico, who found himself in dire straits, abandoned all the concepts of chivalrous honor that might have bound him in the West. He became an early example of what is to follow: the Western man behaving in Asia in a fashion that would be unacceptable back home.

In the flourishing world of Renaissance humanism that Ludovico came from, the official doctrine governing matters of love and sex was that of the Catholic Church, leavened by the heritage of medieval chivalry, though many conflicting attitudes coexisted. A generation after Ludovico, the irreverent and scabrous French author François Rabelais would write parody-filled masterpieces that were proscribed by the church, so if Ludovico himself was not a paragon of knightly loyalty, he would not be alone. The world was divided between the sexually righteous and the sexually rakish, and Ludovico decidedly belonged in the latter category, and he had to have known it. According to the Western ideal, in which Ludovico was certainly schooled, the knight—the *cavaliere* in Italian—strove to win his lady's love in battle, gladly risking his life for her sake, accepting sacrifice if necessary, at least in theory. "The knight and his lady, that is to say, the hero who serves for love, this is the primary and invariable motif from which erotic fantasy will always start," Johan Huizinga wrote. "It is sensuality transformed into the craving for self-sacrifice, into the desire of the male to show his courage, to incur danger, to be strong, to suffer and to bleed before his lady-love."

The chivalrous ideal got its most common expression in the medieval tournament, with its aristocratic sports like jousting, in which two armor-clad men rush at each other on horses with lances pointed at each other's breasts while some fair damsel looks on breathlessly from the castle ramparts. One suffered for love; indeed, the willingness to suffer extended to the desire to save the fair virgin from great danger—"defending imperiled virginity," as Huizinga put this. In its fairy-tale version, it was the lady in the tower—Rapunzel being the most famous example—rescued from the wicked witch by a handsome prince. Of course, the ideal and the reality were not identical, and for those who were not knights, especially the bourgeois inhabitants of the towns, such activities as jousting and noble suffering for one's ladylove all seemed ridiculous upper-class affectations, and they seem a bit ridiculous to us in our world today, where chivalry has become a Dark Ages relic.

In that context, Ludovico's account of his amorous adventures, which take place in a sultan's court, comes across as a rather modern parody of courtly love, in which the only dragon to be slain, witch to be outwitted, or rival to be knocked from his horse is precisely the danger of being ensnared by the lady's love. He depicted himself as a character in an adventure story in which the hero has been liberated from the virtues of love, honor, and fidelity and is free to save his own neck no matter what—a narrative vastly less romantic, but psychologically far more realistic, than the narrative of chivalrous self-sacrifice.

Moreover, Ludovico's East is a place where virtue can be dispensed with altogether. It is a domain where the constraints on behavior, imposed by chivalry and bolstered by the church, are replaced by a freedom to do as one pleased. From Ludovico in what he called Arabia Felix to American soldiers in Indochina was a long and twisted route of nearly five hundred years. The places and the times were as different as the styles and the languages of the women and the men. But the essential ingredients, which include the elimination of restrictions and the freedom to do what one can't do back home, are common to both. In Ludovico's amorous adventure, moreover, we find other ingredients that supposedly did not exist in the West, not least of them a hot-blooded, highly sexual woman who, in making no secret of her passion for the presumably superior Western man, stands at the opposite extreme of the chaste, pure, essentially sexless idealized female love object of Europe.

LUDOVICO, BORN ABOUT 1470, is best known as the first non-Muslim to make the pilgrimage to Mecca and Medina, which he did by becoming a member of the Mamluk garrison that guarded the caravan from Damascus in 1503. He must have converted to Islam in order to pose as a Mamluk, the Mamluks being foreign slaves captured by some sultan or sheikh and, after converting to Islam, trained to be soldiers, the most famous of whom became a powerful military caste in their own right, ruling Egypt from the thirteenth to the sixteenth century. One wonders whether, in order for Ludovico to become a Mamluk, he would have undergone circumcision, an excruciating procedure for a grown man, especially before the invention of local anesthetics. He didn't say. But if he managed to pose as a Muslim with an uncut member, his charade would not only have been highly dangerous but also consistent with a more general knack for dissimulation, which he practiced whenever he saw an interest in doing so. Whether involving circumcision or not, Ludovico's conversion to Islam would have been no more sincere than his later protestations of love and fidelity to an Arabian queen.

Whatever his personal qualities, Ludovico produced descriptions of the holiest places of Islam that are deemed by experts to be remarkably accurate. But Mecca and Medina were only the beginning of his great adventure. From Mecca, he went to Jidda for a boat that would take him down the Red Sea and through Bab el Mandeb to Aden, where he embarked on a ship that went first to the Persian Gulf and then to India. He spent many months exploring South and Central Asia, including what is now Afghanistan and Iran. He returned to India, went to Ceylon, and sailed on to Sumatra, Java, and Borneo, the farthest points east that any Italian voyager had reached until that time. He turned back west, visited the Malabar Coast of India, became a soldier in the Portuguese garrison at Cannanore, crossed the Arabian Sea to Tanganyika, went on to Mozambique, which was already a Portuguese outpost, and finally returned to Europe via the Cape of Good Hope and the Azores.

It was quite a trip, and Ludovico was well aware of the interest it could generate, publishing his *Journey of Ludovico de Varthema of Bologna* in Rome in 1510, giving an account of the territories he visited that, according to the great nineteenth-century British explorer Richard Burton, put him in "the foremost rank of the old Oriental travelers." His book went through dozens of editions in all the major European languages, which means that many literate Europeans became familiar with a savory tale that prefigured a great deal in the subsequent erotic and romantic history of East and West. That tale unfolded after Ludovico left Mecca and stopped in Aden on his way to India.

Aden, which is now the capital city of Yemen, was a lively port of call in what Ludovico, following the Romans, knew as Arabia Felix, a country, he said, "subject to a Moorish lord" and "very fruitful and good, like Christian countries." On his second day in Aden, "some Moors" overheard one of his companions call Ludovico a "Christian dog," whereupon Ludovico found himself accused of being a spy for Portugal, which had recently seized some native ships in the Arabian Sea. Ludovico was put into irons and, the sultan being absent, taken "with great violence" to the palace of the next-highest authority, the vice sultan. He was held there, by his own count, for sixty-five days, until after the sultan returned from one of his many wars, when he was taken into the royal presence for an interview.

Ludovico, who had learned some of the local language, told the sultan that he was a Roman but had become a Mamluk in Cairo and, having been to Mecca and Medina, was now "a good Moor" and the sultan's slave. But when the sultan asked him to recite the Muslim creed—meaning, probably, some lines from the Koran—he was unable to do so, and the sultan had him imprisoned in a castle in the city, which Ludovico called Rhada, probably the current city of Rada'a in Yemen, the location of one of the country's most famous medieval ruins.

Two days after Ludovico's unsuccessful audience, the sultan left at the head of his army to make war on the rival sultan of Sana'a, and Ludovico interrupted the story of his imprisonment to provide a detailed description of the army, its shields, uniforms, and arms. When he returned to his own predicament, he introduced himself as one of the first Europeans in history, at least since the fall of the Roman Empire, to make a sexual conquest of the East.

Ludovico, it can be assumed, was in dire straits, having faked his conversion to Islam, having lied about it, and consequently having been imprisoned by a local tyrant, who had no reason to show him mercy. But, fortunately for Ludovico, he was not chained to the wall of some stinking dungeon, forgotten by everyone but the guard who brought him his bread and water. He had the opportunity to exercise in the courtyard of the castle, beneath the windows, as Ludovico described it, of "one of the three wives of the Sultan, who remained there with twelve or thirteen very beautiful damsels, whose color was more near to black than otherwise." Ludovico recounted that he had two companions in prison and that together they determined that one of them "should pretend to be mad, in order the better to assist one another." When it came Ludovico's turn to be mad, a task he found "exhausting," he noted that his performance attracted the attention of the queen and her attendants, whom he saw watching from their windowed vantage point above.

Knowing that the queen was looking on, Ludovico displayed his mad courage, strength, and audacity. He even parodied the sultan's interrogation of him by commanding a sheep to recite the "Muslim creed" and then breaking its legs to punish it when it didn't respond. He cudgeled a Jew, Ludovico said, leaving this evidently less-than-human person for dead, and he got into other fights, all the while dragging his heavy chains behind him until, finally, the queen had him brought to the palace and placed in a chamber, still with his leg irons attached, and she began a close, admiring examination of him.

"She, being a clever woman, saw that I was not at all mad," Ludovico wrote, "and began to make much of me; ordered a good bed after their fashion to be given me, and sent me plenty of good food. The following day she had prepared for me a bath according to their custom, with many perfumes, and continued these caresses for twelve days. Afterwards, she began to come down to visit me every night at three or four o'clock and always brought me good things to eat."

Soon the queen was showing signs of love for the strange European prisoner. She looked at him, Ludovico wrote, "as though I had been a nymph, and uttering a lamentation to God in this manner: . . . 'O God, thou has created this man white like the sun; thou has created my husband black, my son also is black, and I am black. Would to God that this man were my husband. Would to God that I might have a son like this man.' "

Overcome by emotion, the besotted queen wept. She passed her hands over Ludovico's body, promising him that when the sultan returned, she would see to it that his shackles were taken off. Then, on the next night, she offered herself to Ludovico altogether. If she didn't appeal to him, she said, he could have one of her maidservants. When Ludovico replied that accepting her offer would get his head cut off, she assured him that he was safe, "for I will stake my own head for your safety." But Ludovico—at least in the version of the story that he offered to his European readers—declined the queen's offer of love, thinking to himself that though she would give him gifts of gold, silver, and horses if he accepted, she would also provide him with a guard of ten black slaves, and then he would never be able to leave Arabia Felix.

"I should never have been able to escape from the country, for all Arabia Felix was informed of me, that is to say, at the passes," Ludovico wrote. "And if I had once run away, I could not have escaped death, or chains for life." In that sentence, Ludovico established a kind of complicity with his European readers. The queen may have fallen in love with Ludovico, but while the queen was sincere, she was naïve in the fashion of primitive people. Ludovico, by contrast, was sophisticated, but he needed to be deceitful, as when he told the sultan that he had become a Moor. By falling in love with him, the queen saved him from a lifetime in an Arab prison, but her love threatened a prison of another sort, and Ludovico played for time, looking for a way out.

Finally, the sultan returned and Ludovico was granted an audience with him. The queen, who was present, demanded his release. When the sultan agreed and asked him where he wanted to go, Ludovico pretended to want nothing more than to stay in Arabia Felix and serve as the sultan's slave for life. The queen took Ludovico away. Once again, she showered him with kisses and she told him, "If thou wilt be good thou shalt be a lord." Ludovico engaged in his usual strategy. He told the queen that he was too weak and hungry to think of love. The queen brought him "eggs, hens, pigeons, pepper, cinnamon, cloves, and nutmegs" every day. He went on a hunting expedition with the queen, and when they returned, he pretended illness for eight days. Finally, he told her that, as "a promise to God and to Mahomet," he was obligated to visit a holy man in Aden. The queen was pleased with this show of religious devotion, and so, guileless as always, she sent Ludovico off with a camel and twenty-five ducats of gold.

Once in Aden, Ludovico contacted the captain of a foreign ship and arranged, after a further tour of Arabia Felix, to go with him to his next destination, Persia. Needless to say, the queen never saw him again.

LUDOVICO'S TRAVELS, in the first years of the sixteenth century, took place early in the age of exploration, just a few years after Vasco da Gama opened the sea route around the Cape of Good Hope to India and a decade or so before another great contemporary, Ferdinand Magellan, embarked on a mission to circumnavigate the globe. It was, in other words, the very beginning of the colonial era, when Portugal was setting up trading posts on the Malabar Coast as well as in China, Japan, and South America, though nearly another century would pass before the British East India Company was formed, and it would take yet another century for Europe to achieve its territorial conquest and political dominion of the East. And yet already Ludovico's picaresque tale has a paradigmatic quality to it. How many stories would there be in the centuries to come of the Western adventurer who wins the love of a winsome and exotic princess? Pocahontas and John Smith come to mind as a New World variation on this theme. Both the American Indian princess and the unnamed queen of Arabia Felix save the neck of a strange foreigner by interceding with the ruler, a father in one case, a husband in another, and both of them are willing to offer up their own head to guarantee the safety of the man they would save.

How much truth there is to either of those tales is open to question, but surely whatever actual events may have inspired them, they are projections of a particularly Western erotic fantasy. Chinese literature, drama, and opera are full of stories of imperial princesses being sent to faraway and barbarian places to placate the animosity of dangerous potentates. There are many stories of women in Asia who sacrificed themselves for love, refusing, in a common variation on this theme, to serve as an emperor's concubine out of loyalty to the ordinary man they truly love. But there are no stories of Asian men who win the affections of some Western princess. One reason is that Asians simply didn't explore. They didn't travel to the West. They essentially weren't interested in it, except when it concerned their foreign policy. And the men didn't express longings for Western women. Many European books purported to reveal the secrets of the Asian harem, but no Asian books pried into the love lives of the kings of France and England. In the Western imagination—as, for example, in *Madama Butterfly*—the Eastern woman falls for the virile, white-skinned Western man, not the other way around. In the collective mind of Europe and America, it would seem implausible, if not entirely impossible, for there to be a story of, say, a Frenchwoman who falls in love with a Persian or Arab adventurer (except perhaps one of fabulous wealth and royal standing) and remains loyal to the point of self-destruction when he turns out to be unfaithful to her.

Ludovico de Varthema's tale in all these ways anticipates the inner erotic workings of the experience of Westerners in the East. There's many a European or American man who spent a few years of his bachelorhood in Asia and left a local girl behind when it came time for him to go home. He might have professed undying love for this girl, and his expression might have been quite sincere because she was charming and beautiful and had rescued him from his loneliness, his isolation, his sense of not belonging, his sexual frustration. But then, after a year or two, he needed to return to what he saw as his real life, and his Asian companion didn't have a place in this life plan.

This situation is embedded in Western culture. Nearly a century after *Madama Butterfly* was first performed, a latter-day reincarnation,

called *Miss Saigon,* in which a Saigon bar girl reenacts the fate of Puccini's tragic Japanese heroine, opened on Broadway. It seemed a credi-
ble story, given the amorous entanglements of Americans in Vietnam
in the 1960s and early 1970s, the kind of story—minus the bar girl's
self-sacrifice when her former lover returns with the American wife he
has married in the meantime—that could really have happened.

Ludovico's adventure with the queen of Arabia Felix is a predecessor
to these modern stories of tragic love. Indeed, it is possible to believe, if
there is any truth at all to his story, that the Arabian queen's love for
Ludovico was just as dangerous in its way as the virtuous Cio-Cio-San's
love for the adventurer Pinkerton in *Madama Butterfly,* because it
involved a risky, possibly even mortal act of disloyalty to the sultan.
Ludovico himself didn't tell us whether the queen endangered herself
by showering him with "caresses," though surely this act of infidelity
would have compromised her with the sultan, whose seraglio she
inhabited. Ludovico's implicit assumption is that the queen could do
what she wanted, perhaps because the sultan had other wives and often
went off to war, but this assumption had to be wrong. In falling for
Ludovico, the queen risked sacrificing herself, as other Asian women
later were willing to do for the sake of other Western paramours who
had journeyed from afar into their lives. And yet after his escape from
her embrace, Ludovico showed no concern for her. Certainly, he didn't
express any curiosity about her fate; he didn't mention her again in his
Travels. Surely, at the very least, the queen, who saved his life, would
have felt the heartbreak of his disappearance, as well as sadness at his
deceitfulness and ingratitude, but Ludovico showed no concern for
that either.

The queen's love was for him purely instrumental. He exploited it
with false declarations and promises in order to escape his predicament,
and who can blame him? The early Western explorations of Asia
involved great danger to the solitary travelers in the East, and therefore
we forgive them whatever trickery, flattery, or false shows of love they
resorted to in order to surmount that danger. Who among us in hostile
situations abroad would have behaved differently?

Ludovico's story assumes the desirability of the Western man who
traveled in Asia. He gave, perhaps for the first time, implicit expression
to the idea of the superior masculinity of the Westerner: he attracted

the attention of the beauteous sultana with his physical prowess, his daring parody of the sultan, and, not least, the whiteness of his skin. Even before his encounter with the sultana of Arabia Felix, Ludovico had noted "the partiality of the women of Arabia for white men." Later the assumption was that the masculine West, materially advanced, white, and Christian, would seduce the East and that, but for a few extreme cases, like those in *Madama Butterfly* and *Miss Saigon,* the East would be better off for it. The East would become Christian through the teachings of missionaries. It would become materially progressive through trade. And it would become democratic as a result of Western political tutelage. There is tremendous arrogance in this vision, a kind of sentimental imperialism to accompany gunboat imperialism. It's the idea that the West will get control, and it will also get the girl, because it is better than the East.

But there was more to Ludovico's story, especially in his pose of Muslim piety, in his false declarations of love for his savior, the sultan's wife, and in his frank acknowledgment of his deceitfulness to his European readers, who, he knew, would not condemn him for it. What mattered here was not the sultana's broken heart but the safety of our hero-adventurer. And in this there is a kind of inversion of the usual notions of morality, an acceptance of the fact that in the East, which, in any case, was seen to be full of artifice, superstition, and deceit, it was all right to lie—in matters religious and sentimental. When he journeyed in the East, the Western man was liberated from the chivalrous ideal of true love, even as, in *Madama Butterfly* and *Miss Saigon,* the woman temporarily loved is both admired and pitied by Westerners for remaining true to her love for a false man. In the West, the dominant tale had to do with the gallant knight's rescue of a damsel in distress locked like Rapunzel in a stone tower by an evil witch. In Ludovico's case, it is the damsel in the tower who rescues the knight in distress, and she is rewarded for this with a certain mockery, certainly not with enduring love.

There is an alloy of poignancy in Ludovico's story too, and more than an alloy of poignancy in the many stories, like Cio-Cio-San and Pinkerton's, that his anticipates. Ludovico could have stayed in Arabia Felix enjoying the life of an honorary prince, provided with "gold and silver, horses and slaves, and whatever I had desired," and Pinkerton could have lived forever there in the house overlooking Nagasaki Harbor where Cio-Cio-San had spent her years pining for him. Ludovico passed up a prince's life lived with a queen and her twelve or thirteen "very beautiful damsels" because real life for him involved being a Christian European and an explorer, not a pampered man kept like a prized falcon in a Moor's palace. The queen should have known that, and maybe she did but made her gesture of love anyway.

And so it might also be said that for the Asian women centuries later who defied parental or societal requirements of virginity by giving themselves to a young Western man, a student perhaps, a young businessman, a soldier, or just someone enjoying what the college kids call "a year off." Those women, too, should have known what they were doing, and maybe they did too, even though after a time the young man went home, and like the queen of Aden, the Asian women often never heard from him again.

It is of course almost de rigueur to view stories like Ludovico's as fantasies, projections onto an Eastern canvas of the Western man's erotic imagination, particularly that part about the assumed superior masculinity of the European. Certainly later this assumption is deemed to be a private enactment of the demonstrable military superiority of Western civilization. Why, after all, would a woman married to a king and surrounded by twelve or thirteen maidservants fall for a shackled adventurer over whom her husband enjoyed the power of life and death? Ludovico may have been strong and daring and perhaps even handsome, but in the eyes of the queen there should have been nothing intrinsically superior about him.

One reason could simply have been the boredom of life in the seraglio, where, as we will see, life for a country's most beautiful virgins could entail a hellish sort of uneventfulness. Ludovico's sultana made mention of her black son, which means, obviously, that at one time or another she was called to the sultan's bed and, having produced an heir, would have acquired considerable prestige at court. But she may no longer have been called to the sultan's bed, instead passing her days in pampered monotony. The arrival of the swashbuckling Ludovico could in this sense have been just the thing to reawaken desire in a healthy young woman.

There are other possibilities, including Ludovico's assertion about the whiteness of his skin, though that too seems to be more Western male fantasy than reality, especially in those pre-colonial days, before it had become common in Europe to talk unabashedly about European colonizers as the "dominant race." Pigmentation is probably not the reason for Ludovico's appeal to the sultana, but it is certainly possible that he did appeal to her. He was an exciting figure. He may have been, in her eyes, exotic and manly. In other words, the notion that Eastern women fall irrationally for Western men may not be purely an operatic Western fantasy. It may, at least in some instances, be true—and in enough instances to make it a social and romantic pattern.

I don't know about Ludovico, but certainly in later centuries a young American or European living in Asia did have enough special appeal to make a story like *Madama Butterfly* seem plausible and, because plausible, all that much more poignant. In our enlightened era, the Western male view of the Asian woman as pliant, submissive, and sultry is deemed a racial stereotype, and it is. But there seems to be a reciprocal stereotype in the Eastern woman's view of Western men as representatives of a zone of freedom unavailable to them at home, as less bound by stultifying convention, as more open to a woman's possibility.

In any case, Ludovico's story is an early suggestion that the love affair between the West and the East was not one-sided, involving the passive Eastern woman in confrontation with the exploitative, powerful, and assertive Western male. There were initiatives taken and fantasies fulfilled on both sides.

INTERLUDE 2

"Just a Page in the Book of Your Life"

THERE WAS ONCE A YOUNG WOMAN in Taipei in the days before the United States established diplomatic ties with mainland China, back when American students had to go to Taiwan if they wanted to study Chinese. She was called Miss Lu, and she worked in the Ministry of Education helping Western students get the student identifications that were required for long-term visas. One such student, a young American, fell for her utterly. He found excuse after excuse to go to the Ministry of Education to conduct some item of administrative business with her as he strove to get his visa. She seemed, he thought, or maybe he only hoped, happy to see him, though he couldn't be sure. One day when he knew that his papers would be ready, he went to her office for a final visit, arriving just as the day was coming to an end, figuring that Miss Lu would be leaving work at that hour and it would seem natural for him to ask her to go someplace with him for a cup of tea.

The plan worked perfectly in a way that such plans seldom do.

"This is our last official excuse to meet," Miss Lu said as the two walked out of the office building and into the swirl of Taipei's street life, and the young man's heart leaped.

He was thrilled with the prospect that suddenly seemed to have opened up before him. Behind that official demeanor, behind those eyes that betrayed nothing, there was a mind that had been getting it all along. Miss Lu accepted his invitation to tea even though, she told him, she had never gone out with a boy by herself before. She was twenty-three or so, an age when, especially in those years, the early 1970s, casual sex had become a common practice among many American women. So Miss Lu and the American student sat opposite each other in a teahouse, and he, already envisaging an end to his loneliness, not to mention romantic and erotic evenings with this woman, asked her if she would go to the movies with him the next night.

"Oh, no!" Miss Lu said. She had thought constantly of him, she admitted. She had written page after page about him in her diary, but she confessed that to him with an air of gloom, as if it were bad news.

"But that's wonderful," he said, revealing how he had tried so hard to manufacture small administrative misunderstandings so that he would have to take the bus across town, to the Ministry of Education, to see her again, asking questions whose answers he already knew. It was a moment of both exhilarating frankness and disappointment. Why, if she felt as he did, wouldn't she go out with him?

A few years before, while still a college student, this same young man had been in Japan on an exchange program, and there, at a student hostel, he had met a pretty young woman named Isumi. He paid court to her and she seemed to respond, but when he tried to kiss her, she pushed him away.

This young man had not long before been taken by a male Japanese acquaintance to a steam bath in the Shinjuku district of Tokyo. There, in what, for a young American, was a place of unimaginable exoticism, he had been ministered to by an attractive though not really beautiful woman. "Are you virgin?" the woman had asked, and then, without waiting for an answer, she had anointed his rampant member with warm oil, thereby inducing in him the most pleasurable sensation he had yet experienced in his short and uneventful life.

The lesson then, as he faced the mildly indignant Isumi, was that, as in other cultures of the harem, there are girls for pleasure and there are nice girls, and Isumi coolly declared herself to be in the latter category. "I am a Japanese girl," she said in her excellent English, "and you are in Japan."

And then again, in that teahouse in Taipei, the young American scholar was receiving a similar lesson.

"You are only a visitor here, and one day you will leave," Miss Lu said. "For you, I would be just a page in the book of your life, but for me you would be my whole book."

That might sound like a line stolen from a soap opera script, but Miss Lu really said those exact, never to be forgotten words, and her sincerity gave them an aura of poetic depth and originality. Miss Lu said no and she meant no, but her resolve proved unequal to the task. One day in a local market, passing by the vendors of bananas and mangoes and music cassettes, the young man and Miss Lu saw each other, and they stopped to talk. He noticed that she had had her hair done and that she was dressed more stylishly than she had been in her dour office. They went someplace, to a coffee shop, and talked for a long time, and then the young man invited Miss Lu to his room, down a numbered alley off a street called Amoy Lane.

It was a small room, hardly large enough for two people, with a bed and a desk and a chair. A late-autumn chill was in the air. Miss Lu shivered as she sat on the bed, while the young man stuck to the chair, tormented by the question of what he should do next: move to the bed and risk a terrible embarrassment if Miss Lu rejected him, or accept the evidence of her voluntary presence in his room?

Every evening at that spot in Taipei, a vendor passed by the lane below the student's window, using a haunting minor-key chant to sell his offering of a traditional Taiwanese snack. "*Wu-xiang-cha-ye-dan*" went the hawker's lilting little song, sung in a tremulous tenor that started high and ended low, each syllable lengthened into a sustained sigh of regret: "*Fiiiiive-perfumes-tea-leaf-eeeeg.*" It was a chant that the young man would remember all his life, though he never heard it again after his year in Taipei. The vendor came, the chant drifted into the room, and our student and Miss Lu melted into each other on the room's narrow bed for a moment—or was it an hour?—of tenderly unconsummated intimacy. Afterward she told him that she would never see him again.

"But why not?" the young man cried, genuinely angry at what seemed to him a denial of the very beauty of life.

"Because after a year or so, you will leave and I will stay behind, and you will go on to the next girl, and I will be ruined," she said. Tears were in her eyes.

The young man could have yielded to the temptation to promise her everything on that afternoon when he was overwhelmed by desire and loneliness. He could have promised to take her with him when he left, or in the fashion of Ludovico de Varthema in his direr Arabia Felix straits, he could have promised to stay on in Taiwan forever. There were men who married their Taiwanese girlfriends, and a few even decided to stay on in Taiwan, where they are to this day. But he knew that he wouldn't be among them, and in this she was right. After his year or so was up, he would go home to prepare for a future in America, not Asia. For him, she would indeed have been just a page in his book. He desired her; he longed to have her company and to repeat over and over this molten moment in his room in Taipei. He even loved her and her sleek black hair and Eastern slenderness, her quiet intelligence, charm, her barely controlled passions, and even the breathless way she denied him, characteristics so different from those of the seemingly tougher, more blasé women he went to school with back home, but he loved her temporarily. He wouldn't take her with him when he left.

It was one of the conditions of the Western penetration of the East that many temporary sojourns called for temporary solace. As we will see, in places like Japan and India in the seventeenth to the nineteenth century, a sort of provisional marriage of a Western man with an Eastern woman emerged to satisfy the need for medium-term companionship and erotic pleasure. It was the principle that operated when Pinkerton took Cio-Cio-San to be his wife in Nagasaki, though Cio-Cio-San violated the terms of the deal by wishing for an enduring love. But that was then. By the time our student was on Taiwan, there were no temporary marriages anymore, though there was the unearned distinction that attached to being from the advanced and glamorous West, and there were plenty of broken promises too. Miss Lu in this sense was wiser than Cio-Cio-San and the queen of Arabia Felix.

"But we will have had this time together," the boy pleaded, trying to lure her into a temporary arrangement by using the argument of moral utilitarianism so common in the West at the time. "We can be happy now." She was unconvinced.

He never forgot Miss Lu, and perhaps she never forgot him. From time to time over the years—and this man is now in his mid-sixties—he contemplated with a light sort of melancholy the path that Miss Lu had invited him to take and that he had rejected, feeling as he did the melancholy he would have felt had he taken it. But after that one amorous late afternoon, accompanied by a vendor's chant about perfumed eggs on Amoy Lane, he never saw her again.

CHAPTER FOUR

The Harem in the Mind of the West

I N ABOUT 1668 the British diplomat Paul Rycaut published his book *The Present State of the Ottoman Empire,* which has remained ever since a prime source on the Ottomans.

Rycaut, who had been posted as British resident (a diplomatic agent) in several Middle Eastern countries, was regarded as his country's chief authority on the Turks, who controlled one of the largest empires in the world, certainly a rival in size and grandeur to the contemporaneous Qing dynasty of China. His book is readably encyclopedic, one of those systematic, earnestly pedantic travelogues of a sort that went out of fashion decades ago, and it is usefully replete with descriptions of Turkish politics, society, and customs. Rycaut is at the origin of the later vision of Turkey as the land of what came to be called Oriental despotism, to which, he believed, the Turks were naturally inclined. He influenced the great French philosopher Montesquieu, whose *Spirit of Laws,* so widely read among American revolutionaries like John Adams and Thomas Jefferson, divided the world into several types of government: tyranny (namely, Turkey), monarchy, and republic. Rycaut attributed Oriental despotism to a genetic disposition (though obviously he didn't use that phrase), which was in turn the product of the Turkish way of breeding. "The Grand Signior himself," Rycaut wrote, referring to the sultan ruling from Topkapi Palace in Constantinople, was "born of a Circassian Slave," since the Turks have "many or more Children by their Slaves than by their wives, which without question frames in them a Disposition of bearing the most Tyrannick Yoak, without the least reluctancy."

No doubt among the more avidly read pages of *The Present State of the Ottoman Empire* was Rycaut's description of the harem and the sex life the sultan, which, as the passage just cited indicates, he believed to be closely connected to the Ottomans' political culture. One might assume that people with experience of slavery would be the least likely to accept the "Tyrannick Yoak," but Rycaut evidently thought either that slaves are slaves because they are born that way or that they accept slavery and domination because their experience leads them to believe them inscribed in the natural order of things. In any case, in Turkey, where, as Rycaut noted, very few sultans procreated with their official wives, even the sultan was the son of a slave.

But there is more than a political conclusion here. Rycaut's description of the Ottoman Empire consists of an elaboration of a sensual and social world that must have seemed almost phantasmagoric to seventeenth-century Europeans, a world of a vast and opulent palace of brocade divans, velvet drapes, and marble parquet, whose parapets and balustrades overlooked the turquoise sea and whose very purpose was to permit the fulfillment of desires deemed sinful in the West. Earlier travelers like Marco Polo had written about the harem. With Rycaut, a European tradition of what might be called sensuous detailing began. He was among the first to display the sultan's seraglio as a world apart, with its pages, white eunuchs, black eunuchs, thousands of the most beautiful virgins of the empire, and above it all, the lucky sultan, for whose favor all those beautiful virgins eagerly competed.

> Whenever the Grand Signior has an Inclination to divert himself with some of those Lady's, all the Avenues of the Gardens are Beset by the eunuchs, at which time the Women call all the Dexterity they are Mistresses of, to draw the Grand Signior's Affection, either by wanton Postures and Dancing, or Amorous discourses to themselves.
>
> If he happens to pitch upon one for his Bedfellow, he goes into the Lady's Apartment, who there stand ready to receive him. He throws his Handkerchief to her, whom he has chosen. The Virgin kneeling down and kissing it, puts it in her Bosom, and after she has been washed, bathed and adorned with precious

Stones and rich Cloths, she is conducted by her Companions with Musick and Songs, to the Sultan's Bed Chamber, where being received by the Eunuch then in Waiting, she kneels before the Grand Signior, and then enters in at the feet of the bed, unless he be pleased to put her into the Bed another way.

Rycaut's account is full of additional titillating particulars, about how the women of the seraglio slept (in rooms in which every sixth bed was occupied by a eunuch), how they were trained in music and dance, and how they were acquired in the first place—most were simply the spoils of conquest, "of which are chosen the most beautiful and undoubted Virgins." Rycaut also established what would remain a standard feature of later accounts of the Turkish harem, that the Turks, particularly female Turks (because of the country's hot climate) were more sexually charged than Europeans (and therefore less civilized). The eunuchs were needed because the Turks, like the peoples of most other eastern provinces are "sensible of the Libidinous Inclinations of the women." Some of the more common of these inclinations were "unlawful," Rycaut wrote, especially lesbian love affairs among the virgins. In all, Rycaut said, there are about sixteen hundred virgins housed in the palace, who had little to do but hope against the odds to be the recipient of that fateful handkerchief and to land perhaps one, maybe more, nights in the sultan's bed, and—the ultimate achievement—bear a son for the sultan and thus rise to a vastly higher status.

Other accounts of the Turks are as genial as Rycaut's, seeing the sultan as both a capable and a romantic figure, an empire builder who happened also to lead a dreamy sex life. But particularly after the mid-fifteenth century, when the Ottomans conquered Constantinople, which, as the capital of the Eastern Roman Empire, had been an outpost of Christian civilization for centuries, a scurrilous and bigoted literature depicted the Turks as deviant and depraved. Martin Luther wrote that the Turks' "illicit sexual practices know no bounds." The Turks were reported by various travelers to engage regularly in bestiality—with female fish, according to one narrator—and to be massively addicted to sodomy, for which purpose, according to one writer, they castrated comely Christian boys and men "so not the slightest hint of masculinity appears on their body, and once healed, the arch-enemy uses these poor slaves for ignominious and sodomitical fornication."

The impulse in our post-Freudian age is to interpret this literature, whose ostensible purpose was to portray non-Christians as sexually depraved, as an expression of repressed homoerotic desire. It is a warning of what might happen if the "sodomitical" desires of Europeans were freed. It parallels another literature on the more terrifying Turkey that came after the Ottomans' seizure of Constantinople. As with the Tartars described by William of Rubrouck in the thirteenth century, there is no feminine imagery applied to the Ottomans of the sort that was hinted at by later travelers like Ludovico de Varthema and became a major feature of the West's image of the East once the former had succeeded in colonizing the latter. But the literature that demonized the Turks had one major element in common with the literature and art that portrayed the Ottomans in lush and desirably sensual ways: both depict the world where harems existed as erotic opposites of Europe, where monogamy, chastity, and the control of allegedly wicked impulses were the highest values. The Turkey of bestiality and sodomy was an image of hell on earth, a warning of what would happen when humankind gave in to base impulses. It was a place that might be immoral precisely because it gave free expression to the most fundamental desires.

The literature exemplified by Rycaut promised to disclose what was often called the secret of the harem. In fact, while there was really no secret of the harem, since its dual purpose, to provide pleasure to the sultan and heirs to his throne, was hardly unknown, it nonetheless had many meanings in Europe, including those in the numerous works of art and literature that it inspired. The play *Bajazet* by Jean Racine and Mozart's opera *Abduction from the Seraglio* use the seraglio and the Turkish court as settings for psychological drama and farce, respectively. But particularly after the seventeenth century, the scholar Leslie Peirce has written, the European image of the Ottoman sultan changed from one of admiration to one of contempt, Mozart notwithstanding. The sultan turned from great ruler and conqueror to "the embodiment of depraved tyranny, in whose moral degeneration the seductive and corrupting feature of the harem figured prominently." This was the case with regard not just to Turkey but to other countries of the greater

Middle East. For writers as varied as Montesquieu, in his *Persian Letters,* and Byron, in *Don Juan* and other poems, the harem was a powerful emblem of political tyranny and sexual domination, a warning of what the consequences would be if monarchy and conservative politics weren't curbed in Europe.

In a less politically charged fashion, the harem was an important theme in Western painting, from Ingres and Delacroix to the painter John Frederick Lewis and the cartoonist Thomas Rowlandson. Ingres, whose *Odalisque with a Slave* among his most celebrated paintings, returned to the harem and its decorated sensuality time and again.

Odalisque shows a woman whose alabaster skin indicates that she is a slave from one of the Caucasian provinces of the empire, her red hair cascading over her arm and onto a brocade bedcover. She is supine and naked but for a sheet of gauze draped casually over her hips, her arms thrown back over her head in a pose of submission to desire. Beyond her is a palatial décor, red column and drapery, an inlaid balustrade, and intricately painted walls. A black eunuch in turban and brocade

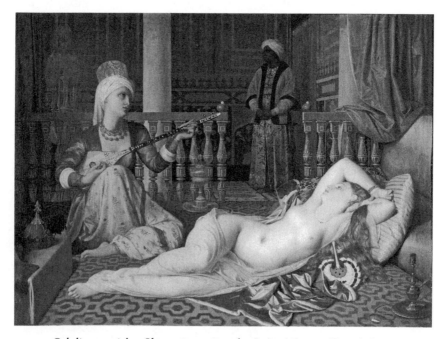

Odalisque with a Slave, 1839–1840, by Jean-Auguste-Dominique Ingres.

Harvard University Art Museums

robe stands guard in the near background, while seated at the foot of the bed another female slave, this one fully, luxuriantly clothed, plays a long-necked lute. It is an image of what one scholar called "cloistered sensuality." And because Ingres, like every man but the sultan and his eunuchs, was banned from the harem, forbidden on pain of death even from seeing a single one of the sultan's concubines, his *Odalisque,* like his many other harem paintings, is entirely imaginary. He "neither did what he made, nor saw what he thought," the Marquis de Custine said in 1840.

But that's the point. The cloistered quality of the harem is one of the things that gave it its allure and shrouded it in an aura of secrecy. The word *cloistered* is particularly apt. It illustrates the way in which the harem formed a kind of libidinous parallel to the European ideas of family and sexuality. The cloister in Europe was a nunnery, whose virginal inhabitants presumably remained virgins, married only to their Lord, Jesus. The European cloister illustrated the Christian notion that sexuality was sinful and that the purest devotion involved sexual renunciation. In Christendom, the cloister was a place where girls and women were protected from the sexual dangers that lurked outside. In the harem, it was the inverse. The Turkish, or the Persian, or the Egyptian cloister was a place where, true, virgins were shielded from the everyday world of work and war, but it was also a place where they were reserved for the pleasure of the man of power. The sultan himself had the biggest and most elaborate and best-protected harem, but in Turkey, as in Persia or China or other of what Rycaut called the Eastern principalities, any man of wealth or power was entitled to his harem. "Each Turk is allowed four wives," Rycaut wrote, "to whom he must pay a dowry, but he is also allowed as many women slaves as they are able to maintain, the Turkish wives being well enough satisfied on this point, provided the Husband does not neglect to perform his conjugal Duty to them, which they claim once a week at least by the law."

If he thought of it deeply perhaps, the average European of wealth and power would have found this formal arrangement to be more physically demanding than entirely pleasurable. For those of the sultans whose orientation was homoerotic, and there were several of them, tending to the harem must have been more ceremonial and physical obligation than sexual fulfillment. Some Western scholars argue that the harem's status as a palace of pleasure is a wild misunderstanding. "The word *harem* is a term of respect, redolent of religious purity and honor, and evocative of the requisite obeisance," one such scholar has written. The word itself means "sanctuary" and refers to a sacred precinct, which suggests that it was not mostly or even all that much about sex but about family relations and politics. Most of the women of the harem did not occupy the sultan's bed. It was more nunnery than bordello "in its hierarchical organization and the enforced chastity of the great majority of its members." In other words, the harem as a "site of Muslim promiscuity" is a Western myth.

Still, whether myth or reality, the harem as a place of both pleasure and reproduction was one of the institutions that divided the world into two parts, not just into East and West, Western Europe and the Levant, Christendom and heathen domains, but also into the world that contained the harem and the world for whom the harem was a sinful curiosity. The cultures of the harem, which represented the vast majority of humankind, stretching from North Africa to East Asia, took as an element of the natural order of things practices that inhabitants of the Eurasian peninsula known as Europe believed were decreed mortally illicit by God himself. Among them was the notion that sex and procreation for the most powerful members of society did not generally take place within a monogamous relationship, that sex and love were separate concepts and one did not necessarily entail the other. A second notion was that the greater a man's power, the more women he was entitled to. Indeed the very physical arrangement of the Ottoman court—as well as that of other imperial domains, like the palaces of China's emperors—suggested the relationship between power and sexuality. There were the public areas where government was conducted and the inner zones, forbidden to all other men, where, as an Italian visitor to the court of Mehmed II wrote, "the most splendid, well-kept, and beautiful women that could be found in the world" were lodged. Furthering the connection between power and sex was the fact that a majority of these beautiful women, in the Turkish case, were the spoils of war, a tangible sign that the women and girls seized for the pleasure of the conquering sultan were precisely the women and girls whom a defeated ruler had been rendered powerless to protect.

Power everywhere has translated into sexual opportunity, but this truism, informal in the West, was polygamously institutionalized in the East, where the assumption was not only that the ruler needed sexual companions for relaxation but also that it would be dangerous for the security of the ruler if, in engaging in this relaxation, he were to become emotionally attached to the giver of pleasure. Manuals on government were very clear on this rule: concubines were to have no influence on the affairs of state, and the more the sultan actually loved a concubine, the more the state would be in jeopardy. In fact, the lore of the harem gives considerable influence to the person called the Royal Mother, namely, the former concubine whose son actually became the sultan, so power acquired via sex was not unknown in Ottoman Turkey. Still, in its separation of sex from love, the culture of the harem once again represents an inversion of the culture of Christendom, wherein love was a religiously endorsed requirement of sex. Suleiman the Great was exceptional as a sultan in that he remained faithful to only one woman, a fact so strange that Hurrem, the woman in question—very likely a Russian or Pole seized in battle—was widely deemed to have been a sorceress whose use of potions, charms, and magic arts explained her complete capture of the sultan's heart. Suleiman was roughly a contemporary of Henry VIII, who, of course, took England out of the Catholic Church so that he could divorce one wife and marry another—unlike the sultan he could have only one wife at a time. The irony is in the way each royal figure shattered the expectations of his subjects. Henry broke with Rome over a divorce, while Suleiman shocked his countrymen with his faithfulness to one woman.

It could be argued that the culture of the harem, while less reverential about marriage, was more realistic about human nature, certainly more accommodating than the Christian West to the weaknesses of the male of the species, for whom, as countless episodes of infidelity over the centuries attest, monogamy has been a vexed institution. To be sure, seen especially from the standpoint of today's values, the harem was powerfully regressive, a device that was made by and for the patriarchy and ensured its dominion over women, whose own desires for pleasure and perhaps for variety went unrecognized. Montesquieu and Byron were correct that the harem was an instrument of both sexual and political absolutism. The Ottomans came to prefer concubines to legal wives as the mothers of heirs to the throne because concubines didn't have to be treated with the deference due queens. In addition, by elevating slaves to the status of royal mothers, rather than marrying the daughters of other powerful men or neighboring kings, the Ottomans reduced the stature of the houses from which the wives would otherwise have come—again enhancing the sultan's power.

Certainly by contrast with the polygamous East, the institution of monogamous marriage, however it may have been violated over the centuries, was an ideal that gave Western women vastly greater dignity and pride of place. It was also an institution that circumvented a source of political instability in the Eastern provinces, because the intrigue of the harem, the literally murderous competition among the branches and factions spawned by rival consorts, was absent in the courts of Christendom. Still, the Ottoman system endured for a very long time. In part this is because the existence of the harem enabled it to avoid an intrinsic weakness of monogamous Western monarchy, which is that the only legitimate successor was the offspring of the king and his queen. If that union produced no male offspring, the succession was threatened. The Ottomans perpetuated an unbroken line of sultans through thirty-six generations. And one of the reasons is that any child fathered by the sultan—and most children were produced by concubines, not wives—was legitimate, with the concubine becoming one of the most influential figures of the realm, the royal mother.

THE IMPORTANT POINT IS that the Ottoman harem enchanted Europeans for centuries, tickled their imagination, inspired works of literature and art, all in appreciation of the existence of an alternative sexual world. The literature that illustrates the Western fascination is voluminous and somewhat repetitive, even if different writers, men and women, strove to differentiate their description of the harem from the descriptions of other writers and to claim for themselves the honor of having uncovered the harem's true secret. "I will not only trace the Sultans to his amorous Pastimes with the Virgins of his Pleasure," Aaron Hill, a British traveler and playwright, wrote in 1709, "but admit the Reader to the closed Apartments of the fair SERAGLIO LADIES, nay and into the retir'd Magnificence of the Bedchambers, but shew him all the various Scenes of Love and Courtship, which are practis'd daily by their Lord and them, even to the Consummation of their utmost Wishes."

Hill was a wealthy, eccentric, high-minded, and irritating Englishman who, as a young man just out of school, had traveled through the Middle East, producing in 1709 a volume with an almost identical title to that of Rycaut, if a bit grander: *A Full and Just Account of the Present State of the Ottoman Empire.* Unlike Rycaut, Hill claimed to have visited the seraglio at some moment when the sultan was not present. That assertion, given what we know about the death sentence supposedly meted out to any man except the sultan himself and his eunuchs who even accidentally viewed one of the seraglio ladies, might well have been a fib. Nonetheless, Hill used his supposed intimacy with the sultan's establishment to claim his book to be more accurate than Rycaut's, saying, for example, that Rycaut's story of the handkerchief was "erroneous." This set into motion a debate about that detail that continued for centuries, a debate of consuming and enduring interest similar to the debates that animated the Royal Geographical Society over such matters as the source of the Nile or the existence of a Northwest Passage. Later Hill corresponded with Alexander Pope, edited a two-penny half sheet called *The Prompter,* which chronicled the world of the London theater, and was deemed literarily important enough by the time of his death, in 1750, to warrant burial in Westminster Abbey.

Hill, like Rycaut, in short, had credibility. He laid out for his English readership a wonderful, fulsomely described world replete with "paths of love" and "labyrinths of pleasure" of the sort that would be the nighttime fantasies of any young or not so young man. Again, all of this literature exposes the unidirectionality of transcontinental erotic interest. Mozart, Racine, Montesquieu, Byron, Puccini, even Gilbert and Sullivan wrote operas, plays, parodies, epic poems, and musicals inspired by the harem, but few if any Turkish works are placed, for exotic, humorous, or admonitory effect, in Versailles or the Court of Saint James's. Suleiman's contemporary Henry VIII and Louis XIV, who lived a century later, at the time of Mehmed IV (whose mother was a Russian concubine of the "mad" Sultan Ibrahim), had famous mistresses, and historians have written a great deal about them. It does not seem as though the Turkish residents in London or Paris at the time of Suleiman or Mehmed wrote vivid descriptions of the Western boudoir to satisfy some curiosity back home, but the West's fascination with the harem produced a literature that lasted for centuries.

A few years after Hill published his book, in the second decade of the eighteenth century, Lady Mary Wortley Montagu, the wife of the British ambassador in Constantinople, entered the secret-of-the-harem sweepstakes, claiming that as a woman she enjoyed an access that no man could dream of. Although Lady Montagu lived in Turkey and traveled in the Ottoman Empire in 1717 or thereabouts, her book, in the form of a collection of intimate letters to various women friends, wasn't published until 1763, after her death. Her ostensible goal was a scholarly one, to set the record straight and correct "the falsehoods" contained in the descriptions of other authors, but her book further aroused the collective erotic interest of the West for the East. Ingres copied lengthy extracts from her letters into his notebooks, so although Montagu's letters are not especially distinguished from the literary point of view, they helped to inspire masterpieces in the depiction of the erotic and exotic world of the East.

This is the case even though one of Lady Montagu's messages is that the erotic culture of the Ottomans and that of Christian Europe are less different from each other than other writers suggested. She discounted the ideas, for example, that Turkish men not only could but actually did have four wives and that they casually defied the wishes of their wives by having as many mistresses as they wanted. "When a husband happens to be inconstant (as those things will happen) he keeps his mistrisse in a House apart and visits her as privately as he can, just as tis with you," she writes in one letter.

Montagu called that business about the sultan throwing a handkerchief to the bedmate he had chosen for the night "altogether fabulous," and so, she contended, were those stories of the girl of the night creeping into the sultan's bed. Still, she portrayed a world of feminine beauty on naked display within an institution that could never have existed in the Christian realm. In one of the passages transcribed by Ingres, she spoke of "a Beautifull Maid of about 17, very richly drest and shineing with Jewells, but was presently reduce'd . . . to the state of nature."

The scene, which was actually part of a wedding ceremony, was entirely decorous in Montagu's description. There was no sexual slavery here, not even any sex. Montagu bemoaned the "extreme Stupidity" of previous writers for depicting Turkish ladies as shut up and miserable. They were, she said, "the only Women in the world that lead a life of uninterrupted pleasure, exempt from cares, their whole life being spent in visiting, bathing, or the agreable Amusement of spending Money and inventing new fashions." For Montagu, in such striking contrast to the view of this matter in today's West, the veil was not a mark of subjugation but an aide to freedom, because the "perpetual Masquerade" allowed women to "go abroad" in complete anonymity. "You may easily imagine the number of faithfull Wives very small," she writes in one of her letters.

Lady Montagu, who corresponded with some of the leading women's rights advocates of her century, herself had a scandalous love affair after returning home from Constantinople, so there is likely a bit of wishful thinking in her portrayal of Turkish women as free and unburdened by the cares of the world. She was the daughter of an earl who rejected her wish to marry her longtime paramour, Edward Wortley Montagu, arranging another marriage for her instead. But she broke off that engagement with the wedding plans in an advanced stage and eloped with Montagu, an act that certainly showed an independent spirit on her part, even as her letters from the Ottoman Empire show a striking lack of concern for the possibility that the aristocratic Turkish women whom she believed to be so free were similarly constrained by such things as arranged marriages. Lady Montagu was also a gossip and careless with her facts. She became an object of considerable contempt and derision in her later life, much of which she spent in self-imposed exile in Italy, after she and Edward Wortley Montagu went their separate ways.

She was, in other words, a complicated and tragic figure, this English aristocrat and protofeminist who believed the veil to be liberating and life in a harem to be free. And just as she accused other writers on the harem of being ignorant of their subject, Lady Montagu was accused of the identical fault by a later group of female writers who also made the harem their object of study. An early-nineteenth-century writer, Julia Pardoe, for example, upon visiting the baths where Lady Montagu had seen nothing but alabaster nakedness, saw "none of that unnecessary and wanton exposure" that Lady Montagu had seen. Perhaps, Pardoe speculated, Lady Montagu was present for some "peculiar

ceremony, or the Turkish ladies have become more delicate and fastidious in their ideas of propriety." In midcentury, Emmeline Lott, who
worked as a governess in Eastern harems, a position that "gave her
access to those forbidden 'Abodes of Bliss,' " wrote her own account of
the seraglio, contending in it that Lady Montagu had seen pretty much
nothing of "the daily life of the Odalisques."

The literary rivalry continued as different female writers competed
with one another to substantiate their claims to have discovered, at
long last, the true secret of what took place inside the harem. But the
women who disagreed with one another on certain specifics tended
with Lady Montagu to see the harem as a zone of feminine freedom
and possibility rather than female enslavement.

One of them, Elizabeth Craven, another aristocrat who went to
Constantinople, in her case a generation after the publication of Lady
Montagu's letters, envied Turkish women because, she believed, they
were "perfectly safe from an idle, curious, impertinent public." The
harem protected their privacy and even their sexual freedom. Just as the
sultan's putative handkerchief became a talisman of the European
imagination, the female writers on the seraglio who dismissed the
handkerchief as a fiction made much of the slippers of Turkish women.
Craven wrote that if a husband saw a pair of slippers at the door of his
harem, he would not enter, a custom, she said, that provided a sort of
protection for a woman's lovers. Julia Pardoe seized on the slippers, but
as the scholar Ruth Bernard Yeazell has written, she and other female
travelers "associate them not with sexual freedom but with a freedom
from sex—or at least from sex-on-demand—conspicuously absent
from home." The harem in the imagination of Victorian women was
almost entirely transformed, from a place reserved for the sexual pleasure of the sultan to a place serving as a retreat, a haven, for its female
inhabitants.

But while women wrote books and argued with one another, it was
the men who later went to the East to become little sultans with little
harems of their own, and it was the notion of the harem as a place of
limitless erotic possibility that prevailed in the Western imagination. In
the East, as Western men surely noticed, not only did worldly success
bring multiple sexual opportunities, but the sexual opportunities came
with no requirement of love. The harem was the place where women

chosen for their beauty and purity were cloistered so that they would be available to satisfy the sexual desires of men of power. For Europeans, this was a remarkable fact. We're not talking about Secret Service agents looking the other way as one of John F. Kennedy's mistresses was infiltrated into the White House or about some back door to the palace of power surreptitiously kept open so that the king's illicit bedmates could be let in for the night and let out again in the morning. In the West, an extramarital relationship for a president or king required a clandestine complicity on the part of the power holder's inner circle. But there was nothing clandestine about sex outside marriage in the East. The culture of the harem required a large bureaucracy whose sole purpose was to recruit and maintain hundreds of women for the delectation of the supreme ruler, this person being unburdened by any expectation of fidelity to any single woman, least of all his wife. Wisdom, of course, teaches that the greatest sexual pleasure for a man comes in a healthy monogamous and loving relationship with one woman. Monogamy in this sense is moving. It is an emotional as well as a sexual enhancement. Still, let's face it, men frequently do not live in accordance with what wisdom teaches, and for many Western men the harem represented an alternative world, one free of what they saw as the burden of monogamy, the ennui of just one woman, and redolent of the possibility of sexual plenitude amid maidens who stayed young even as wives and husbands grew old.

THE DREAM OF THAT alternative erotic world was, no doubt, one reason for the European fascination with the harem and its supposed secrets. But the harem also inspired another keen Western desire: to know what is supposedly forbidden to know. Like many of the women of the colonized world depicted in travelers' tales and paintings, the harem itself was veiled, and the desire to tear away the veil and see what lay beneath it remained a European desire for centuries.

The veil in this sense was a provocation, and the ability to see what lay behind it was a chief mark of the power and prestige of the sultan, who, in accounts like Rycaut's, was alone privileged to do so. The French romantic poet Gérard de Nerval, writing in his *Voyage to the Orient,* focused not on Turkey but on another Levantine domain of enduring interest to European visitors, from Gustave Flaubert to Lawrence Durrell—namely, Egypt. These days, Egypt is probably deemed by most Westerners an anti-erotic country of political dictatorship, squalor, beggars, and touts. But to Nerval, as to Flaubert, it was a place of tantalizing sensuality, "a country of enigma and mysteries" that both discouraged the visitor and stirred an attempt to "lift a corner of the stern veil."

Nerval provided this enticing description of what can be seen of the Egyptian woman: "Beautiful hands ornamented with talismanic rings and silver bracelets, sometimes pale marble arms completely escaping the large sleeves rolled up underneath the shoulder, bare feet loaded with rings that the babouch [oriental slipper] abandons at each step, and which reverberate around the ankles with a silvery noise . . . : here is what is permissible to admire, to guess, to surprise, to discover without the crowd getting nervous about it or the woman herself seeming to notice."

The Orient, as one scholar put this, provoked "an erotic urge to see the imaginary nakedness behind the veil." It is, he continued, "a more literal wish to tear the veils of the Oriental women in a voyeuristic attempt to see their hidden bodies." The key was power, the power to lift the veil, to reveal its not very secret secret, which gave rise to at least three activities on the part of Westerners. One was to chronicle the harem itself, as writers like Rycaut, Hill, and Montagu did, competing with all the others to reveal ever more of the life hidden within. The second was to engage in a kind of sexual tourism—and Flaubert, as we will see, was an early illustration of this practice, which has gone on in different guises for at least the past two hundred years as men from Europe and America have explored the erotic possibilities available in the East but denied in the West. And the third was to acquire the power to exploit those possibilities. Colonialism and military victory accomplished this. The allure of the veiled East combined with the power of colonial conquest to make what started as pure fantasy an everyday reality, achieved in more recent times on a massive and vulgar scale.

The Fantasy Comes True

AROUND 1812, the British cartoonist Thomas Rowlandson published a pornographic drawing titled *Harem,* which illustrates the dreamworld that the Ottomans' peculiar institution was for the West. Rowlandson, born in 1756, had never traveled to the Levant, so his drawing had to have been based on the harem's reputation rather than its reality, and the imagination of what Ruth Bernard Yeazell called "the dream of infinite possibility that inspires so many masculine fantasies of the East." It shows a turbaned man, evidently the sultan, looking at two tiers of naked women lined up to a vanishing point on the drawing's edge, each striking a pose of come-hither seduction.

The only person with clothes on in this drawing of teeming life is the sultan himself, who sits on a rug beneath a canopy, a gracefully curved pitcher and bowl by his side. He is wearing a turban and an elaborate robe, and the robe is open in front, revealing both to the viewer of the drawing and the women within it a fully engorged penis. The sultan's member seems almost like a divining rod, an implement to assist the otherwise baffling decision of which woman to choose, baffling because the depicted women are so similar to one another that, in Rowlandson's vision, the infinite number of women actually presents no real choices. "As if the alternative to monogamy were indeed gratification without limit, bodies and pleasures multiply endlessly in harems of the mind," Yeazell wrote of Rowlandson's work. Like Ingres' and Mozart's and Byron's harems, Rowlandson's is imaginary, an illustration of the erotic possibilities of elsewhere. He didn't intend it to be taken as reality.

Thomas Rowlandson's drawing *Harem,* ca. 1812.

But down a well-known narrow lane in Bangkok, a hundred yards or so from one of the city's broad commercial thoroughfares, is another sort of harem that is decidedly real, of the here and now and the entirely possible. A neon sign identifies it as the Darling Massage Parlor, one of many such establishments in Bangkok, and although this now-famous emporium of pleasure didn't exist in Rowlandson's time, the caricaturist perfectly anticipated it in his work. The Darling Massage Parlor, you can learn on any of the many Web sites that provide information about it, is open daily from 3 p.m. to midnight. Inside are men standing in a sort of foyer looking at women who sit on tiered wooden banquettes in a sort of goldfish bowl of tinted glass. The women are dressed in diaphanous pastels. Most of them are not especially young or pretty, though a few of them are. They can see the men looking at them, and they try to make eye contact in an effort to attract a customer, like Rycaut's virgins striking "wanton Postures" to attract the attention of "the Grand Signior."

The manager of the place will tell you which woman specializes in which particular service. He will let customers know which of them sucks and who among them fucks, and he will urge customers to take two of the girls so that they can have a little of both and be in the middle of a sort of Oriental sandwich, one girl on top, the other on the bottom and both lathered with soap and warm water. Whatever choice the customer makes, he will be given a bath, then massaged a bit, and finally, after some negotiation, given what is marvelously called a happy ending, the different forms of which command different prices.

The Darling Massage Parlor is one of many such places in Bangkok and far from the most opulent, luxurious, or popular. It is said that that distinction belongs to Poseidon, at 209 Ratchadapisek Road, which, according to its Web site, has three levels of women: fishbowl, sideline (women who sit outside the fishbowl), and models, ranging in price from about $70 to $180 for an hour and a half, the price going up with the beauty of the masseuse, the happy ending extra. Other such establishments are Ceasar's, Mirage, New Cleopatra, and Victoria's Secret, and they all offer a close approximation to Rowlandson's fantasy. These are harems available to every man, present-day realizations of the fantasy propagated by Ludovico de Varthema and Paul Rycaut centuries ago, the life of the sultan democratized.

CHAPTER FIVE

The Eternal Dream of Cleopatra

Like the ocean, this river sends our thoughts back almost incalculable distances; then there is the eternal dream of Cleopatra, and the great memory of the sun, the golden sun of the Pharaohs.

—*Gustave Flaubert,* Flaubert in Egypt

In 1850, the young Gustave Flaubert wrote to Louis Bouilhet, his pal back in Le Croisset, Normandy, of seeing the Red Sea at Kosseir (modern-day Quseir), the Egyptian port where the caravans of pilgrimaging Muslims "take ship for Jidda, whence it is only three days to Mecca." Kosseir was not one of the places that inflamed Flaubert's imagination, which was especially inflammable during his year and a half in the Middle East between 1849 and 1851, though he did note for Bouilhet's benefit that among the pilgrims he observed was "a whole veiled harem [that] called out to us like magpies as we passed." And there was a moment in Kosseir when Flaubert became the sensualist he is famous for being. He swam in the Red Sea and told Bouilhet that "it was one of the most voluptuous pleasures of my life; I lolled in its waters as though I were lying on a thousand liquid breasts that were caressing my entire body."

Flaubert probably didn't know that just a couple of years before, another European traveler, Richard Burton, had stopped on the Egyptian shores of the Red Sea and did take ship for Arabia and Mecca, an exploit that would make his reputation. Burton was in some ways the opposite of Flaubert. He was the Platonic ideal of the tireless danger-seeking explorer of the exterior world; Flaubert was a danger seeker in his own way, but except for his journey to Egypt (and a later trip of a few weeks to Libya), he led a sedentary existence, exploring the psychological and moral interior, driven to expose the pathetic frailty and the ridiculousness of the human endeavor. While Burton was impatient whenever he was home in England and always plotting some arduous expedition in Asia or Africa, Flaubert, the private sensualist and public literary realist, was content to stay at home in France, living with his mother in their cottage on the Seine and turning out masterpieces of French literature. He famously said, "Be regular and orderly in your life, so that you may be violent and original in your work." Burton, the British soldier, the linguist extraordinaire, and possibly the greatest traveler-explorer of the nineteenth century, was a man of practical deeds, unrelenting activity, and unsurpassable physical bravery. He was as violent in his life as Flaubert was orderly, and while not a literary genius of Flaubert's rank, he was gifted, stylish, and original as a chronicler of his adventures and an observer of foreign lands.

They were similar in many ways too, not least in that both of them had enormous libidinous energy, frequented prostitutes wherever they were, and, indeed, suffered most of their lives from venereal diseases contracted during some exotic sexual adventure. Both also were addicted to the scrutiny of the facts, to the world as it was in all its magnificent and smelly detail, rather than to the world that the Romantics and, worse, the sentimentalists of the time wished for. Both were original thinkers impatient with convention, especially intellectual convention—the received ideas, as Flaubert famously put it. And both spent their time in "the Orient"—Burton spending far more of it than Flaubert—taking advantage of the erotic possibilities that the East offered.

The literary scholar Edward Said, author of the enormously influential book *Orientalism,* believed that both men illustrated what he described as the Orientalist fallacy: not seeing its reality but rather affirming a preexisting prejudice formed by earlier reading and the stereotyped exoticism that was part of the imperialist enterprise. As we will see, there is both insight and blindness in this theory. But Said was correct when he observed that Flaubert and Burton illustrated the clear association "made between the Orient and the freedom of licentious sex." "Virtually no European writer who wrote on or traveled to the Orient in the period after 1800 exempted himself or herself from this quest," Said wrote. The difference is that, for Said, this association was merely part of the stereotype by which the West both understood and diminished the East, whereas for Flaubert and Burton the freedom of licentious sex was neither fantasy nor stereotype but an affirmable reality.

What make Flaubert and Burton especially valuable in this regard are the frank records of their exploits. Both loved prostitutes, unabashedly, at home and abroad. One of Flaubert's biographers, Francis Steegmuller, who compiled a book of his letters and notes from Egypt, cited Flaubert himself to this effect: "It may be a perverted taste, . . . but I love prostitution, and for itself, too, quite apart from its carnal aspects. . . . The idea of prostitution is a meeting place of so many elements—lust, bitterness, complete absence of human contact, muscular frenzy, the clink of gold—that to peer into it deeply makes one reel."

Taken together, Burton and Flaubert, who never met and never referred to each other in any of their writings, perfectly illustrate a crossing of paths, not surprising because thousands of less-celebrated others were on the same paths. Both exemplify the Western fascination with the Orient not only as a domain of dream and fantasy about the harem but also as a place for a sensual realization and an experience of manhood unavailable at home. Both celebrated the sexual East in word and in deed. Unwittingly, probably, in Flaubert's case, more knowingly in Burton's, they gave expression to the relationship between power and sexual advantage that characterized the imperial era and, to a great extent, the era that came after it and continues today. Wealth and power were sought as ends in themselves, but coincidentally wealth and power procured plenty of girls (and boys) for the soldiers, explorers, writers, and adventurers who embodied those attributes in the colonized and otherwise dominated portions of the globe.

SINCE FLAUBERT HAD PLENTY OF EXPERIENCE with prostitutes in Paris, where there was no shortage of them, what was so special about the Orient? What opportunity did Egypt offer that wasn't offered at home? Certainly whatever it was, it was not sex by itself. "The next two days I lived lavishly—huge dinners, quantities of wine, whores," Flaubert said in his travel notebook, referring to October 22, 1849, when his Egyptian expedition was about to begin. But he was writing about two days he had spent in Paris, often tearful because of the separation from his mother that had taken place at his uncle's house in Normandy a few days before. He lived with his friend and traveling companion Maxime Du Camp, who, until *Madame Bovary* was published seven years later, was a better-known figure in the French literary world than Flaubert. Indeed, up to that point Flaubert had hardly published anything of note. He was twenty-eight years old in 1849, "almost six feet tall, muscular, a blond 'Viking,' " as Steegmuller put it, the son of a surgeon who had died four years earlier, leaving the family enough money for the young man to pursue his travels and literary ambitions without having to work for a living.

He was a young, ambitious sensualist who had the resources to live a life of considerable ease, writing until late at night, having breakfast with his mother at noon. Du Camp was about the same age as Flaubert, and wealthier. It was he who dragged the stay-at-home Gustave with him to Egypt, with plans to go on to Palestine, Greece, and Persia, though in the end the Persian part of the journey was scrapped. Flaubert had read the classic works that evoked a romantic and exotic East—Byron, Victor Hugo, and *The Arabian Nights,* though not in Richard Burton's celebrated translation, which didn't appear until decades later. "Oh, how willingly I would give up all the women in the world to possess the mummy of Cleopatra" is an example of what Steegmuller called his "youthful 'oriental' effusions." Flaubert was, in addition, smitten with the cult of antiquity, which affected many young French and English men of the nineteenth century. When he arrived at the Sphinx, which at the time was a much less viewed and even more fabled sight than it is now, he almost expired in a paroxysm of nostalgia for the disappeared splendors of the past. "I am afraid of becoming giddy, and try to control my emotion," he wrote in his journal, and later he said in a letter to his bosom friend Bouilhet back home, "We don't have emotions as *poétique* as that every day, thank God; it would kill us."

He was a man, in short, who loved the Orient before he got there and in this sense exemplifies the view of Said and other writers of the Orientalist persuasion. In their view, Flaubert and most other travelers of the Romantic era in Europe "were especially inclined to such hallucinations of memory, as if they were not so much viewing the Orient for the first time as re-viewing it through the representations of the past." This is the case even though Flaubert, despite the power of his exotic yearnings, almost decided not to take the trip, so pained was he by his departure from his mother and his anticipation of her suffering in his absence. Leaving Le Croisset, he wept into his handkerchief over this separation, and once he got to Paris, he continued to wrestle with his decision, agonizing for hours with Du Camp until, finally, he elected irrevocably to go. There was a final dinner in Paris, during which Flaubert described Bouilhet "gnaw[ing] at the end of his cigar after enjoining us to think of him if we should find ourselves in the presence of some relic of Cleopatra." Once he did arrive—by train, stagecoach, and Rhône River steamer from Paris to Marseilles and then "eleven days of rolling and pitching, of wind and heavy seas" on a steam packet called the *Nil*—Flaubert slowly made the Orient his own, closely observing the details even as he continued to think of Cleopatra, who linked his antiquarian interest to his sensual appetite. In Egypt, he found a world of heat, color, privilege, dust, decrepitude, disease, desperation, music, eroticism, and sex that, taken together, could never have been duplicated in Paris.

And this is the main point. If prostitution for Flaubert was a fabulous meeting place of the sordid and the sublime (and Flaubert loved the sordid especially), Egypt was too. "The psychological, human, comic aspects are particularly plentiful" was the way Flaubert summed this up in a letter to Bouilhet from Constantinople in 1851, a few months after his departure from Egypt. "One meets splendid types, pigeon's-breast existences very iridescent to the eye, highly diversified as to rags and embroideries, rich in filth, tatters, and fancy braid. And, underneath always the same *canaillerie* [roguishness], immutable, unshakable. . . . Ah! How much of it there is to be seen!" Egypt offered a spectacle that was "febrile and intoxicating" for Flaubert. Among other things, it offered a life in imitation of that of a sultan or a pasha or a sheikh or some other Oriental potentate, the life of a sort of conqueror without arms following in the path of Napoleon (who conquered Egypt in 1798, ostensibly to liberate the country from Ottoman rule) and enjoying power and prestige conferred on him simply by virtue of being a foreigner. "It is unbelievable how well we are treated here—it's as though we were princes, and I'm not joking," Flaubert wrote to his mother. And later, to Bouilhet: "The pasha at Rosetta gave us a dinner at which there were ten negroes to serve us—they wore silk jackets and some had silver bracelets; and a little negro boy waved away the flies with a kind of feather-duster made of rushes." And again to his mother, who was worried about his safety, he marveled at the power that he enjoyed as a Westerner, at "the respect, or rather the terror, that everyone displays in the presence of 'Franks,' as they call Europeans. We have had bands of ten or twelve Arabs, advancing across the whole width of a street, break apart to let us pass."

This is not to be underestimated in the private lives of otherwise very ordinary or, certainly, not very powerful European men when they traveled or lived in the East, from Algeria to China, this psychological advantage that they held over native men, an advantage that was a reflected glory stemming from the superior military force of the countries they were associated with. When Napoleon seized Egypt half a century before, some six thousand Mamluk troops were killed but only three hundred French soldiers. Flaubert, in his reference to the thousand liquid breasts of the Red Sea, suggests this transformation of the East into a woman even in its very physical characteristics, its sensual warmth, its agricultural fertility. But it is sexual too, in the way its society is organized to offer such a multitude of opportunities, some of them involving a kind of sexual obsequiousness whose deeply poignant and melancholy aspects Flaubert appeared not to notice. Flaubert cheerfully recounted an encounter "with a boy of six or seven and two barefoot little girls in blue smocks, their pointed woolen caps on the ground beside them. . . . The boy was excellent—short, ugly, stocky: 'If you'll give me five paras I'll bring you my mother to fuck. I wish you all kinds of prosperity, especially a long prick.' " Among the enticements to pleasure that he mentioned more than once to Bouilhet was the ready availability of *bardashes,* or catamites, boys who engage in sexual relations with men, perhaps, though he didn't say this, a sort of resurrection for Flaubert of Greek antiquity. "It's at the baths that such things take place," Flaubert reported in one letter. "You reserve the bath for yourself (five francs including masseurs, pipe, coffee, sheet and towel) and you skewer your lad in one of the rooms. Be informed, furthermore, that all the bath-boys are bardashes."

This, in other words, is what the East proffered to Western visitors, and it is hard, especially with an observer as brilliant and original as Flaubert, to see what he saw as mere "re-viewings" of earlier writings. What he viewed and touched was real, and it was catalogued by Flaubert (and his English counterpart Burton) with a concreteness and vividness worthy of the author of *Madame Bovary*. He saw and smelled everything, the "rolling and stony" terrain, the "large plaques of yellow sand that look as if they were varnished with *terre-de-Sienne*-colored laqueur," "the Arab boats, with their outsize sterns," "the ghastly odor of soap and rotten eggs," the young eunuch, "bare-headed, wavy hair, a small dagger stuck in his shawl-belt, bare arms, thick silver ring on one finger, pointed red shoes," the "little red-haired girl, wide forehead, great eyes, nose slightly flat with wide nostrils, strange face full of fantasy and animation," the pearl fishers who go out in their canoes in pairs, "one to row and one to dive," with the diver returning "bleeding from ears, nostrils, and eyes," the slave traders' boats drawn up on a beach on the Red Sea and the slaves themselves "walk[ing] in groups of fifteen to twenty, each led by two men," the "white birdshit" that "streaks down" an otherwise perfect obelisk at Luxor forming "a flat mass at the bottom, like a dribble of plaster." ("Inscriptions and bird-droppings are the only two things in the ruins of Egypt that give any indication of life," he wrote to Bouilhet.)

And, as always with Flaubert, there is an intentionally and strenuously anti-Romantic indulgence in the seedy and even the disgusting, a hardheadedness and skepticism, a sense of the vanity and folly of it all appropriate to a man who once said that "the dream of democracy is to elevate the proletariat to the level of bourgeois stupidity." He was irritated that he was obliged by Du Camp, whose main purpose in Egypt was to apply his knowledge of the new science of photography to ancient places, to visit so many Egyptian temples, which, Flaubert allowed, "bore me profoundly." He gave a purposefully flat account of the use of the bastinado, his very lack of emotional involvement intensifying the effect of cruelty and sensuality: "When a man is to be killed, four of five blows suffice—his lower back and neck are broken; when he is only to be punished, he is beaten on the buttocks: four or five hundred blows is the usual number; five or six months are required for the healing—until the lacerated flesh falls away. . . . The Nubians greatly dread this punishment, since after it they are never able to walk again"—this unsentimental, unhorrified description from a twenty-eight-year-old man who had wept inconsolably upon saying good-bye to his mother a few months earlier. Flaubert always stayed just a bit detached, an observer both of the exotic world of Egypt and of himself and his changeable moods. Again, in contrast to the Romantics whom he would reject in his literary depictions of the world, there was a deep, almost perverse pleasure in the corruption, the seediness, the horrible that he saw around him, as when he described the boy offering him his mother to fuck as "excellent" and "ugly." He told Bouilhet that, finally, he had experienced anal sex with a bath boy, describing him as "a pock-marked young rascal wearing a turban." (Jean-Paul Sartre, who wrote a long biography of Flaubert, believed this episode did not actually take place, but who knows? Flaubert said that it did.) When his mistress Louise Colet expressed disgust at the bedbugs that Flaubert, apparently in an earlier missive, mentioned in his encounter with a prostitute, Flaubert's reply was that their "nauseating odor" was "the most enchanting touch of all," especially as it "mingled with the scent of her skin, which was dripping with sandalwood." There was another girl, Flaubert told Bouilhet, "fat and lubricious, on top of whom I enjoyed myself immensely and who smelled of rancid butter." When he wrote to Bouilhet, in his long post-Egyptian letter from Constantinople, that he and Du Camp both had chancres on their sexual member ("I sus-pect a Maronite—or was it a little Turkish girl?—of having given me this present"), his reaction was ironic: "Nothing's so good for the health as travel."

Flaubert's first sexual encounters in Egypt, beginning in Cairo at a place called la Triestine, after la Triestina, the madam of the establish-ment, were special not so much because they were enjoyable but because they were strange. He described two women at la Triestine, not especially beautiful; one played the *darabukka* (a kettledrum) while the other did what he called an Alexandrian dance. "A litter of kittens has to be removed" from Flaubert's bed—the kind of detail that he would have savored. Flaubert, who described everything he saw, described

Hadely, his partner for the night, as if she were a trinket to be purchased in the bazaar: "firm flesh, bronze arse, shaven cunt, dry though fatty." In a letter written shortly afterward to Bouilhet, he said they had "a strange coitus, looking at each other without being able to exchange a word, and the exchange of looks is all the deeper for the curiosity and the surprise."

More important to Flaubert was his visit to Kuchuk Hanem, the one perfumed with the smell of bedbugs. Musicians played, Kuchuk Hanem danced, and, Flaubert said, her dance "is brutal," full of "marvellous movement," something that he'd seen "on old Greek vases." There were "four women seated in a line on the divan singing," while "the lamps cast quivering, lozenge-shaped shadows on the walls." He named two of the others: Safiah Zugairah (Little Sophie) and Bambeh. Flaubert, having already had "a little entertainment" with Kuchuk Hanem, had what he called a *coup* with Little Sophie (who was "very corrupt and writhing, extremely voluptuous"), then again coupled with Kuchuk Hanem. "Her cunt felt like rolls of velvet as she made me come. I felt like a tiger." Flaubert spent the night with Kuchuk Hanem, boasting to Bouilhet later: "My night was one long, infinitely intense reverie—that was why I stayed. I thought of my nights in Paris brothels—a whole series of old memories came back—and I thought of her, of her dance, of her voice as she sang songs that for me were without meaning and even without distinguishable words. . . . As for the *coups,* they were good—the third especially was ferocious, and the last tender—we told each other many sweet things—toward the end there was something sad and loving in the way we embraced."

There was more. He told Bouilhet, in the same letter in which he described Kuchuk Hanem, "I have lain with Nubian girls whose necklaces of gold piastres hung down to their thighs and whose black stomachs were encircled by colored beads—they feel cold when you rub your own stomach against them." He saw Kuchuk Hanem again and felt "infinite sadness" on leaving her. At Kena (today's Qena), he wrote, he "had a beautiful whore who liked me very much and told me in sign language that I had beautiful eyes." On the very night, July 19, 1850, that he took ship in Alexandria for Beirut, he experienced a sadness that, especially for Flaubert, that most emotionally realistic of men, seems almost maudlin: "The boat left while I was asleep; I did not see the land of Egypt disappear on the horizon. I did not bid it my last farewells. . . . Shall I ever return?"

As Steegmuller noted, he didn't return. He went home and within six years had produced the imperishable *Madame Bovary*, which would seem to be as far from Egypt as it is possible to be in its setting, theme, and characters. But Egypt, as Steegmuller reminded us, remained in Flaubert's mind, and even in 1880, shortly before his death, he wrote to his niece expressing "the longing to see a palm-tree standing out against the blue sky, and to hear a stork clacking its beak at the top of a minaret." It was the persistent Western dream of the Orient as a place of what Flaubert called a bellyful of colors, intoxicating, vivid, richly perfumed, a place of a plenitude of being and a sensual intensity impossible in the West.

CHAPTER SIX

Enlightenment from India

All was voluptuous with gentle swellings, with the rounded con-
tours of the girl-negress.

—*Richard Francis Burton*, Zanzibar: City, Island, and Coast

S URROUNDED BY IMMINENT DANGER in a place where no
European had ever ventured before him, living "under the roof of
a bigoted prince whose least word was death, amongst a people
who detest foreigners," the British explorer Richard Francis Burton
might well have been entirely preoccupied with getting out alive. The
emir in question was the absolutist ruler of Harar, a city on a hill in
Somalia, now Harer, in Ethiopa, and largely forgotten to the outside
world. But in the middle of the nineteenth century, Harar was legendary not only as a great center of Islamic learning but also, like
Mecca itself (which Burton had already reached a year or so earlier, disguised as an Afghan wayfarer), as a place forbidden to non-Muslims.

Harar was the perfect destination for a European eager to unveil the
secrets of the Orient—as Burton thought of Africa even if it was,
strictly speaking, not the Orient. Burton arrived in 1854 after a long
and risky trek through the wilds of East Africa disguised for most of the
journey as an Arab named Haji Mirza Abdullah, but he grew increas-
ingly concerned that his light complexion would give him away, so
once he was in the presence of the emir of Harar, he admitted that he
was a British soldier and had come "to see the light of H. H.'s [His
Highness's] countenance." Then, in a reflex typical of this man of many
death-defying adventures, as his weeks of effective imprisonment at

Harar slipped by, he not just noted but also closely experienced the charms of the women.

"Stars are tattooed upon the bosom," Burton wrote of the slave girls, who had been captured, it seems, in wars with the Galla, one of Somalia's major tribes, and with whom he dallied. "The eyebrows are lengthened with dyes, the eyes fringed with Kohl, and the hands and feet stained with henna." Burton did with the Galla what he did with many other women he met on his far-flung adventures. It is almost certain that he slept with them, for starters. But Burton, the participant-observer par excellence, also described them with anatomical exactitude, and in the tradition of one of those Renaissance travelers telling tales of the marvels of the East, he detailed the strange and exotic practices to which they were devoted. In the case of the Galla slave girls, this was an erotic technique that he had noted elsewhere in East Africa and especially Egypt, one, as he put it later in a footnote to his translation of *The Arabian Nights,* involving "the use of the constrictor vaginae muscles, the sphincter for which Abyssinian women are famous." The female partner in this practice, known as the *kabbazah,* which is Arabic for "holder," "can sit astraddle upon a man and can provoke the venereal orgasm, not by wriggling and moving but by tightening and loosing the male member with the muscles of her privities." This is a power that all women have but that many women do not use. The Arab slave dealers pay handsomely for a woman who does.

It's remarkable that a man traveling in a place where his kind is supposedly forbidden and not free to leave without the consent of a ruler can enjoy languid afternoons with local courtesans. As the experience of Ludovico de Varthema showed two and a half centuries earlier, this is a privilege that only the Orient offered to imprisoned visitors from faraway. To be sure, Burton's sexual explorations were only a part of his more general explorations. He was a man who in his long career as an explorer and agent of British colonialism swallowed whole worlds, providing remarkably detailed and voluminous reports on just about everything he saw, from Sindh, a province in current-day Pakistan, and Tanganyika to Salt Lake City—on local history, the flora, the fauna, physical and moral characteristics of the peoples he encountered, their histories, diseases, architecture, cuisine, fortifications, customs, religious beliefs, courtship and marriage customs, and much else. No detail was unworthy of note and no occasion to show off his immense learning missed. "The Hig is called 'Salab' by the Arabs, who use its long tough fibre for ropes," he noted in a footnote in *First Footsteps in East Africa,* which contains his account of his Harar expedition. "Patches of this plant situated on moist ground at the foot of hills, are favourite places with sand antelope, spur-fowl and other game." Despite his erudition and his deep appreciation of the poetry and philosophy of the East, Burton at times exemplifies standard mid-nineteenth-century imperial British prejudices. Some of his descriptions of Africans and Middle Easterners are jarring by today's standards. " 'Conscience,' I may observe, does not exist in Eastern Africa, and 'Repentance' expresses regret for missed opportunities of mortal crime," he wrote in his account of his Harar expedition. "In character, the Eesa [a Bedouin tribe that Burton observed in Somalia] are childish and docile, cunning, and deficient in judgment, kind and fickle, good-humoured and irascible, warm-hearted, and infamous for cruelty and treachery.... Robbery constitutes an honorable man: murder—the more atrocious the midnight crime the better—makes the hero. Honor consists in taking human life: hyena-like, the Bedouins cannot be trusted where blood may be shed. Glory is the having done all manner of harm."

Late in his life, when he was bitter and disillusioned, beset by enemies and haunted by his failure to advance beyond captain in the army or minor consul in the diplomatic service, Burton wrote a tract on the Jews that Adolf Hitler would have admired.

Among his closest observations, always, are those of the women he encountered. His writings are full of esoteric and intimate bits and pieces of lore—that, for example, the Yemenis derided the Somali women for their swelling hips, while, Burton wrote, the Somalis compared "the lank haunches of their neighbours to those of tadpoles or young frogs." He noted that there were no "harlots" among the Somalis, but that "because of the inactivity of their husbands," the Somali women preferred "amourettes with strangers, following the well-known Arab proverb, 'The new comer filleth the eye.' " And as one of his biographers noted, "Who but Burton was the 'newcomer'?"

There is more, using just the example of *First Footsteps in East*

Africa, which is one of the forty or so books Burton wrote. He informed his readers that "the Somalis have only one method of making love," namely, lying side by side, the woman on the left, the man on the right. And he is meticulous and thorough in his description of infibulation, "this barbarous guarantee of virginity and chastity" practiced by most of the tribes of East Africa. It consisted in "sew[ing] up the lips of the girl's private parts either with a leather lace, or, more often, with one of horse-hair." Burton, also almost certainly drawing on his real-life experience, knew the ways women got around this practice: "Those who suspect their wife's fidelity, when they go on a journey will sew up again the aperture of the pudendum; but a woman who is so minded will break the suture with the greatest ease and sew it up again when her desires are satisfied." This detail is accompanied by a sweeping generalization: "The fair sex lasts longer in Eastern Africa than in India and Arabia: at thirty, however, charms are on the wane, and when old age comes on they are no exceptions to the hideous decrepitude of the East."

Burton in many ways echoed the accounts of earlier travelers to the East, from Marco Polo to Ludovico. He depicted a world of wonders and cruelties just as his predecessors had, the difference being that he was writing about peoples no longer so remote from Europe, peoples who were, or soon would be, what the colonizing world regarded as "natives," and this gives some of the most vivid of his descriptions a realism that still makes for chilling reading. He was a hands-on collector of information, an avid and indefatigable seeker of objective knowledge, and if he failed here and there to achieve objectivity, that was nonetheless his consistent standard. "I have forgotten as much as many Arabists have learned," he once wrote.

And Burton was unsparing in his findings, though he admired much about the non-Western world, especially when it came to the elements of sensuality that he believed were lamentably missing in Europe. He waxed lyrical in Egypt, where he discovered the Arab concept of *kayf,* which, to Burton, illustrated all the difference between East and West. It is "the savoring of animal existence; the passive enjoyment of mere sense; the pleasant languor, the dreamy tranquillity, the airy castle-building, which in Asia stand in lieu of the vigorous, intensive, passionate life of Europe." The other side of this admirable, feline hedonism is the casual, unreflective cruelty of Asia, which Burton described in fastidious detail. For Burton, Asia was different, a separate and distinct cultural realm, and it was experience and observation not bigotry or stereotype that was involved in its elaboration.

He told his commanding officer in Sindh, Charles Napier, of the local men who had agreed to be executed as substitutes for wealthy convicted murderers. They did this, Burton reported, in exchange for a lavish final meal and a cash payment to their poverty-stricken families. He knew about the fathers and brothers who hacked off the heads of daughters and sisters on suspicion of infidelity. In a famous report to Napier in 1845, he described brothels offering up boys and eunuchs for the satisfaction of their customers. Being the only officer in the English encampment who could speak the local language, he was assigned to look into these brothels, because Napier worried they might have a corrupting influence on his soldiers. Disguised as a local, Burton "passed away many an evening in the townlet" (meaning the newly founded city of Karachi), learning that there were three such brothels in operation and that within them boys were valued more highly than eunuchs. "The scrotum of the unmutilated boy could be used as a kind of bridle for directing the movements of the animal," he explained. Burton was not horrified by prostitution, quite the contrary, but he was by slavery, which was still a highly visible and lucrative practice in East Africa, carried on largely by Arab traders and often involving a mutilation as unspeakably cruel as it was widely practiced. Always it is his absorption of rich, graphic, and sometimes horrifying detail that sets him apart. A traveler like Flaubert, just passing through, might have noted the presence of slave traders. At one point in his Egyptian sojourn, Flaubert described a scene at Assiut (Asyut), capital of the Upper Nile, where the slave caravans stopped for "a compulsory rest, which the *gellabs* (slave traders) take advantage of to mutilate their young negroes, fitting them for service in the harems." But whereas Flaubert's account is touristy, hasty, and abstract, Burton, the traveler and anthropologist, told the whole gruesome story. In a note that he wrote in his great compendium of sexual practices and published in an appendix to his translation of *The Arabian Nights,* Burton provided this account of the surgical procedure used to castrate boys and young men forced into slavery to serve as eunuchs in Eastern harems: "The parts are swept off by a single cut of a razor, a tube (tin or wooden) is set in the urethra, the wound is cauterised with boiling oil, and the patient planted in a fresh dunghill. His diet is milk; and if under puberty, he often survives."

Burton, in other words, was no starry-eyed romantic so enamored of non-Europe that he ignored the many ways in which non-Europe was truly benighted. This must never be forgotten. Much of the world of sexual opportunity presented by the East has always been, and still is, based on exploitation and injustice, and Burton, unlike many of today's sexual travelers, remained keenly aware of that fact even as he fully engaged in the possibilities. He made even a contemporary fellow exotic traveler like Flaubert seem naïve in the ways of the world in which he took his pleasure.

Burton is not important mainly because he enjoyed the sexual opportunities of Africa and Asia. He was far from the only Englishman to frequent Sindh's *lal bazaars,* or native red-light districts (*lal* being the Hindi word for "red"), or to have a steady supply of *bibis,* as native Indian mistresses were called (the Hindi word *bibi* meaning "honorable lady"), or to dally with African girls of "rich nut-brown" skin and "perfect symmetry of limb." Numerous British and other foreign travelers did that too. If Flaubert privately espoused the special thrill of exotic sex, Burton became the chief exponent of the idea of exotic sexual superiority. It was the one area of life where Burton believed the East was vastly superior to the West, the vaginal athleticism of Galla slave girls being one of the many illustrations of this that he provided in his voluminous works.

For Burton, India, the Middle East, and Africa were all places of sexual "artists," where the cultivation of love far surpassed the low and unsatisfactory levels attained in frigid, Christian Europe. The East was a place where the erotic and the poetic mingled, where, stripped of its taint of immorality, it could be the subject of a kind of connoisseurship, a learned cultivation. During Burton's years in the East, his ceaseless exploration of sexual practices was made up of about equal parts actual dalliance and serious scholarship. "A conviction was born in him—perhaps intensified by failures in his own life, or by sampling the wide variety in the sexual market—that there was in the East a reservoir of experience against which the West, especially England, foolishly barricaded itself with dams of false modesty and shame," Fawn Brodie wrote in her biography of Burton. Burton belonged to a small avant-garde in Britain, whose members wanted to liberate the West from its sexual self-denial. Burton and his cohort took legal risks to do this, since the publication of explicit sexual writings of the sort they translated and printed was punishable in Victorian England by lengthy terms of imprisonment. In championing Eastern sexuality, Burton became a sort of early exponent of the sexual revolution that would come many decades later in Europe and the United States and would find part of its inspiration in the erotic rites, real and imagined, of the East.

BURTON WAS BORN IN 1821 in England, but his father, a retired British army officer from Ireland, took the family to Europe, where Richard, his brother, and his sister were educated largely by tutors. He learned several European languages early on and may even have learned the Gypsy language during an affair with a Romany girl he is rumored to have had. He went to Oxford University, where he began his lifelong study of Arabic, but was expelled when he challenged to a duel a fellow student who had mocked his military-style mustache. This circumstance led him to buy a commission in the army of the East India Company and to go to India, thereby beginning his extraordinary career as a soldier, intelligence agent, spy, explorer, linguist, writer, and translator. His list of accomplishments is staggering. One of his first, his journey to Mecca, and his vivid account of the experience, made him a household name in England.

Not long after that, he made his expedition to Harar, partly in the company of John Hanning Speke, an almost equally famous explorer and, in later years, a bitter enemy of Burton's. The Harar expedition was followed by Burton's most famous expedition of all, to discover the source of the Nile, which he also made in the company of Speke. That expedition failed in its main purpose, though it did result in the discoveries of both Lake Tanganyika and Lake Victoria. Burton's book on that journey, *The Lake Regions of Central Africa: A Picture of Exploration,* would have been enough all by itself to establish him as one of history's greatest geographers and anthropologists.

Later in his life, Burton, who is said to have mastered twenty-nine languages, made an unexpurgated translation of what is commonly called *The Arabian Nights,* which he translated as *The Book of a Thousand Nights and a Night,* whose elaborate footnotes and lengthy appendix are the fruit of Burton's lifelong accumulation of often-arcane data. He also translated what has become the two most widely read Indian love manuals, *Kama Shastra* (also known as *Ananga Ranga*) and *Kama Sutra.* In what seems a striking contradiction to the ensemble of his preferences in life, he married a religiously Catholic English aristocrat named Isabel Arundell, the only white woman he seems to have known intimately, who wrote an extremely admiring biography of her husband but also burned his huge collection of diaries and letters, presumably because of their erotic and salacious content.

As a result, Burton's biographers have had to read between the lines of Burton's published texts to form an image of him as sexually voracious. On an early stage of his Mecca expedition, for example, he stopped in Alexandria for a month or so and wrote in his *Personal Narrative of a Pilgrimage to Al-Madinah and Meccah* that he took advantage of "an opportunity of seeing 'Al-nahl,' the Bee-dance, . . . for it would be some months before my eyes might dwell on such a pleasant spectacle again." The assumption drawn from this brief reference is that Burton must have spent some of his time visiting prostitutes, as he seems to have done almost everywhere he went, and that seems a reasonable assumption. Flaubert, too, had written about the bee dance, and from his accounts it is clear that the dance itself was a preliminary to a sexual encounter. Later, in his book on the Gypsies—and most of the bee dancers were Gypsies—Burton described them as "arch-seductresses whose personal beauty makes them dangerous."

In many respects, his life and his marriage, and the apparent contradiction between the two, disclose something about the complexities of Victorian life—and in that sense illuminate the moral background against which Burton and his confederates in the publication of Indian love manuals operated.

BURTON ENTERED THE SCENE during the age of emerging bourgeois hegemony, the era of great fortunes being made by men who were dynamic, confident, rich, and imperial in their ambitions. They were called merchant princes or captains of industry, a nomenclature that revealed their status as a new aristocracy in European society, but, as the historian Peter Gay has written, the mass of the new classes was not so grand. Its members were the "bourgeois proletarians," the small merchants, the clerks, and other white-collar workers who were financially and socially insecure, had no claim on aristocratic status, and yearned for respectability. "It was precisely because most of them clustered around the lower edges of the pyramid that they were all the more intent on upholding middle-class morality and middle-class styles of living," Gay has written. Respectability was one of the concepts that differentiated the members of this middle class from the proletariat, from whom they ardently wished to be differentiated, and, even more so, from the urban poor who lived around them. A major attribute of respectability was the repressed, retrograde attitude toward sexuality that has over the decades become the standard image of Victorian society, involving three elements (in Gay's formulation): "purposeful propriety, diligent self-censorship, and tense moral preoccupations."

In fact, the bourgeoisie may not have been as obsessed by prissy decorousness as we imagine. Still, by economic necessity, its members had to be champions of postponed gratification. Indeed, they saw the unchecked urge for sexual pleasure as a proletarian vulgarity. "Sexual intercourse was a deed of darkness," one historian has written of the attitude of the English middle class; "sexual desire was something the well-bred man and woman should not have." A certain Dr. James Copeland, author of the widely read *Dictionary of Practical Medicine*, warned of the "pollutions" caused by what he called *manustupration* (masturbation), among them being decreased life expectancy. William Acton, another doctor and perhaps the best-known Victorian-era authority on matters of sex, was clear and uncompromising. Masturbation, he wrote, caused the body to be "stunted and weak," its muscles to be "undeveloped," complexions to be "sallow, pasty, or covered with spots of acne," and intellects to be "sluggish and enfeebled."

More generally, according to Acton, fulfilling sexual desire outside marriage was "fatal." It led to a "house of death." Young men needed to be taught that "every sexual indulgence is unmitigated evil," not only because of the danger of syphilis, a common Victorian-era scourge, but also, and more predictably, because of an ebbing away of the life forces that, in the scientific Victorian view, were preserved through the retention of semen. In his most ultra-Victorian finding, Acton propagandized the view that women didn't enjoy sex at all, or, for the sake of their mental and physical health, they shouldn't. This learned man of science (in what might seem a paradox, Acton was known for his scientific approach, his open-mindedness, and his liberalism) believed that what he called "overindulgence" led to cancer of the womb and to madness. Many of "the best mothers, wives and managers of households," he wrote in his major work, *Functions and Disorders of the Reproductive Organs,* "know little of or are careless about sexual indulgences. Love of home, of children, and domestic duties are the only passions they feel. As a general rule, a modest woman seldom desires any sexual gratification for herself. She submits to her husband's embraces, but principally to gratify him; and were it not for the desire of maternity, would far rather be relieved of his attentions."

Whether middle-class Victorian women actually experienced sex the way Acton said they did cannot really be known, though, given the reality of sexual pleasure, much actual behavior must have failed to conform to Dr. Acton's description of it. The truth is that prostitution flourished in Victorian society, wealthy men proudly flaunted their kept mistresses, who were badges of worldly success, and a trade in child prostitutes, both male and female, kept on despite all the efforts by societies for good works to suppress it. "At mid-century," the historian Ronald Hyam has written, "there were almost certainly more brothels in London than there were schools and charities put together." The aristocracy carried on with its affairs and infidelities as it always had and still does. The working classes were lewd, drunken, and indecent. The older, stronger public school boys coolly sodomized the younger, weaker ones. Pornography, although illegal, was easily available, like illegal drugs are today. A mid-century attorney general, Lord Campbell, whose definition of obscenity included anything "offensive to modesty or decency or expressing or suggesting unchaste or lustful ideas or being impure, indecent or lewd," saw to it that laws were passed punishing pornography. Nonetheless, it flooded into England, largely from France, even as the Society for the Suppression of Vice campaigned to have the works of the likes of Rabelais banned and one well-known publisher was imprisoned for twelve months for having produced an English translation of Émile Zola's novel *La terre*. And surrounding it all was a vast conspiracy of silence, an absence of all but the most prudish, Acton-like discussion of sex and sexuality.

But as the prevalence of prostitution and pornography indicates, Victorian society was complicated and, especially in the last third of the nineteenth century, in transition in the realm of sex. "It would be a gross misreading of the bourgeois experience to think that nineteenth-century bourgeois did not know, or did not practice, or did not enjoy what they did not discuss," Gay has written. Dr. Acton himself can be credited with having opened up for discussion matters of sexuality that had previously been subject to the vast Victorian conspiracy of silence, most conspicuously prostitution, which, though he believed that it was bad, he also believed that it was inevitable and therefore needed to be legislated. He wrote a learned compendium on prostitution, which led in the 1860s to the passage of three contagious diseases acts, which regulated prostitution at military encampments in England, requiring prostitutes to be examined and, if infected, forced to stay in hospitals for treatment. The law was extended to India in 1897. Though his writings on female sexuality make him seem an unbearable prude, he was actually a liberal activist who, for example, recognized both "the dull stupidity that shuts its eyes to well-known evils" and the right of a woman "to make a profit of her own person" if she so desired.

Enter Eastern sexuality, partly in the form of Richard Burton's translations of Indian sex manuals, his great "Terminal Essay" to *The Arabian Nights*, and many other works—the information about sex often in lengthy, learned footnotes. Unexpurgated, *The Arabian Nights* translation was published in two limited editions of sixteen volumes in the 1880s. Burton in this sense belonged to a sexual and cultural liberation movement that, a century before a remarkably similar movement, used the examples of the East to illustrate the life- and pleasure-denying restrictiveness of the West. The surrounding sensibility was what Gay has called bourgeoisophobia, hatred of the bourgeois, its presumed prudery, vulgarity, hypocrisy, and sentimentality, its willful ignorance of sex, and its repression of desire. Flaubert was perhaps the most caustic of the bourgeoisophobes, and his indulgences during his trip to Egypt, and the earthy and explicit letters that he wrote there, illustrate a consciously chosen alternative sexual lifestyle (even though the word *lifestyle* hadn't been coined yet). Flaubert wanted to be different, and speaking in bawdy terms to his friends—to talk about "pricks," "whores," "cunts," and "Nubian girls whose necklaces of gold piastres hung down to their thighs"—was to include them in the club of the anti-bourgeois. It is an "axiom," Flaubert wrote to George Sand, that "hatred of the bourgeoisie is the beginning of all virtue." Burton, probably unknown to Flaubert, who before the publication of *Madame Bovary* was certainly unknown to him, expressed a strikingly similar sentiment: "The prospect of a book which can produce horripilation is refreshing."

Flaubert's sexual adventures in Egypt were exceptional in his life and not repeated. For Burton, however, Eastern sensuality was a lifelong preoccupation. To be sure, it was always a fascination among a minority of Western men, with the vast majority falling in love with, marrying, having affairs with, and being sexually drawn to Western women. But Burton prefigured something that would happen when the mixing of the civilizations became common and some men would develop a veritable cult of the Asian woman, who seemed to them naturally more sensuous, less inhibited, more sultry, slender, fragrant, feline, and languid, less competitive, less demanding of absolute fidelity, and for some or all of those reasons, more desirable than Caucasian women. Burton felt that way. The cult of the Asian woman among Western men—her erotic elevation—didn't originate with him, but it received validation from his writings and his experience. From the very beginning in India, he and others like him extolled the virtues of the *bibi* over the white woman back home, both because she caused less trouble and because she was better in bed. None other than the Anglican bishop of Calcutta, Reginald Heber, admitted that he had difficulty keeping his eyes off the local Bengali women he saw bathing in the river at dawn, confessing that "the deep bronze tint was more naturally agreeable to the human eyes than the fair skins of Europe." With slightly different reasoning, first Viscount Garnet Wolseley, field marshal in the British army, admitted that he consorted with an "Eastern princess" who fulfilled "all the purposes of a wife without any of the bother" and that he had no intention of marriage with "some bitch" in Europe, unless she were an heiress.

Burton had three important love affairs during his seven years in

India, all with native women, and it was clear, given his later activities, that compared with them he found European women literally and figuratively colorless. Flaubert's descriptions of his encounters with writhing, oiled, and scented dancer-whores carries the implicit message that the women back home were antiseptic by comparison, erotically insipid. Flaubert, unlike Burton, never said so explicitly, but then again he didn't write tumescent notes to Bouilhet about his sexual encounters with prostitutes in Paris. For Burton and other Englishmen with experience in India or Ceylon, the East represented a reservoir of wisdom and, as Burton suggested in connection with those Galla slave girls, an artistry whose absence in the West was a cause of something more important than missed opportunity: frigidity, lack of fulfillment, a lack of the ability to be wholly alive.

IN THE EFFORT to shatter the thick ice of Victorian morality, Burton was a natural partner to a group of mostly wealthy bohemian English aesthetes, pornographers, and admirers of the Marquis de Sade who would, under other circumstances, probably have had little in common with a swashbuckling explorer and agent of British imperialism. In 1853, when Burton was in Egypt preparing for his undercover expedition to Mecca, he encountered a young man named Fred Hankey. Both were guests of an Italian, Galeazzo Visconti. Hankey was, as one historian has put it, "a notorious libertine" who spent most of his time in Paris collecting pornography and supplying the erotic collections of other wealthy Englishmen. In a letter to the secretary of the Royal Geographical Society, Burton provided strong evidence that the Italian engaged in orgies in Egypt, describing the Visconti home as "a center of depravity, showing what Cairo can do in a pinch, and beating the Arabian Nights all to chalk."

Years later, after Burton had returned to London and married Isabel Arundell, one of his closest friends was Richard Monckton Milnes, later Baron Houghton. Milnes was a patron of the arts at whose country estate the likes of Benjamin Disraeli, Thomas Carlyle, and Algernon Swinburne, as well as Burton, frequently gathered. He was also an avid collector of erotica, whose trove of the works of de Sade, as one historian has written, "was well known through the upper reaches of

English literary society." Another member of the circle was Henry Ashbee, a wealthy businessman and habitué of brothels from London to Algiers who, under the pseudonym Pisanus Fraxi, compiled three immense indexes of pornographic literature with the Latin title *Index librorum prohibitorum.* These men were not patrons of seedy sex shops of the sort that would come to most Western cities decades later. They were literati for whom pornography was an emblem of liberation from the dead hand of respectability. Ashbee, another good friend of Burton's, was probably the author of one of the more remarkable books written in Victorian England, the eleven-volume *My Secret Life,* which recounts with a Sadean cruelty and lack of inhibition an English gentleman's adventures with 1,250 women. Both Milnes and Ashbee were clients of Hankey, who was living his dissipated life in Paris in conscious imitation of de Sade—indeed, Ashbee called him "a second de Sade without the intellect."

This was the group, minus Hankey, that supported Burton in what became the great project of his later years: to instruct his countrymen in the pleasures of sophisticated sexuality by translating into English the two Indian love manuals and *A Thousand Nights and a Night,* complete with his great compendium of sexual practices. With Milnes providing a good deal of the financing, Burton and Foster Fitzgerald Arbuthnot, an Indian-born student of Indian literature, created the Kama Shastra Society in 1882. That organization, an imaginary publishing house situated, supposedly, in Benares (present-day Varanasi), India, was a device to publish the Indian sex manuals while avoiding England's strict laws against pornography.

"Our ignorance of aphrodisiacs is considered the most remarkable phenomenon: there being scarcely a single oriental work on physic that does not devote the greater part of its pages to the consideration of a question which the medical man in the East will hear a dozen times a day," Burton wrote in one of his travel adventures, illustrating his lifelong ambition to raise the erotic consciousness of the English, an ambition that reached its highest expression with his late-in-life translations. Many years later, in a note to his translation of the *Ananga-Ranga,* Burton provided a poignant afterword to his Indian experiences, admitting indirectly that his own lack of education in the art of love was duly noted by his mistresses. Europeans "are contemptuously compared by

Hindu women with village cocks; and the result is that no stranger has ever been truly loved by a native girl," he wrote. Among the techniques of the Hindus, he continued, was the "retaining art," the ability not to finish too quickly and thereby leave one's partner satisfied, and the secret of this "art" is to think and do something else during the sexual act so as "to avoid over-tension of the muscles and to pre-occupy the brain; hence in coition the Hindus will drink sherbet, chew betel-nut and even smoke."

The "Terminal Essay" and Burton's other works contain a great deal along these lines and for that reason stand as an expression of Burton's vision—of the East as a place of natural openness toward sex and the West as a place of "silly prejudice and miserable hypocrisy." "Among savages and barbarians the comparatively unrestrained intercourse between men and women relieved the brain through the body," Burton wrote, continuing with a vision of Western people living without that natural relief, forced "to dwell fondly upon visions amatory and vene-real," to live in the "rustle of (imaginary) copulation." In a view that seems surprising today, Burton felt that "Moslems who do their best to countermine the asceticism inherent in Christianity are not ashamed of the sensual appetite; but rather the reverse." He was talking especially of the Sufi brand of Islam, which he admired and whose poetry he translated, not the strict and puritanical Wahhabism from Saudi Arabia, which dominates much of Islamic discourse today. Burton, along these lines, told the story of a saintly Persian lodged by a disciple at Shiraz who came out of his room and demanded a woman, "whereupon he was given a slave girl to marry and satisfy the demands of the flesh.

"By contrast, the England of our day would fain bring up both sexes and keep all ages in profound ignorance of sexual and intersexual relations; and the consequences of that imbecility are peculiarly cruel and afflicting," Burton wrote, sounding very much like the early advocate of sex education that he was. In writing clearly and unmistakably about female pleasure (and the denial of it through female circumcision and infibulation), Burton not only contradicted the prevailing Victorian prejudice on this matter but also anticipated the scientific writings of Freud and Havelock Ellis at the end of the nineteenth century. He was no Dr. Acton in this regard, writing in the "Terminal Essay," "In England some mothers are idiots enough not to tell their daughters what to expect on the wedding night. Hence too often unpleasant surprises disgust and dislike. The most modern form is that of the chloroform'd bride upon whose pillow the bridegroom found a paper pinned and containing the words 'Mamma says you're to do what you like.' "

Burton in these ways is an early illustration of what would become a continuing literary theme in Britain, the exposé of the arch moralist, often a missionary, whose life's goal was to force the "natives" to give up their lewd and provocative behavior, like dressing scantily in the tropical heat, and to reserve sex for procreation, not pleasure. The later prototypes for this kind of figure are Mr. and Mrs. Davidson in the short novel *Rain* by Somerset Maugham, the Davidsons' being missionaries in the South Pacific who have had great success eradicating the shocking immorality of the natives. By today's standards, the suffocatingly prudish, unbearably self-satisfied Davidsons seem to be caricatures (until, of course, Maugham's last lines reveal Mr. Davidson's terrible secret). Who can imagine someone talking these days like Mrs. Davidson when she tells Maugham's narrator how they managed to eradicate the locals' native dress in favor of "Mother Hubbards" for women and "trousers and singlets" for men? Or when Mr. Davidson announces, "I think that was the most difficult part of my work, to instill into the natives the sense of sin."

But, as we will see later, the truth is that couples like the Davidsons were common in the world of nineteenth- and early-twentieth-century proselytism in Asia and the Pacific Islands, and they shed light on another aspect of the erotic relationship between East and West, namely, that if in many instances Westerners exploited sexual opportunities to enhance their own enjoyment, in other instances they stamped out the enjoyment of the peoples they colonized. Burton (and, of course, Maugham, though much later) belonged to the exploiters, of course, not to the prosyletizers.

This was the situation when the Indian love manuals were translated, and the indications are that they fell into receptive hands. Burton and the fictitious Kama Shastra Society brought out two very limited and expensive editions, the first in 1883 with 250 copies in seven parts, all but one of them supposedly printed in Benares and all of them marked "For Private Circulation Only." A smaller edition, bound in one volume, was brought out later, and that was that as far as Burton and the Kama Shastra Society were concerned. But the numerous pirated copies probably made Burton's *Kama Sutra* one of the biggest best sellers of all time.

Then came *A Thousand Nights and a Night,* a much vaster work of editing, translation, and commentary. Burton published an edition of one thousand sets of ten volumes, and when he sent out solicitations to some thirty-six thousand prospective buyers, he was, as one of his biographers, Edward Rice, put it, so "swamped with returns" that he hastened to do another edition, which he called *Supplemental Nights.* Burton's original *Nights* is one of the few widely read books whose footnotes are as appreciated as the main text, though the main text itself is a story of the very Eastern harem that had titillated Europeans for centuries. It tells of King Shahryar who, cuckolded by his wife and his ten favorite concubines, not only has the unfaithful women slaughtered but also refuses to marry again. Instead, he takes a different queen every night for three thousand nights, having each of them beheaded afterward. Then, having slept with and then beheaded three thousand queens, King Shahryar finds that no more women are willing to accept his arrangement—and he is kindhearted enough not to force any to do so. In response to the king's predicament, his vizier offers his own daughter Shahrazad to consort with Shahryar, and she plots to save her life by telling the king a different story every night until, 1,001 nights and three children later, she is spared the fate of her predecessors and becomes the new queen—for life.

Burton, in his footnotes, never loses a chance to enlighten his countrymen about the sexual customs of other people. When Shahryar discovers his queen in the embrace of "a big slobbering blackamoor with rolling eyes which showed the whites, a truly hideous sight," Burton informs us in a footnote, "Debauched women prefer negroes on account of the size of their parts." Not satisfied with that, he gives the results of his own research on penis size, in which he found, indeed, that both the men and the animals of Africa are well endowed (though, Burton added, "the pure Arab, man and beast, is below the average of Europe"). More often, however, his *Arabian Nights* is an object lesson in the superior sensuality, the erotic connoisseurship, that he found in the East, as he did, for example, in the story of Ali Shar and the slave girl Zumurrud, rendered with rich sensuality in Burton's translation:

So saying, she lay down on her back and taking his hand, set it to her parts, and he found these same parts softer than silk; white, plumply-rounded, protuberant, resembling for heat the bath or the heart of a lover whom love-longing hath wasted. . . . Then he sheathed his steel rod in her scabbard and ceased now to play the porter at her door and the preacher in her pulpit and the priest at her prayer-niche, whilst she with him ceased not from inclination and prostration and rising up and sitting down, accompanying her ejaculations of praise and of "Glory to Allah!" with passionate movements and wrigglings and claspings of his member and other amorous gestures.

Burton, in these writings, is perhaps the last of the great European travelers to the exotic East, bringing to a sort of final point of observation the science and pseudoscience that had begun hundreds of years before with the likes of Marco Polo, John of Mandeville (if he existed), and Ludovico de Varthema. But if Burton marks the final step in one literary tradition, he is in the very middle of a new era of erotic relations between East and West. One aspect of that era was the commercialization of Eastern sensuality, a phenomenon that continues to this day in the vast explosion of "Asian" pornography, that large portion of the business of porn in which Asian women have sex on camera, frequently with Western men. Burton published his first edition of *Nights* very worried that it would cause him legal troubles. The irony is that the brisk sales of *A Thousand Nights* made Burton a wealthy man. "I struggled for forty-seven years," he wrote, and "I never had a compliment nor a 'Thank you,' nor a single farthing." Clearly he had in mind here his many enemies who kept him from rising above the rank of captain and consigned one of his country's greatest explorers to remote diplomatic posts. Indeed, even as he worked on his translations of the great works of Eastern sensuality, he embarked on ill-fated expeditions in Africa in an attempt to get rich by discovering gold mines. Burton continued: "I translated a doubtful book in my old age, and immediately made sixteen thousand guineas."

Burton was representative of another aspect of the new era as well, in which fantasy and speculation were replaced by the actual experience of Western men, who, beginning with British and French colonialists in Africa, India, and Southeast Asia, began going east by the tens of thousands and then by the hundreds of thousands. No longer did European men have to read books about the East. They could go there, and they discovered, to their great delight, that what had only been dreamed about by earlier generations could be a daily reality.

CHAPTER SEVEN

Colonialism and Sex

COLONIALISM HAS ALWAYS produced sexual opportunities for the colonizers, or at least it is difficult to find an instance when prostitution and concubinage didn't ensue from the conquest of an Eastern country by a Western one. The paradox here is enormous, given that the Christian West was the domain where sex was deemed a sin and the morally benighted and lewd portions of the globe were expected to benefit from the introduction of Christian civilization. In fact, sex was a pleasure avidly pursued by the builders of empire going places where it was generally readily available, and that has been the case since the very first of the European trading expeditions to Asia, which led eventually to European conquest and rule.

The Portuguese led the way in imperial initiatives in the final years of the fifteenth century and the early decades of the sixteenth, sending their ships down the coast of Africa and all the way to India, China, Malaysia, Japan, and Indonesia, and although their dominion of the seas was short-lived, their sexual activities are an indelible part of the record.

One British sailor in the Moluccan Islands (now part of Indonesia) in the sixteenth century was struck by the joyful life of a Portuguese settler he met there, a man, the Englishman noted, who lay "with as many women as he pleaseth. . . . He will sing and dance all day long, nearly half naked . . . and will be drunk two days together." Like other Europeans, many Portuguese were attracted to India, where Vasco da Gama first arrived by ship on May 20, 1498, and the attraction, as one student of this subject has put it, was to "the delights of a society in which slavery, concubinage and polygamy were widespread and entirely accepted."

After the Portuguese commander Afonso de Albuquerque had, in 1510, conquered the trading port of Goa, which Portugal held for the next 451 years, he ordered his soldiers to marry the widows of the Mughal soldiers they had killed. Presumably the widows also had to be ordered to marry the slayers of their husbands. Albuquerque himself presided at the weddings, which were aimed at forming Catholic families that would beget Portuguese children who would serve on future Portuguese ships. Within a few years, however, the Goans weren't becoming Portuguese, but the Portuguese were becoming Goan— dressing in Indian silks, drinking cow's urine for their health, smoking hookahs, and establishing harems.

A hundred or so years later, after the British East India Company had embarked on what was to become British rule in India, the first recorded British-Indian love affair took place. A letter from 1626 in the company's files tells of a certain John Leachland, who, "in spite of all persuasions," had for some years "kept a woman of this country." Leachland refused, in the letter's words, "to put her away," and his defiance led to a debate within the company over whether to relieve him of his duties. In what might have been a historic move, it was decided to tolerate Leachland's sexual transgressions, and on very practical and realistic grounds: firing him, the company decided, "would only lead to his marrying her and forsaking his country and friends." Therefore, "it is resolved not to adopt this extreme course in the hope that time will reclaim him."

The record is very clear that many of Leachland's countrymen followed his example and did so for the next three hundred years, even though the practice by which Englishmen took on the attributes of Indian nawabs and maharajas earned continuing disapproval back home and, after about two hundred years, did come to an end. In the late eighteenth century, the political philosopher Edmund Burke sponsored an effort to have the colonial governor of Bengal, Warren Hastings (one of the epochal figures in Britain's Indian conquests), removed from office because of what Burke termed his promotion of the literal rape of Indian women. Sex with native women wasn't the main thing that bothered Burke; it was the generalized corruption, in which company officials seized great wealth from local people, that troubled him most. But seizing women and seizing wealth were part of the same process by which the British slowly became the masters of India, and Burke, who lost his suit against Hastings, was powerless to prevent either of them. "Virgins who had never seen the sun . . . were violated by the lowest and wickedest of the human race," he declaimed in a speech before Parliament. Robert Clive, the first significant commander of British troops in India and the figure given the most credit for Britain's early conquests there, has been controversially depicted as a sexual glutton who took full advantage of the availability of local women. Most of the stories about Clive are unconfirmed, and some have been determined to be fraudulent. But one remnant from the historical archives—a letter to Clive from a close friend referring to a rich record of sexual adventures they undertook together—is strong evidence that Clive lived an Indian life very far from chastity.

And Clive was only the beginning. Francis Day, the pioneering company official who founded the fort of Madras on the Indian Ocean, is said to have chosen the site because it was near his Indian mistress's home. Richard Wellesley, Earl of Mornington, governor general of Bengal from 1797 to 1805, who was unaccompanied by his wife during his years in India, consoled his lonely days by visiting the brothels, something he would have been unable to do had he been governor general of Canada. Wellesley's younger brother, the Duke of Wellington, he who defeated Napoleon at the Battle of Waterloo, was so shocked at Wellesley's lifelong "profligate habits" that he wished he could be castrated. Perhaps Wellesley was not an example of what, by the late 1700s, Englishmen back home were sarcastically and pejoratively calling *nabobs*—East India Company officials who, in the view of the time, had learned the ways of corrupt and vice-ridden India, lived like maharajas there, and then used their dubiously earned lucre to buy seats for themselves in Parliament—but Clive certainly was. Like the nawabs, actual Indian aristocrats, the nabobs kept harems in India, or certainly many of them did. "A lass and a lakh a day" was a favorite toast among the company's rakish buccaneers, a lakh being the Hindi term for one hundred thousand rupees. By the seventeenth century, *bibi* had become the common term for an Indian mistress, and it remained part of the language for the entire colonial epoch.

In 1971, I had the occasion to spend a few days with an English family in the Western Ghat Mountains in southern India. The master of this household was one of the last British managers of a tea plantation in India, and all the accoutrements of colonial life seemed to be present. He lived in a hilltop house whose broad verandas hung with orchids and whose rooms were busy with servants, who called him *sahib,* the Hindi word that means "master" and was the common form of address for white men in India for three hundred years. He spent his evenings in the wood-paneled Indian club—formerly an English club—where the tea-plantation aristocracy gathered to eat, play tennis, and get drunk. He expressed nostalgia—and engaged in racism-tinged conversation about the good old days, when, he proclaimed, "we had the niggers by the balls." And not only by the balls. Years later in New York, I met a daughter of the family whom I hadn't seen since that week in the Western Ghats. She told me, among other things, that like most of the other British managers of the tea plantations (and to the chagrin of her mother), her father for many years had kept an Indian mistress. She was known as his *bibi,* the daughter said.

This erotic involvement of the British in India is not an unchanging tableau. The nabob phenomenon occurred early in the East India Company's history and was a product of the most freewheeling, swashbuckling time, when, as one British historian has put it, "Those responsible for India underwent a moral transformation, abandoning British habits of mind and codes of public behavior and embracing those of the subcontinent." Among the habits of the subcontinent most eagerly adopted were graft, by which many company officials waxed wealthy, and the keeping of native mistresses, on whom they spent some of their loot. In time, many company officials, British army soldiers, and colonial officials were to bring wives and family to India, where they led perfectly boring semitropical conventional lives, socially and physically separate from India and the Indians, for whom they had more contempt than admiration. Fewer native mistresses were kept, or fewer were kept openly, to the satisfaction of churchmen and others who had always condemned the practice. Still, John Leachland and my friend's father, separated by more than three centuries, had what many British colonialists had in common for almost the whole of the several hundred years of British colonialism—and they had it in common not only with one another but with the colonial-era emissaries of other countries in other empires, whether the Dutch on Dejima Island near Nagasaki in Japan or the French in North Africa and Indochina. They had the sexual privileges that came with colonial dominion, especially in the territories of the harem culture, where those privileges were seen as normal and natural, part of the order of things. And they often had these privileges not as dark family secrets to be revealed in hushed tones years later but with a certain conspicuous display and panache.

The early representatives of the East India Company lived it up in India, unabashedly adopting the habits of the Mughal princes who were still very much a part of the scene. Among the preferred entertainments of the company's representatives was the nautch, a sensuous performance by musicians and silk-bedecked dancing girls.

One seventeenth-century German visitor called the nautch "the greatest entertainment imaginable." David Ochterlony, the British resident in Delhi in 1803 and a commander in the Indian army, not only illustrates the way the English adopted the styles and manners of Mughal princes but was, as it were, illustrated in doing so. Ochterlony reportedly had thirteen wives, one of whom was identified in his will as "beebee" Mahruttun Moobaruck ul Nissa Begume, alias Begum Ochterlony. It is worth noting that this woman, whom Ochterlony said was "the mother of my younger children," was presented to him, or perhaps sold to him, when she was twelve years old. Ochterlony had served the empire well, commanding the troops during the punitive military expedition to Nepal in 1814–15, an exploit that presumably gave him some credibility when he insisted that he be addressed by his Mughal title, Defender of the State. He also liked to parade around Delhi with his wives following behind, each on her own elephant.

Ochterlony's example is of particular note because a Persian-style miniature, painted around 1820, shows him in his Oriental splendor. He reclines on a carpet, leaning on pillows and bolsters, wearing an Indian costume—a white robe with gold and black brocade trim and a red turban. Servants, also wearing turbans, stand behind him while a group of musicians and the inevitable dancing girls perform in front. In a superbly sardonic gesture, the miniaturist shows four portraits of what appear to be Scottish and American ancestors (Ochterlony was born in Boston), some in uniforms, and one European woman looking

Early-nineteenth-century watercolor showing the British resident in Delhi, David Ochterlony, at home smoking a hookah and watching a nautch.

British Library

very prim and dour compared with the dancing girls, all seemingly shocked as they peer from a high wall at the spectacle below. Ochterlony once received the bishop of Calcutta, Reginald Heber (who, as we have seen, was an admirer of the bronze skin of local women), in just such a scene—wearing a loose robe and a turban, sitting on a divan, a *punkah wallah* stirring the air with an ostrich-feather punkah (a kind of bellows).

As late as 1906, in a report to the British Foreign Office, a certain A. J. Bucknill, wrote, "Of course, the lascivious-minded man of European race can always, in any part of the world, find means of gratifying his wishes." These lascivious-minded men were served well by the British practice of recognizing reality and attempting to accommodate it. Particularly in the nineteenth century, as imperialism reached its zenith and the number of colonial civil servants and soldiers swelled to the hundreds of thousands, what one official called "promiscuous and hazardous intercourse with profligate women of the bazaar" led to a dramatic increase in venereal disease. The infection rate among British soldiers in Bengal, for example, fluctuated between 16 percent and 31 percent of the total. What to do? Reality dictated, as the British surgeon general of Bombay put it in 1886, only two means of "satisfaction" for unmarried men. These were masturbation—which, "as is well known, leads to disorders of both body and mind"—and "mercenary sex," the hazard of which is venereal disease.

The solution, though fiercely criticized by various churchmen and writers, one of whom called it "an attempt to make sinning safe," was to foster two complementary institutions: one was the "lock hospital," a medical clinic with origins in Britain, where infected prostitutes were confined until they were cured, and the other was the *lal bazaar,* a supervised red-light district for Europeans, whose employees could be regularly checked.

The *lal bazaars* were intended for the members of the British lower classes, who were, in the view of the time, less able than their betters to control their physical desires and more inclined to descend to the level of the heathen natives they were meant to govern. One scholar has counted seventy-five cantonments of Britain's Indian army in which "regulated prostitution" was available. This practice led to the creation of some large establishments. The brothel in Lucknow had fifty-five rooms. But as the erotic engagements of Clive, Wellesley, and Ochterlony amply demonstrate, plenty of upper-class colonial civil servants and ranking officers also "descended" to that level. Not all of them went quite as comprehensively native as Ochterlony, but many dressed in Mughal robes, smoked hookahs, and kept native mistresses, the famous *bibis,* who served as unofficial wives, managing the household, nursing the sahib when he was sick, and satisfying his sexual desires.

British life in India in these ways was certainly different from life in Britain itself, though of course not in the sense that sex was available in India and not back home. In the years before the full onrush of Victorian morality, sex was widely enough available back home that young Englishmen going to India expected it, demanded it, and found it easily attainable. Still, the pursuit of sexual pleasure in India brought fewer restrictions, less official supervision, and more latitude than it did in England, and the visual sensuousness of Indian life itself, as seen in so much painting and sculpture familiar to better-educated and better-traveled Europeans, had its effect on the Western consciousness. Some colonial civil servants and officers resisted local temptation. A fair number of celebrated colonial-era figures, Charles Gordon and Cecil Rhodes among them, seem to have been asexual and to have embodied one of the great colonial-era ideals: the great man who gives up the pleasures of domesticity for the sake of Crown and empire. The truth is that many, if not most, colonial officials exchanged conventional domesticity for sexual lives of far greater variety and excitement than conventional domesticity would have offered. "The empire was a Moloch, created by men not of a moral class," declared the writer of the previously cited 1887 letter to the *Pall Mall Gazette*. The fact was that, as one scholar has noted of the British, "the result" of their encounter with India "was the creation of a heathen, ribald sensual class of Britons absolutely unbound by convention."

And they were abetted in this by the circumstances of colonial life—the boredom and spareness of barracks life and even of life in the councils of administration and the absence of most other forms of entertainment. There was also the surrounding sensuousness of India, whose society attached no opprobrium to the woman who sold her body for money or position. In Europe, prostitutes and mistresses may have been numerous, and some well-bred courtesans even achieved a certain celebrity, but they were viewed as having sold their virtue for a few coins, as morally degraded, partially or even fully criminal. The Indians tended much more to accept that there would be a class of women whose role in the world was to satisfy male sexual desire and that the satisfaction of male sexual desire was natural and moral. No doubt by today's standards, the Indian attitude was deeply demeaning to women. And yet it makes sense to suppose that prostitutes internalized the surrounding attitudes. If you are regarded as a normal member of human society, depicted in painting and sculpture and in the literary classics of your country, you are going to have a certain pride that those who are reviled and criminalized will not have.

And this explanation accounts for a common belief among Western men in Asia to this day, many of whom would never consider visiting a prostitute at home but make a regular habit of it when they are in the East. To some extent, they do so simply because it is always easier to engage in sin far from the prying eyes of people who know you. Thai men have a bit of conventional wisdom about this, which is never to visit a prostitute in your own neighborhood. But European, Australian, and American men who would never visit prostitutes in their own countries visit them in Asia also because Asian prostitutes don't fit the image of prostitutes in the West, as sleazy, mercenary, cold, depraved, and vaguely intimidating. They seem, actually, sweet, affectionate, unmarred by the businesslike qualities of common sex-for-sale workers in the West. There is, to be sure, self-delusion on the part of Western men in this, because the Thai bar girl is in it for the money, just as her counterpart in Paris or New York is, but it is a self-delusion very much encouraged by the prostitutes themselves, who are charming, eager to please, kittenish, and at the same time, skillful.

In any event, whether this view of Asian prostitutes is delusion or reality, many men certainly are persuaded that it is accurate, and many British in India certainly harbored the same view of the women in the colonies who offered them the pleasures of sex. The better prostitutes—those who charged five rupees rather than two—"are a very different set of people from their sisterhood in European countries," wrote Edward Sellon, a self-described philanderer who spent time in India as a captain in the army in the mid-nineteenth century. "They do not drink, they are scrupulously cleanly in their persons, they are sumptuously dressed, they wear the most costly jewels in profusion, they are well educated and sing sweetly, accompany their voices on the viol de gambe, a sort of guitar, they generally decorate their hair with clusters of clematis, or sweetly scented bilwa flowers entwined with pearls and diamonds."

Captain Sellon admired the Indian women for many reasons, not least because they shaved or plucked out their pubic hairs so that, until you took in the fullness of their breasts and hips, "you fancy you have got hold of some unfledged girl." More generally, Sellon, who spent ten years in India, advanced the view, seconded by Richard Burton and others, that Indian women "understand in perfection all the arts and wiles of love, are capable of gratifying any tastes, and in face and figure are unsurpassed by any women in the world."

For a brief time, Sellon lived in a compound that offered a view of a school for what were called half-caste girls—"nut-brown maidens," he said—and he recounted a conversation with his butler about obtaining one of them for his pleasure. The conversation has a certain ring of authenticity as an illustration of the way things worked in India—how the white man assumed that he was superior, that Indian girls were available to him, and that money oiled the wheels of the transaction. "S'pose the Colonel Sahib, or the Major Sahib, or any other burra sahib [great man], happen to cast his eye that way," the butler said, nodding in the direction of the girls' school. "And him say, 'but, go, bring me such a girl,' ah, that bhote brabher [very proper]. Him you say, 'Bhote eucha, sahib' [very good, sir] and him run to old lady mistress and say, 'The burra sahib wantee such a girl, put a veil over her and let her come.' Then old lady mistress askee, 'You money got?' 'Yees!' him answer, 'How much rupee?' 'Very good baksheesh, ma'am, fifty rupah.' 'Fifty rupees not 'nuff, must have eighty rupees, you tellee Colonel Sahib dat girl one virgin.' "

As Sellon told the story, the butler did go to the schoolmistress to procure a girl for Sellon whom Sellon had admired from his window. He struck a deal, and later that night the schoolmistress came to his quarters and presented "the beautiful creature naked to me." What ensued, Sellon continued, was "a most delicious night," with his "companion" even promising to escape from the school and join him in Cannapore, where he was due to join his regiment. That was not to come to pass, however, because the regimental commander found out about Sellon's conquest and protested to the schoolmistress that she had allowed one of her prettiest girls to go to one of his men rather than to him. An ugly story—or, to be more accurate, an even uglier story—followed. The colonel demanded that Sellon's girl be brought to him. She was, and when she refused to submit to his advances, he had his servants tie her to his bed, where he raped her, a crime that led to his court-martial and imprisonment. Or so went Sellon's tale, not that he cared very much, certainly not about the Indian girl, whom he called Lillias. In his narrative, he passed quickly and cheerfully on to Canna-

pore, where, as he discreetly put it, "I now commenced a regular course
of fucking with native women."

WHAT WERE THE REASONS for this remarkable correlation of sex
with empire? One, of course, was simply the presence of Western men
with plenty of ready cash on the lookout for pleasure and the willingness of Eastern societies to provide the wherewithal—at a price, of
course. These were rich men put in the proximity of an abundance of
pretty, poor girls in places with a long tradition whereby pretty, poor
girls served the sexual needs of the rich. In Ho Chi Minh City, the former Saigon, I asked Nguyen Ngoc Luong, a former translator and
reporter for *The New York Times* bureau in Vietnam who has lived in
that city since 1954, why the bars and cabarets, the dance houses and
massage parlors, were always concentrated on and around the big street
running roughly from the colonial governor's mansion to the Saigon
River—called rue Catinat under the French and Tu Do (Freedom)
Street when the Americans were in Saigon in large numbers. His
answer was that it would be precisely near the centers of power and
commerce that high society and low society were most apt to mingle.

"Here was Norodom Palace, where the governor general of
Indochina's office was," he said, drawing a rough map of Saigon during
the rule of the French. "Next to it was the courthouse, and next to that
was the police station. Nearby was the cathedral. On either side were
the French schools, the Chasseloup-Laubat School for boys and the
Marie Curie School for girls, and behind was the Cercle Sportif, the
tennis and swimming club." Just in front of the Norodom Palace were
the main hotels, like the Caravelle and the Continental, and near them
were the restaurants and the cafés. Naturally, the streetwalkers were
drawn to the same district, and the nightclubs and cabarets were set up
nearby. The colonial administrators and traders were here, so why
should the girls they were happy to have for their pleasure be far away?

The French were particularly lax in enforcing in their colonial territories the laws that applied back home. The French concession of
Shanghai is a good example of this. Shanghai was in any case an almost
lawless city, a near safe haven for criminal gangs, opium dens, gam-

bling, and prostitution, and these vices flourished in particular in the city's two districts where the unequal treaties of the mid-nineteenth century had given foreigners extraterritorial rights, including their own police forces and courts. Chinese law did not apply in either the French concession or the International Settlement, which was run mainly by the British. Again the question is why vice was so rampant in the very areas controlled by the relatively law-abiding and sexually conservative Europeans, those who, as we've seen, agonized back home about intimate relations with "the heathen" and sent their do-gooders and social reformers to crack down on both vice and misguided religious beliefs. The answer is certainly in part that the empire builders were more inclined to take advantage of illicit opportunity in the colonies than engage in Christian moral enforcement, which they left to their more conscious-stricken countrymen. The great influx of foreigners added to, rather than subtracted from, the atmosphere in which the culture of the harem was already strongly rooted. They brought with them all the loose pageantry of urban life—their movies, movie stars, and culture of celebrity, their lipstick and rouge, and the money they had to spend on the pleasures of the night. The presence of so many Europeans liberated from the inhibitions of home encouraged the rise of gambling casinos, dance halls, racetracks, theaters, and nightclubs, where they and the moneyed Chinese elite, liberated from their own government's controls, could cavort together. "By 1936, there were over three hundred cabarets and casinos in Shanghai's foreign concessions alone," the historian Frederic Wakeman has written. The Chinese love to gamble, and the foreigners, who loved to also, gave them large, gaudy casinos— the biggest and most luxurious of which were often registered with the consulates of Latin American countries in Shanghai to escape Chinese law—in which to take their chances. The biggest casino of them all, the Fusheng on Avenue Foch in the French concession, "even provided its big-stake customers with chauffeured pickups and returns in the latest model limousine," Wakeman has written.

The foreign concessions, which, given the warlordism and social disorder in China during much of Shanghai's heyday, might have been expected to be more efficient at controlling crime, were actually havens for it, especially opium use and prostitution. Criminals wanted by the Chinese police needed only to slip across the boundary of the French concession or the International Settlement to evade the operation of Chinese law, and this was the case even after 1928, when the revolutionary Nationalist government under Chiang Kai-shek, seized with the fervor to remake China morally as well as politically, attempted to clamp down on vice. One English-language newspaper noted the contradiction between the "announced reasons for maintaining the present foreign régime in Shanghai"—namely, that the city would go to the dogs if the Chinese controlled it—and the reality, which was "a spectacle of public prostitution" greater and more conspicuous than in any other city of China.

The foreign concessions of Shanghai were centers not just for the "normal" crimes of prostitution and narcotics sales but also for such very abnormal crimes as the sale of young girls and women into sexual slavery. Some of the victims, most of whom were from China's impoverished countryside, were sold by their families; others were kidnapped, and until they could be sold to brothels, the kidnappers were able to hide them in safe houses in the French concession that were disguised as small hotels. The foreigners' response to this moral degradation was inconsistent in the extreme. Public do-gooders rescued more than ten thousand women and children sold to brothels between 1913 and 1917. Later, a League of Nations report citing Shanghai as a major center for prostitution prompted expressions of opposition to prostitution by the colonial authorities, even as these same authorities issued 1,155 brothel licenses in 1939 alone.

The British-run International Settlement was no model of probity in this regard, but the French concession was even worse. "The tendency at the present time is that when anything socially unsound is discovered in the International Settlement, it is immediately removed to the French Concession, where it can comfortably settle down, and therefore the French Concession in Shanghai has become, morally speaking, the dirtiest spot in the Orient," one Chinese journalist wrote in 1932. Undoubtedly there was racism in France's casual attitude, a sense that in any case the colonies were places where it was natural and normal for a different moral standard to exist. But it was a different moral standard dearly desired by the foreigners who lived in those colonies and who delighted in the opportunities they presented. "Shanghai was the place to give a bachelor all the fun he could possibly ask for," Ernest Hauser said in *City for Sale*. It was a place where the party went on through all the years of turmoil and revolution between the fall of the Manchu Empire in 1911 and the Communist takeover of 1949. The empire issued both pro forma and sincere protests, but for the most part the imperialists wanted things that way.

Moreover, the case can be made that the sinfulness of empire was not merely a sidelight, an added-on amenity, but was a necessary condition for its functioning. Ronald Hyam of Cambridge University, has argued that sexual relations between the British and the Indians "crucially underpinned the whole operation of British empire and Victorian expansion." The empire wasn't created so British men could sleep with nut-brown maidens, nor did the impulse to discover the East and seek national glory there derive from an excess of sexual energy. But the ease of sexual opportunities made it far easier than it would otherwise have been to maintain the large military and bureaucratic establishments needed to govern and control the colonized territories, and surely that is one reason colonial and post-colonial administrations, whether the British in India or the Americans in Vietnam, never attempted to impose on the East the sexual regulations that were in force back home. To be sure, the harem culture combined with local poverty created the erotic possibilities, but political and military leaders in the field were only too happy to have their soldiers and administrations take advantage of them. "The expansion of Europe was not only a matter of 'Christianity and commerce,' " Hyam wrote, "it was also a matter of copulation and concubinage."

It is difficult in this sense to find a colonized territory that was not to some degree colonized sexually as well as militarily and commercially, not as a matter of official policy or intention but as a function of the way the world works. This explains, for example, how Shanghai, largely under foreign control, became, as Wakeman put it, "the vice capital of the world." It explains why, on the other side of the planet, in the West Indies, it was rather exceptional for a white man not to have a black concubine. "Many are the men, of every rank, quality, and degree, who would much rather riot in these goatish embraces than share the pure and lawful bliss derived from matrimonial, mutual love," one eighteenth-century observer, Edward Long, sourly noted of the British colony of Jamaica.

At its worst, sexual exploitation was an adjunct of slavery, and an inevitable one. "There is no slavery without sexual depravity," wrote Gilberto de Mello Freyre, the great Brazilian sociologist. Freyre had Brazilian slavery particularly in mind, but the dictum applies elsewhere as well. In the Dutch Cape Town colony in South Africa, as Hyam noted, the leading and highly visible brothel was a hostel for slaves. The harem culture itself, whether in China or the Ottoman or Mughal empires, was nourished by slavery, though slavery was not a necessary part of the sexual opportunity presented by East to West. Abundant sexual opportunities existed in places where the colonizing powers did not practice slavery, like French Indochina and British India and, indeed, took measures aimed at curbing the abuse of women—abolishing, for example, the practice of suttee in India. A certain eroticism was part of the way things worked, with both blatant and subtle consequences. In French Indochina in the nineteenth century, the *me-tay*, the name given to local Vietnamese women who served as wives and mistresses to French soldiers and administrators, formed a new and influential caste because of their closeness to the foreign power. "If you get into trouble, you depend on Miss Hai [a prostitute] escorting you to report to their honors, for only then is the case settled," a Vietnamese villager was recorded as saying. Needless to say, this considerably undermined the authority of traditional Vietnamese village chiefs.

In both the French and the British colonial enterprises, the local mistress, the local clerk, and the locally recruited soldier were all elements in the subjugation and administration of territories with vastly bigger populations than those in the colonizing countries. In India in the early decades, the East India Company, like earlier Portuguese officials, formally encouraged marriages between British soldiers and Indian women so as to build up a pool of locally born male children to serve as soldiers—the company gave a cash christening present to each such child born. The French, too, married often, though more in Indochina than in North Africa, where Islam discouraged marriage to non-Muslims. There, taking a local mistress was the more common arrangement. Like the British in India, the French in North Africa set up a system of brothels near military encampments, and always for the same reasons: they wanted to keep the prostitutes under control in order to attempt to control the spread of venereal disease, and they wanted to reduce friction with the local people by removing the incentive to molest "nice" local girls.

One French scholar who has studied the North African case concluded that in introducing essentially European-style brothels in countries like Algeria, "the traditional Muslim slave market was replaced by a French-based prostitution commerce." No person concerned with the equality of women could find very progressive the pre-French sexual practices of Algeria, which were based on the prerogative of men to have up to four wives and as many concubines as they could afford, concubines, as the historian Christelle Taraud has said, "usually bought on the market of female slaves who came from sub-Saharan Africa."

For that reason, European-style prostitution involving streetwalkers and brothels was largely unknown in Algeria, where men had a different way of indulging their desires for women not their wives. The French changed this. They banned slavery, normally an unobjectionable thing to do, but what that meant in Algeria was that many former slaves were "liberated" from the harem but forced to work as prostitutes in the new French system. Some liberation! The French were concerned that having Muslim women service non-Muslim men would offend Islamic sensibilities, so they required prostitutes to live in "reserved neighborhoods" segregated from the rest of North African society. But it didn't work. "For the local people," Taraud concluded, the French way of providing sexual release for soldiers and administrators "represented the very essence of colonization in that it degraded local traditions, institutions, and social norms." When Algerian nationalists formed the National Liberation Front to wage war against the French, prostitution as practiced under the French was seen as "bodily collaboration," and indeed, there were bomb attacks against some brothels patronized by French soldiers.

It is easy to understand the nationalist point of view—that prostitution under the French was a particular colonialist humiliation. Indeed, when in 1946 the French abolished controlled brothels in France itself, the new law did not apply to the North African colonies on the grounds that they represented a "condition of inferior civilization," certainly another insult to nationalist sentiment. Still, it is not so easy to distinguish morally between the traditional sexual slavery as practiced

A French postcard from Algeria, ca. 1920.
University of Minnesota Press

under the Ottomans before the French arrived and the European-style prostitution that came afterward. In any case, with the exception of the brothels set up by the colonial administration, the North African harem culture seemed to adapt quite well to the arrival of Europeans with desires and the money to satisfy them. In the words of the French writer Ernest Feydeau, best known for the erotic comedy of manners *Fanny,* "The French arrived in Algiers hungering for Moorish women." One peculiar French practice was the production of postcards showing what were called *femmes Mauresques,* Moorish women in various sexualized poses, presumably within the very harems that were closed to prying European eyes.

These postcards were produced by the thousands, and thousands of them were sent back to *la métropole* by the tourists who came from Europe to enjoy the beaches and casbahs of the Maghreb (the term used by the French to refer to Muslim northwest Africa). The pictures were posed by the French photographers who took them, and they are roundly denounced by Algerians today as a means of perpetuating the European fantasy of the Eastern woman—or, as the Algerian scholar

Malek Alloula has put it, "the sweet dream in which the West has been wallowing for more than four centuries." The pictures, he has written, are "fantastic representations of western designs on the Orient." And "there is no phantasm, though, without sex, and in this Orientalism, a confection of the best and of the worst—mostly the worst—a central figure emerges, the very embodiment of the obsession: the harem."

In a world that denounces colonialism as a crime against humanity, the use of "Moorish" women to titillate the Western imaginations seems, as Alloula has put it, "degraded, and degrading." Certainly, this photographic practice was unidirectional, and in this sense it incarnated the power of the West to do what it wanted in the subjugated world, including using its women, whether for pleasure directly or for the pleasure of manipulated portrayal. There were no photographs of Frenchwomen in seductive poses being sent home by Algerian visitors to France for the simple reason that the French had the power to prevent it. It was Moorish women who were subject to French scrutiny, just as Algeria was as a whole. And a crucial aspect of the colonial vision of the colonized was sexual. One postcard is particularly striking in this sense. It shows a man looking at a woman through a barred window. The bars seem to represent a kind of prison in which the woman is confined. Her breasts are bare, her eyes downcast, her posture one of resigned submission. Her hair is held in a printed kerchief that falls back and disappears behind her exposed shoulder. Like almost all the paid models who posed for these photographs, she is unveiled, and this perhaps is the most important indication of the power of colonialism to subject the colonized to its scrutiny. Algeria of course was a Muslim society, in which women were concealed from the prying eyes of outsiders. Among males, only the husband and sons of a woman were allowed to see her face. But the colonized lost the power to conceal their women, while the colonizers gained the power to expose them to view.

The anguished and angry reaction to these pictures among postcolonial Algerians is understandable. But the claim that such artifacts as postcards of Moorish women represented phantasm alone seems only part of the story. The postcards, with their highly sexualized images suggestive of a sexual paradise, tell a truth not about Moorish women but about the sexualized status of colonies in general. For the French in Indochina and North Africa, sexual fantasy could become reality, and did. In Saigon, it was in places like the Arc en Ciel and other nightspots, many of them given by Emperor Bao Dai to criminal gangs to control, where Frenchmen went to find beautiful women for the night, or for life. The femme fatale figure in Graham Greene's novel *The Ugly American* comes from just such a place, and Greene seems to have accurately reflected the way of life in Saigon in the early 1950s, when French control was about to give way to American. Imagine being a young man in Vietnam in 1930 or 1950, where you can dance whenever you want with a beautiful perfumed girl with jet-black hair falling over the white silk of her *ao dai,* the sheer shaped traditional dress of Vietnamese women. And after you have danced with her, she will accompany you home and spend the night in your arms. A fantasy? Yes, to be sure, a kind of dream. But many Frenchmen and other Europeans saw in places like Indochina and North Africa a place to realize erotic dreams of every variety, including the dreams that would have been unmentionable perversions back home.

A Secret Life in Algiers and Paris

HER NAME IS RAHMA, though her French lover calls her Ram, and she is "about 14, with straight shoulders, newly formed breasts, strong feet, and eyes that could set a bale of straw on fire from 30 feet." Lucien Auligny, a lonely and bored young officer in the French colonial army, sees her while riding through a village in southern Morocco. Until his fateful meeting with Ram, Auligny has made do with the services of "the coarse, seedy Arab wench" named Ftoum, who "does for the others too" at the French encampment in the dreary town of Birbatine. Now he asks a local merchant to introduce him to the girl with the fiery eyes. He proposes a price. Rahma's answer arrives the next day, and the day after that she and Auligny have their first meeting.

"It all happened as if he were buying a horse," the narrator of this tale says near the beginning of the story. But what starts as a vulgar sexual transaction becomes a powerful and even poignant erotic drama, a sort of *Lolita* of the desert set against the strange background of French colonialism in North Africa. In one way, the novel *L'histoire d'amour de la rose de sable,* translated into English as *Desert Love,* simply gives fictional form to the fact that French colonialism, like British colonialism, produced its own variation on the special attractions of the East for Western men. Auligny's arrangement with Ram is what the French in real life called *mariage à l'indigène,* "native marriage," a partnership of convenience almost always between a European man and a "native" girl or woman (never a "native" man and a European woman) stripped of the fullness of enduring romantic love and friendship.

And because the *mariage à l'indigène* between Auligny and Ram involves a child mistress, *La rose de sable* exemplifies another way in which the East made opportunities available to men that wouldn't have been available back home. Many men might have engaged in unrewarded fantasies about a girl with "newly formed breasts," skin of "satiny smoothness," and breath smelling of "spice and orange," but few would have had the occasion to enjoy one. And, it has to be remembered, *La rose de sable* is a work of fiction. Still, it is the pedophiliac element that is immediately striking in this lubricious tale of French army life in North Africa. And the historical truth is that in life as well as in fiction, pedophilia was among the offerings that the colonized East made to the colonizing West.

"At a certain time, everything was permitted, even what could never be admitted in the West, for example, an attraction to young, even very young girls," a French scholar has written, relating literary depictions of European life in North Africa to the social reality there. "What would have been a scandal in the home country (in what is today the grave crime known as pedophilia) is at the very least relativized in the Orient."

In fact, *La rose de sable,* a fine, complex, and unexpected literary work, is a lot more than an erotic desert fantasy, one, indeed, in which the author treated the theme of pedophilia rather lightly, as just a normal part of life in the out there that was the French colonial empire. In fact, whether it was considered criminal or normal, the relationship between Auligny and Ram is not entirely one between an all-powerful European man and a compliant, powerless child prostitute. Within the secret confines of their *mariage à l'indigène,* Ram has power, and she exercises it through a kind of passive resistance. Her agreement to become Auligny's mistress is conditioned on his vow to keep her virginity intact, which adds both a certain sexual tension to the story and a dimension of submission on the part of Auligny. He is permitted to caress Ram's naked body with his hands and lips, but what he wants is a response of pleasure from her, and until, finally, he is allowed to possess her fully, she doesn't give him that.

La rose de sable has been read as an anti-colonialist novel, in part because it gives to the Arab girl a fullness of character foreign to the objectifying and demeaning stereotypes that existed in the colonialist French mentality. At first, Auligny is perturbed by Ram because she is so much more passive and seemingly inert than any European girl would be, but over time he comes to love her for those very qualities—yet another illustration of a Western man coming to see an Eastern girl as more fully feminine than a Western girl would be in her response to male sexual passion. There is no fussiness in Ram, no guilt or remorse, no coquettishness, no artifice, no demands, no social pretensions, no competitiveness. She is an entirely natural being even as she knows how to turn her weakness into a strength. Through Ram, Auligny comes to perceive what he regards as the unrecognized grandeur of the Arab soul, and therefore, also through Ram, he comes in his thinking to be an adversary of French colonialist assumptions.

La rose de sable is anti-colonialist in one other, more interesting sense: it puts the lie to the official justification for France's colonial enterprise—namely, that it was an effort to bring the blessings of enlightenment to benighted natives, the famous civilizing mission. This hypocrisy is explicit in the case of Auligny, who is shown early on as a standard French patriot, influenced by the standard French books depicting his soldierly role as heroic and self-sacrificing. But his experience with Ram illustrates the fraudulence of the French colonial self-presentation. The French back home in *la métropole* sent their letters and gifts to their brave young troops in North Africa to help them get through the supposed austerity and grimness of their lives, so devoid of the comforts of home, when, in truth the French in North Africa were indulging themselves with child mistresses in ways that would have been criminally prosecuted in France. A civilizing mission indeed.

But what is perhaps most interesting about *La rose de sable* is the book's author, Henry de Montherlant, a twentieth-century literary figure not well-known in the Anglo-American world but celebrated as one of the century's greats in France, up there in the same exalted rank as André Gide and Albert Camus. His North African novel, for which he collected information during five years he lived in Algeria when he was in his early thirties, is one of his first novels, but for reasons that remain a bit unclear, he didn't publish it until after World War II. Montherlant himself proclaimed the book to be an exposé of the concealed realities of French colonialism, and it was that. But it was also an act of concealment, and as such it was an element in a lifelong act of concealment, a lie by conscious omission. For Montherlant may have intended his book as a novelistic condemnation of French colonialist prejudice, but during the years he lived in Algeria he was himself in active, obsessive, nonstop pursuit of the colonialist sexual advantage, though in his case the pedophiliac interest wasn't in young girls but in young boys.

North Africa opened up a vast realm of sexual liberation and excitement for Montherlant. His years there defined the identity that was his for the rest of his life but a secret until his death. Only three people are believed to have known the real Montherlant and his obsession with young boys. And in this sense, Montherlant illustrated two things: that along with commercial profit and national glory, the sexual relationship was an important part of France's decades-long encounter with its colonies and that French colonialism involved a strenuous, sanctimonious effort to deny that such a relationship existed.

MONTHERLANT WAS ONE of the more interesting and disturbing French literary figures of the twentieth century, a brilliant adventurer and novelist who received just about every high honor that could be bestowed by the French republic. He was a member of both the Legion of Honor and, as of 1960, the ultraprestigious French Academy, whose members are known as "the immortals" of French culture. His life was a blending of elements from Hemingway, Nietzsche, and Mussolini. One of his early works is the *Funeral Chant for the Dead of Verdun,* a valedictory for soldierly heroism—Montherlant had been wounded and decorated as a very young man in World War I.

Above all, Montherlant celebrated masculinity and despised everything that he found to be feminine in the European context. He learned bullfighting as a young man and once, while practicing with a bull at a farm in Spain, was gored. Not so admirably, along with a few other writers of his generation, most notably Louis-Ferdinand Céline and Robert Brazillac, he welcomed the defeat of the Third Republic by the Nazis in 1940, though not so much out of overt sympathy for the Nazis as out of what one critic has called an affinity for "aesthetic fascism." For Montherlant, French democracy represented a kind of feminine mediocrity, what he called in a speech in 1938 "shopgirl morality."

He used the term "useless service" to describe what he regarded as the highest human attainment. It had to do with dying for a cause in which one does not believe in recognition of the impossibility of finding true grandeur—a silly and sophomoric idea if ever there was one, a nonsense Nietzscheanism. A related bit of nonsense involved Montherlant's activities during the German occupation, when, along with writing plays that were produced by the Comédie-Française, he had the bad taste to write in a Nazi-sponsored journal, *La gerbe,* about "low Europeans"—this at a time when the self-appointed master race was murdering Jews and other so-called low Europeans. Montherlant was accused and convicted of collaboration with the enemy after the war, though the sentence meted out to him was so light as to be symbolic: he was prohibited from publishing his work for one year.

That, of course, was years after he had written *La rose de sable,* which in turn was based on his years in North Africa, from 1927 to 1932. It was in North Africa that Montherlant was able for the first time in his life to seek to satisfy his homosexual desires, something he continued to do, dangerously and clandestinely, after he returned to France, where he lived for the forty years until his death. There is nothing very surprising in this. Today, after years of civil war, military dictatorship, and a revival of conservative, ultrapuritanical Wahhabi Islam in the Middle East, Algeria hardly has the image of a place where one would go for a languid holiday under the palm trees. But from the 1890s through the 1930s, French North Africa was a tourist-poster destination of desert oases, bazaars, shady gardens, and Moorish exoticism, enthusiastically written up in travel books and visited by well-off Europeans on fashionable holidays. Unmentioned in the tour guides was that it was also a domain within which wealth and power translated into erotic pleasure. It was a zone of sexual freedom, a distorted mirror of the prohibitions and inhibitions of Christendom. For the majority of sexual tourists, the culture of the harem offered the favors of young girls without the obligations of love, marriage, or Western-style legality; for the homosexual minority, it offered boys. As always in the East, in North Africa, too, Europeans blended into an existing pattern, pederasty being well established and tolerated in Arab and other Muslim cultures of the Middle East and South Asia. North Africa made the practice available to European men, and since the French were the colonizers of North Africa, they were among the principal beneficiaries. The poet W. H. Auden coined the term *homintern* to refer to the homosexual globalism that thrived during the colonial era.

The French novelist André Gide, twenty-seven years older than Montherlant, spent time in Algeria in 1893 and from 1894 to 1895, and he described in his autobiography an evening with Oscar Wilde in Algiers when a group of French and British literati had gathered to enjoy the weather and the erotic possibilities. On the evening in question, Lord Alfred Douglas, Wilde's lover, announced that he was leaving for Blida, a walled town about thirty miles away, where he and Wilde had spent time together. Blida was the site of a French military encampment and a place where European men went for long walks with local boys in the orange groves outside the town's walls. Douglas's purpose was to "elope" with a young *caouadji,* or coffee server, who had struck his fancy on the earlier visit he and Wilde had made together. And so, left on their own, Wilde and Gide embarked on an evening of touring cafés and music bars in the casbah. For Gide in particular, later than Wilde in coming to terms with his homosexuality, what followed was an episode of life-transforming delirium, involving, in the early morning hours, a prolonged and blissful tryst with a boy musician. Decades later, in 1931, while on a return trip to Algiers, Gide shared an apartment with Montherlant, though it seems that Montherlant was put off by Gide's flamboyance, and they soon split up.

The French were not the only ones for whom Asia allowed the pursuit of desires whose fulfillment would have been illegal in Europe. We have, for example, the complete records of one Kenneth Searight, a captain in the British army in India who was a friend of the novelist E. M. Forster and gave him a remarkable 137-page detailed journal of his sexual encounters with young boys written in rhymed couplets. Searight's journal lists 129 boys who were his sexual partners between 1897 and 1917 and tells in detail exactly what he did and how often with each. It is clear from this that although Searight certainly knew of his sexual inclination before going to India and had had a couple of schoolboy encounters in Britain, India for him was, as Ronald Hyam put it, "a problem-free paradise where all inhibitions were dissolved." Or as Searight put it, speaking of his dalliances with Pashtun boys in and around the present-day Pakistani city of Peshawar:

> *Each boy of certain age will let on hire*
> *His charms to indiscriminate desire,*

To wholesale Buggery and perverse letches. . . .
To get a boy was easier than to pick
The flowers by the wayside. . . .

. . . .

Scarce passed a night but I in rapturous joy
Indulged in mutual sodomy

Why Montherlant's lifelong secrecy, especially at a time when others, like Gide himself, were forging a new understanding of homosexuality? Montherlant, of course, never explained himself. Still, it is not difficult to understand him. Living at a time when homosexuality was regarded as both diseased and immoral, he wanted to receive every honor his country could bestow on a writer, to remain a public figure of unassailable respectability. And, of course, one has to add to that already powerful incentive the fact that Montherlant was a practitioner of pederasty, which was both frowned upon and illegal in France. He is likely the only member of the French Academy who spent his days receiving the accolades of the French literary establishment and his nights on the prowl for young boys.

The danger wasn't only in being recognized. In 1968, while trying to pick up a young boy outside a movie theater in Paris, he was assaulted by the boy's older friends and left blind in one eye, a blindness he vaguely attributed to an accident. Montherlant was seventy-two years old at the time, rather old to be trolling for boys under movie-theater marquees, but after he accepted his predilection for underage boys some forty years before in Algeria, he never let up. Four years later, in 1972, fearful of going entirely blind, Montherlant shot himself, taking a cyanide pill before he pulled the trigger just to make sure.

Since his death, a great deal of information has surfaced about Montherlant. He fully confided his secret to Roger Peyrefitte, a French diplomat who had met him in 1937 at a games arcade in the Clichy neighborhood where both had gone to try to pick up boys. Peyrefitte was in many ways the opposite of Montherlant, at least in his treatment of his own sexuality. Whereas Montherlant desperately hid his homosexuality, Peyrefitte wrote novels and essays about his seeing himself as a champion of what would now be called gay rights. Some of his sharpest polemics involved exposing what he saw as the hypocrisy of those who condemned homosexuality even while secretly practicing it, high officials in the Catholic Church among them. In 1977, he published a sensational book of revelations, *Propos secrets,* in which, among other things, he outed his friend Montherlant, who had died five years earlier.

"In my opinion," Peyrefitte wrote, "never did pederasty play as important a role in the life of a man. . . . With Montherlant it especially played such a role because of the complications that it brought in its train for him. Not only did he live in terror, but he invented terror out of his imagination."

Once, Peyrefitte said, Montherlant called the police when someone rang his bell at night. It turned out to be an English admirer of his books eager to meet the great writer, but Montherlant imagined him to be a blackmailer seeking a payoff. He never brought his lovers home to his apartment on the quai Voltaire but, rather, brought them to a succession of maids' rooms that he rented for the purpose. When he went out "on a hunt," which was often, he put on an old coat, pulled his hat down over his eyes, and wore black sunglasses. After he achieved renown as a novelist and playwright, he didn't allow photographs of himself to be published, for fear he would be recognized as he wandered the streets and hovered in movie-theater entrances and game parlors where teenage boys congregated. Among his ploys was to offer a ticket to a boy, telling him that he had bought it for his nephew who hadn't shown up. Despite Montherlant's many precautions, from time to time he ended up in a police station with one boy or another crying that Montherlant had put his hand inside his fly.

Claude Gallimard, his editor, was once woken up in the middle of the night and asked to pick up Montherlant from a suburban police station. According to Peyrefitte, Maurice Papon, the Paris chief of police, told Henri Flammarion, another legendary French editor, that he had seen Montherlant pulled into the police headquarters about five or six times, always white as a ghost. Papon (who was later convicted of crimes against humanity committed when he was the wartime secretary general for Nazi-occupied Bordeaux) seems to have offered some protection to Montherlant, perhaps out of respect for his literary stature. Still, Papon said, "it was frightful. I was feeling his shame."

Peyrefitte's revelations were followed by a definitive two-volume

biography of Montherlant by Pierre Sipriot, a friend of twenty-five
years, suitably enough titled *Montherlant sans masque* (*Montherlant
without Mask*), whose main theme is Montherlant's sexuality and the
lengths he went to, to conceal it. Even during his years in North Africa,
according to Sipriot, Montherlant feared exposure. Once in Fès, upon
seeing some French military officers, he was gripped with fear that he
would be recognized. Still, as Sipriot put it, using the present tense to
describe Montherlant's life in North Africa, "Every day he takes a little
more risk following his taste for fortuitous encounters. To conquer his
fear and 'take the plunge,' as he says, he thinks of himself as a bull, a
faun or a satyr."

There are further details on the extent of Montherlant's obsession,
how he moved constantly from place to place in North Africa, in part
to avoid being found out but in part to search for his dream boy. At one
point he left Algiers to spend a few days in the Atlas Mountains because
he had heard about a tribe where "all you needed to do is smile and you
could have anybody you wanted." Montherlant here was writing a passage in *Aux fontaines du désire* (*At the Springs of Desire*), previously
unknown to be autobiographical. He would spend entire days walking
the same limited number of streets in the hope of seeing a face he'd seen
once before, convinced as he was that his persistence would pay off.
Whenever he wasn't writing—and he did write a great deal in North
Africa—he would be outside looking. As soon as he arrived at a new
destination, "I wouldn't even brush off my clothes," he once wrote,
"because that would take two minutes more, and my hopes wouldn't
hold for two more minutes." What is critical in this, and what suggests
the importance of France's colonies as domains of illicit sexual liberation for many French and other men, is Sipriot's description of Montherlant in North Africa as "giving himself over to every pleasure while
observing no restraints." Montherlant "truly felt in North Africa that
sensual pleasure and love were distinct from each other. Before, only
love was pure. Pleasure, when it wasn't shameful, was different, surrounded as it was with all sorts of prohibitions."

Montherlant had gone to Algeria in 1927 out of what Sipriot, quot-
ing an essay by Montherlant, called "a great greed for the flesh." He
started this sexual exploration rather late, at thirty, Sipriot wrote, but
then went at it with tremendous energy, day and night, roaming from

Tunis to Fès, from Constantine to Algiers to those villages in the Atlas Mountains. "In Paris, Montherlant didn't dare," Sipriot said. Naming a town in northwestern Algeria, he continued, "In Tlemcen adventure was around the corner."

In those days even more than today, all a Westerner needed to do was go out onto the street and the native hawkers of everything from hashish to carpets, songbirds to little girls, would make their approach. Montherlant wrote at one point of sitting in a café in a North African city when a young boy came up, lifted the carafe of water on the table, filled Montherlant's glass, and drank it. He remembers seeing another boy who kissed the reflection of his own lips in the glass of a storefront window, a gesture that Montherlant didn't explain but seems to illustrate the sense of sensual possibility that he loved about North Africa.

In the mid-1930s, Montherlant wrote an essay, unpublished at the time but revealed decades later by Sipriot, in which he pretended to be a critic analyzing his own writing, referring to himself in the third person. "Montherlant's sensuality is oriental even in its details," he wrote, identifying two of those details: "A) An oriental conception of women. B) Love of youth and even of extreme youth."

In that essay, Montherlant, still writing as if he were another person, identifies himself with an Islamic holy man, arguing, as have others, that in Islam sensual desire and spirituality are linked and mutual, not, as they are in Christianity, hostile and opposed. "Montherlant distrusts and willfully ignores everything that is not either interior life or sensuality, and that seems to be characteristic of the Muslim world," Montherlant wrote of himself. "Numerous are the great muslim mystics (Jelal Eddin Roumi [Jalal ad-Din ar-Rumi] for example) who were as known for their spirituality as for their gallant adventures. The Muslim world moreover suffers from this voluntary double ignorance: confined within God and sexual excess, it ignores the world."

In Sipriot's view, *La rose de sable* is "the fantastic adventure," *The Arabian Nights* of Arab childhood. Montherlant, he said, took notes on Arab children wherever he went, and among the results was his portrait of the woman-child Rahma. But *La rose de sable* is far from the only French novel that takes off from the topic of pedophilia in colonial North Africa. Montherlant's novel was actually something of a late-comer in an already-developed subgenre within the large genre that treated the subject of romantic and sexual liaisons between Europeans and North Africans. One scholar has counted fifty-seven titles by French writers on that subject. Many of them tell about the failure of such relations, with the exoticism and mysteriousness of the Eastern partner a prominent theme.

Pedophilia is well represented among these works, reflecting no doubt that the practice was widespread among Europeans traveling in the colonized world. In *Souna: Moeurs arabes* (*Souna: Arab Customs*), published in 1876, Ernest Feydeau told the story of a French officer named Pierlet, who rescues the adolescent daughter of a fruit merchant from a bandit attack and proceeds to make her his mistress, there being nobody in the poverty-stricken and somewhat complaisant society of North African villages to rescue her from him. The themes of Feydeau's tale are so similar to those of *La rose de sable* that one suspects the second was at least partially inspired by the first. Pierlet is "tired of the rough life, drinking acrid water, sleeping on the hard ground, eating military biscuits, hearing the cries of hate of the Arabs, of battling in the mountains, and so forth." And so, like Rahma with Lieutenant Auligny, "Souna presented herself to . . . [Lieutenant Pierlet] so unexpectedly and in such tragic circumstances, still young, with her beautiful doe's eyes, her casual grace, and her exquisite gentleness. . . . She appeared to him like a spring of fresh water running under a palm grove would appear to an Arab lost in the sands of the Sahara."

In 1912, some four decades after Feydeau's work but still a generation before Montherlant's, in the novel *La fête arabe* (*The Arab Festival*) by the brothers Jérôme and Jean Tharaud, a military doctor becomes attached to little Zohira, who is eleven years old. Learning that she is to be married to an old sheikh, the doctor kidnaps her and has her share his bed. Here, too, the fantasy is a familiar one: the dashing European who saves a young damsel about to be sacrificed for the sake of an old lecher's pleasure, and not just any old lecher but a dark-skinned and autocratic one, a bad bargain compared with an enlightened light-skinned man of science. We've seen how in the sixteenth century Ludovico de Varthema imagined himself to be superior, in the eyes of the queen of Arabia Felix, to the sultan himself. It is the same notion expressed in *La fête arabe* more than three hundred years later—

namely, that a native girl would be better off with a foreign doctor than with a native sheikh, and who is to say that she wouldn't be?

What is different in Montherlant's novel is that the unhappy ending is experienced more by the European man than the Arab girl. Auligny is recalled from Birbatine and asks Ram to go with him. As far as he is concerned, she is his love for life. She says that she will meet him the next day. He goes to the appointed place at the appointed time. She fails to turn up. He never sees her again—no explanation, no note, no message delivered by an intermediary, simply another act of passive power, perhaps even passive resistance to colonial rule. She just isn't there, and Auligny, deprived both of his love and of his faith in French colonialism, performs an act worthy of Montherlant's philosophy of useless sacrifice, dying in a skirmish with Arab guerrillas in a cause— colonial grandeur—he has come to despise.

AFTER MONTHERLANT GOT BACK to Paris in 1932, the years in North Africa must have had a powerful hold on him. They were the years when he had been relatively free and relatively unafraid. But unlike, say, Gide, who returned to Algeria in the early 1930s, when he was already in his sixties, Montherlant never went back. It is difficult to fathom why; perhaps initially it was because of the demands of a nascent literary career and his enormous ambition. It was in the years immediately following his time in North Africa that Montherlant wrote the books that established his reputation: *Les célibataires* (*The Bachelors*), published in 1934, and four volumes commencing with *Les jeunes filles* (*The Girls*), published between 1936 and 1939. Perhaps he was simply too busy to go back to Africa. And then, of course, in 1940 came the war, during which he devoted himself mostly to theater, and after the war he had his fame and his reputation to cultivate and protect.

And so, somewhat mysteriously for a man who had behaved the way he had in North Africa, he stayed at home, living the daily terror of his double life, North Africa a memory of the place where he first broke with his inhibitions. And in his life of seventy-six years, marked by honors, fame, and achievement, it was the only place where, at least partially freed from the constraints of Christendom, he was himself. Peyrefitte, the treasonous friend who revealed the truth about him, clearly believed that Montherlant's terror in being himself in France was itself a product of moral cowardice and hypocrisy. He not only incarnated the dirty little sexual secret of French colonialism, but he also violated the very martial and masculine values that he championed in his novels and in his political pronouncements. His very death by his own hand illustrated the mendacity of his life, Peyrefitte wrote in a harsh final judgment. "For me," he said in *Propos secrets,* "Montherlant's suicide was another theatrical gesture. . . . It was the ultimate mask displaying virile courage on the part of a man who spent his life trembling because of his ways."

The Malacca Blues

NEEDLESS TO SAY, the seed sown by Western men during their sojourns in the East has had an enduring genetic and cultural legacy. In the tropical, weather-beaten, and intensely picturesque city of Malacca (sometimes spelled Melaka) on the southwest coast of Malaysia, I met Martin Theseira, whose ancestors may have been among the Portuguese sailors encouraged by Governor General Afonso de Albuquerque, who conquered the sultanate of Malacca in 1511, to impregnate local Malay women. But if he doesn't trace his ancestry that far back, there is little doubt that among his forefathers was a Portuguese colonist who coupled with a Malay woman, or perhaps a half-Malay woman, sometime before 1641, when Portuguese rule ended.

Martin is in his early fifties, the father of two fine boys, a slender, good-looking man with a graying mustache, copper-brown skin, and straight jet-black hair. He is affable and serious, articulate in three languages, English, Malay, and the mixture of Portuguese, Malay, Arabic, and Tamil known as Kristang. His eyes are more oval than round, but the Iberian cast of his face is unmistakable. There are plenty of middle-aged men in Lisbon who look somewhat like him.

For nearly five hundred years, some twenty-five generations, the Portuguese community of Malacca has endured, remaining Roman Catholic in an overwhelmingly Muslim country. "We've lasted for all these centuries, and we have done it without schools and without any connection to Portugal," Martin said. He meant that Kristang children have always gone to government schools, where the medium of instruction has been English or Malay, with no instruction in Kristang itself. And because Malacca has not been a Portuguese colony since the

Dutch took it over in the seventeenth century, the Kristangs have been effectively severed from what used to be the mother country for more than 350 years.

It's fair to say that the Kristangs have been a modest people, mostly fishermen, farmers, and in recent times, factory workers. Martin makes a living selling jars of what he calls Martin's Homemade—salted fish, picked green mango, preserved roe, and other delicacies, which he does make in his own home. There are probably fewer than two thousand Kristangs in Malacca and another thousand or so elsewhere in Malaysia, not a critical mass that would engender world-class cultural flourishing. There is no Kristang literature. There wasn't even a dictionary until a European scholar compiled one a few years ago. But there are churches, Sunday schools, and a distinctive cuisine, whose signature dish is a deliciously earthy fermented shrimp paste, called *cencaluk,* eaten with chopped onions, chili peppers, and lime. The Kristangs have annual festivals, their own music, and most of all, a sense of identity that, in their minds, sets them apart. They are known locally as the Portuguese. They live in what is locally called the Portuguese settlement, which has changed location from time to time. A complex of sunbaked buildings near their main residential neighborhood is called Portuguese Square. They have family names like Theseira, da Silva, Pintado, Fernandis, and Lazaroo.

There are many such mixed peoples scattered across the zones where Western men traded, conquered, proselytized, and procreated. The Portuguese begat what may have been the first Eurasian population in Goa, on the Indian west coast, where Albuquerque had set up a trading post before venturing on to the Strait of Malacca, Macau, and Japan. As we've seen, Albuquerque ordered his men to marry local women, especially the widows of native soldiers killed in Portugal's conquests, in order to create a population that would serve Portugal's imperial needs. This element in the relations of East and West is a reminder of how strikingly different the world was five centuries ago. Imagine the commander of a conquering army today, or even in the past two or three centuries, ordering his men to marry women whose husbands they themselves have killed in battle! But in centuries past, in the early decades of the erotic encounter of East and West, Eastern women were among the resources to exploit, like cloves or nutmeg. You mow down their husbands with superior weaponry and tactics, and you make the local women your wives, converting them to Christianity.

The result, unintended by Albuquerque, is still with us, in the form of distinct, proud, hybrid populations from western India to eastern Japan, a global mixing of blood, language, and customs. Among them are tens of thousands of Anglo-Indians, usually the progeny of British men and Indian women who mated over the long centuries of colonial rule in India. Centuries later, as a consequence of the sexual free-for-all that took place during the war in Indochina, American soldiers in Vietnam begat many thousands of mixed-race children, the vast majority of whom, growing up in orphanages or with socially ostracized mothers, never knew who their fathers were. There are, in addition, some fifty thousand Amerasians in the Philippines, a product of the many years when American servicemen were stationed there, as well as Amerasians in Korea, where American troops have been stationed since the Korean War.

No doubt it is difficult to generalize about the products of the post-war sexual mingling of Americans and Asians, who in their own way have recapitulated the experience that began with Portuguese maritime expansion at the end of the fifteenth century. But especially in Vietnam, there have been numerous reports of discrimination against Amerasians, who, though living in the country of their birth, have been made second-class citizens, in part because of the sense that they are the product of a shameful act, born to women who practiced a shameful profession. In addition, not a small number of Amerasians are half black, and many Vietnamese display a racist attitude toward blacks that is common in East and Southeast Asia.

Not that mixed populations have always been a product of Europeans or Americans and Asians. Even before Albuquerque arrived with his seventeen ships and twelve hundred men, seizing control of Malacca from the Muslim sultan Mahmud Shah, Malacca was what we would call today a multicultural community. Half a century before the Portuguese arrived, a Chinese princess named Hang Li Po had come with a retinue of five hundred attendants to marry Sultan Mansur Shah, even as the attendants married local people. The marriage was part of an effort by the sultan to forge close ties with China and thereby counter marauding Siamese, who had a habit of making forays down the Malay coast.

The Chinese Malays are known as Baba-Nyonya; Indian Malays, produced by the migration of Indians to the Malay Peninsula during the years of the British Empire, are called Chittys. "But in a way, we are more distinct," Martin told me, referring to the Kristangs, "because the Baba-Nyonya have the Chinese community for support and the Chittys have the Indian community, but we have no larger Portuguese community to attach ourselves to."

Five hundred years is a very long time to survive culturally, and Martin and other Kristangs are proud that they have managed to do so. The Portuguese ruled Malacca for more than one hundred years. The Kristangs stayed put while the Dutch ruled for the next two hundred or so years. The British formally took over in 1824, ruling until the Federation of Malaya (now part of Malaysia) became independent in 1957. For all those centuries, the Kristangs lived in village houses along the coast, netting shrimp and fish, going to mass, congregating under the spreading chestnut trees along the Strait of Malacca to drink, talk, and play cards, holding their festivals, teaching the catechism to their children, listening, perhaps with the sense of alienation that is common to small minorities, to the chant of the muezzin calling the majority Muslims to prayer. They were served by generation after generation of parish priests, dispatched from Lisbon but under the jurisdiction of the bishop of Macau.

"There is one street in Malacca, Harmony Street, where there is a mosque, a Hindu temple, and a Chinese temple," Martin said, illustrating the diversity and tolerance of the Malaccan tradition. We were sitting at a café on Heering Street, eating a lunch of omelets with *cencaluk,* shrimp curry, and wok-fried morning glory greens. Heering Street stretches between rows of two-story wooden shop houses with columned porticoes. It's across the Malacca River from the former Dutch Town, which, complete with windmill, has been preserved as a sort of heritage museum commemorating the two centuries when this part of Malaya was ruled from Amsterdam. Parallel to Heering Street is Jonker Walk, a pedestrian mall at night that has been transformed into a typical, supposedly authentic old town center, lined with cafés, restaurants, and souvenir shops.

But surveying the scene, Martin is not optimistic that the Kristangs will last for many more generations, much less for centuries. "We are not very happy," he said when we first met. "There are so many forces that want to knock us out." Mainly, he believes, there aren't enough people in Malaysia who see the value in the survival of a small Eurasian community, and he also feels that this lack of appreciation is short-sighted, since it robs Malacca of one of its most distinctive and colorful features.

Years ago, land reclamation projects sponsored by the local government separated the Kristang community from the sea, and that was a big blow to the group's identity. Martin showed me his ancestral house, where he makes his Martin's Homemade products but no longer lives. Once it was right on the water. Fishermen's boats were tied up in front of the former Portuguese Settlement where a road now runs, on the other side of which is a stretch of featureless modern structures. The sea, which used to be right there, the sound of the tides soothing the sleep of the coastal residents, is now more than half a mile away.

Slowly the Portuguese moved away, many of them to another sea-coast neighborhood a bit to the south. They were dispersed, and it is difficult for a community so small to maintain a sense of cohesion if it doesn't have its own neighborhood.

"If you separate us from the sea, you destroy our culture," Martin said. "In the past, almost all the Kristangs fished," he said. "Now most of them don't, and that changed everything, the whole atmosphere." If that atmosphere could be restored, Martin feels, it would give back to Malacca a good deal of its lost character. It would be a spur to tourism, since, after all, visitors would be attracted by a vibrant seafront community where fishermen mend their nets and barter freshly caught shrimp for mangrove posts brought by boat from Sumatra, across the strait. Visitors from China, Singapore, and Australia, who now spend their time roaming Jonker Walk and the old Dutch Town, would like that. But there is nothing to see along Malacca's shoreline now.

"In 1998, the government reclaimed a piece of seafront land near the new Portuguese Settlement in order to build a hotel," Martin said.

"They said the hotel would be an extension of the Kristang community, but when the hotel was finished, it was simply taken over by the government."

We visited it, the Lisbon Hotel. It is a kind of Alhambra of the Malaccan Strait, beige stucco wings with red tile roofs surrounding an immense inner courtyard. But Martin said that only two or three Kristangs are employed there—one is a secretary, another a security guard. The hotel is used mostly by government officials on official business, so in proper Muslim fashion no alcohol is allowed on the premises, and how Portuguese can something be if drinking is prohibited?

"It's not compatible with the name Lisbon," Martin said. All it does for the Kristangs is block their view of the sea. "You want the seafront for a hotel? The people should come first," he said. "I would suggest that the whole settlement be moved back to the seafront."

Even if that were to happen, and it probably won't, other circumstances seem to argue against the likelihood of the Kristangs' surviving as a distinct community for much longer, and when Martin talked about those circumstances, he did so with melancholy and resignation. He is not an optimistic man, though he is doing what he can to reinvigorate his culture. He and a friend created a CD of Kristang music; he meets with like-minded people to speak Kristang and to encourage others to speak it to their children. But the circumstance that could spell extinction for the Kristangs is simply the overwhelming size and cultural power of the surrounding Malay population along with the absence of any evident desire on the part of the Muslim-dominated government to preserve the Portuguese community.

Intermarriage is perhaps the biggest issue. Under Malaysian law, if a person marries a Muslim, he or she must convert to Islam for the marriage to be recognized. And many Kristang young people, going away to college or to work—Martin estimates about half of them—are marrying outside the group. Some years ago when Kristang children in a government-run kindergarten were asked to make drawings, several of them drew the crescent, the Muslim symbol.

"In the past, there was always a lot of mingling in Malacca," Martin said, "but there wasn't so much sensitivity about religion or race. Now it's an issue. It's a matter of politics. The political parties vie with one another to be more Islamic," and that has led to enforcement of the laws against marrying outside the Muslim faith.

And so it may just be that we are in the last phase of the long cultural history begun by Afonso de Albuquerque five centuries ago, and that makes Martin sad. He said it over and over: that if nothing is done, the community will be dispersed, and dispersal will mean disappearance. The Iberian-style churches of Malacca will be empty, turned into museums for tourists perhaps, adorned with plaques commemorating the members of the Eurasian community who built them. Or maybe some vigorous leader will emerge to combat the slow Kristang disappearance. Who knows? But if only because their numbers are already so small, the odds are against it.

CHAPTER EIGHT

The Eastern Paradox

THE EDUCATION MINISTER OF RAJASTHAN, one of India's biggest states, said that it was a "disgraceful" idea. It would, he said, "corrupt the minds of the young." Another state official, this one in Madhya Pradesh, declared that in proposing it, the central Indian government had "devalued Indian culture and its values."

These fiercely negative and conservative comments were in reaction to a program, begun in 2007 in all Indian state-run schools, to provide "adolescent education"—that is, lessons in human sexual reproduction—to the country's fifteen- to seventeen-year-olds. In a country with the world's greatest number of people infected with the AIDS virus, 5.7 million, the proposal seemed likely not just to give young people a bit of essential information about how to conduct themselves in their amorous relations but also to save lives. Still, as of May 2007, six of India's twenty-eight states had canceled the sex-education classes in an effort to preserve what was often referred to as "Indian morality."

"Sex education may be necessary in Western countries," Chief Minister H. D. Kumaraswamy of the state of Karnataka told reporters at a news conference, "but not in India, which has a rich culture. It will have an adverse effect on young minds, if implemented."

How remarkably like the response among some American conservatives to similar initiatives in the United States, where notions like sex education and condom distribution to high school students have been greeted by howls of protest against the violence done to what could be called "American values." In the United States, one half of which promotes a sexual culture stressing sin, guilt, and chastity (even as the other half produces a commercial and advertising culture based largely on sexual provocation and desire), it is not so surprising that there would be a powerful belief that public school sex education is contrary to American morality and morality in general.

But India—the country of the *Kama Sutra* and numerous other sex manuals written at a time when Europe was in the Dark Ages, including the dark ages of sex? Only the briefest glance at the religious iconographies of India and Christendom reveals the gulf between these two erotic cultures. On the one side is mother and child, the celebration of the Virgin Birth, procreation without the animal urge of sex, the delicate, pensive, highly spiritual Mary holding the infant Jesus. And on the other is the goddess Lakshmi, consort of Vishnu, the Supreme All-pervading Being, the Creator and Destroyer of all existence. Lakshmi, like other Hindu goddesses—Parvati, the consort of Shiva, is a good example—is commonly depicted in highly sensual poses, bare breasted, full hipped, narrow waisted, her head turned so that she can contemplate the face of her beloved, the image suggesting their congress, which is the primordial act of procreation. The one icon is in the church, the other in the temple, and both are religious, one celebrating chastity as a path to spiritual truth, the other the bliss of sexual union with the divine.

India to be sure has a rich culture, part of which comprises stone carvings of couples in amorous poses, the naked woman gymnastically climbing the thighs of her lover, her head thrown back in ecstasy, her hips swiveled upward to receive his penis. These images are to be seen on the columns or walls of many Hindu temples, all of which have at their physical and spiritual center a lingam, the explicit phallic object that symbolizes life-giving force. The state of Madhya Pradesh, whose chief minister, Shivraj Singh Chouhan, was so worried about Indian values, is the site of the famous erotic sculptures of Khajuraho, one of the country's chief tourist attractions.

Khajuraho teems with sexually explicit sculptures of high artistic attainment. In one, a man is lying on his back, his hands caressing the genitalia of two naked and voluptuous women on either side of him, his engorged member inserted into the vagina of a third woman who straddles his legs. The message of this work of art, created about one

Contrasting Michelangelo's *Madonna and Child*, 1504 (Notre-Dame, Bruges, Belgium), with a typical piece of Indian religious iconography showing the Hindu god Vishnu with his consort, Lakshmi, ca. A.D. 950 (Parshvanatha Temple, Khajuraho).

Scala/Art Resource, N.Y. and Vidya Dehejia

thousand years ago, is certainly not that sex is inherently sinful and should take place only for the holy purpose of begetting new life. The suggestion is that sex is something spiritual, to be celebrated, practiced with skill and abandonment to pleasure at the same time. These sculptures are public documents, not some sort of pornography to be looked at furtively in the hidden quarters of private life.

In the Western tradition, there has been a strict opposition between spirituality and sexual desire, while, as one writer has put the case of India, "the devotional, the metaphysical, and the sexual were not seen as being in any way opposed; on the contrary the three were closely linked." The great sensuous bronze sculptures of the Pallava and Chola kingdoms of south India show "queens, courtesans, and goddesses alike . . . carefree and sensual: bare-breasted, they tease their menfolk, standing on tiptoe to kiss them, hands resting provocatively on their hips." What is immediately apparent in these supple figures is the straightforward pleasure taken in the beauty of the human body. The men are sinuously muscled and well endowed. The women, adorned with bangles, necklaces, and belts wound around their hips, are curvaceous; they smile, they stand in seductive poses. There is also, of course, Western Classical and Renaissance art and sculpture that celebrate the human form, but little that unites the religious and the sensual in the way that Indian art does. The early Hindu scriptures, collected in the *Rig Veda,* show that in the beginning was *kama,* sexual desire—"and desire was with God, and desire was God."

By contrast, the official "Indian morality" of today, exemplified in those statements about sex education, seems to have airbrushed the earlier tradition away, replacing it with an invented tradition of modesty and chastity. The newspaper article that reported on the opposition to sex education in 2007 included a photograph of a group of teenage girls in prim two-toned blue school uniforms, their hair in chaste braids, looking down at supine plaster or plastic models of a man and a woman, the man's chest cavity opened to reveal his plastic organs, each one in a different color. If these rather sexless statues erode "Indian values," what are we to make of the erotic sculptures of Khajuraho and numerous other Indian cities, whose purpose, according to a common scholarly interpretation, was precisely to instruct people in the art of love?

The fact is that in the minds of many prominent Indians, sex education does contradict Indian values, at least according to today's definitions of those values, among which is a wish to keep intimate relations intimate rather than to turn the discussion of them over to bureaucrats. This Indian reaction to sex education illustrates a paradox: the very places where Western men in the past sought pleasures and excitements unavailable at home are today among the most sexually conservative places on the planet—including Communist China, Islamic North Africa, and India itself. At the same time, the former domains of restraint and inhibition have experienced a sexual awakening, a loosening of restrictions that was, in an accompanying paradox, partially inspired by the examples of the East. "The missionaries," Ian Buruma has written of the larger trend, "have taken post in Kuala Lumpur, and the whores of Babylon have moved to London and New York." To be sure, like most countries with a high percentage of poor women, India and China have plenty of prostitutes. There are districts in the major cities of India that are famous in particular for their brothels, which exist in a legal limbo, since prostitution is generally legal in India but brothels are not. In other words, a woman who sells sex to a man is not breaking the law; if she is organized to do it in the same place as another woman who does the same thing, she is. In any case, any foreign man who wants to buy sexual pleasure need only ask a taxi driver in Mumbai, New Delhi, or Calcutta to take him to the red-light district of that city, and there he will find eager strumpets aplenty waiting for him in upper-story brothels or striking poses (remarkably like those of the women figured in the cave temples of Ajanta) behind barred windows.

But publicly, as the sex education-debate showed, India no longer seems to be the place where British soldiers can order their partners from among the schoolgirls next door and where there is a perpetual perfume of the seraglio in the air. What is in the air in today's India is a certain middle-class prudishness reminiscent of Victorian England, and that is probably not a coincidence. Indeed, to compare the vast contemporary movie industry in India—Bollywood—with the bas-reliefs of Khajuraho is to see evidence of India's transformation from a society of open eroticism to one of public restraint. Every Bollywood movie is a love story featuring a handsome man and a beautiful buxom woman, and every one has choreographed dance scenes that are manifestly designed for the prurient interest. It's a pious pornography. But at least as yet, nudity, kissing, and depictions of sex have been forbidden in Indian cinema—in contrast to what was allowed on the concupiscent columns of Khajuraho more than a thousand years ago.

But before we examine this transformation, a fundamental question should be addressed: Is it really the case that the East had a different sexual culture from the West, a culture in which it was viewed as normal and inevitable that men of wealth and power were entitled to both wives and mistresses, a principle that turned out to be very advantageous for colonial-era European men? Was the East at one time more sexually permissive than it is now, and if that is the case, what happened to bring on modern-day prudery? Or is the notion of the East as a zone of special erotic possibilities purely a matter of Western fantasy and wishful thinking, a falsely eroticized image that is itself both a product of and a justification for colonial domination?

THE POLITICALLY CORRECT ANSWER to the question is yes, the putatively different, more openly expressed guiltless Eastern sexuality is a figment of the Western imagination. It is also axiomatic among many academic students of this question that the Western phantasm of Eastern sexuality reduced Easterners to feminized subjects whom it was right and proper to conquer and rule. The grand progenitor of this view is the late Edward Said, whose concept of Orientalism has nearly the status of holy writ among his many followers. Before Said, Orientalism was seen as the activity of harmless bookish philologists, anthropologists, archaeologists, lexicographers, translators, and others who liked to study arcane languages and customs and did so out of an abiding passion for knowledge—knowledge, moreover, that was progressive in spirit because it revealed the magnificent attainments and spiritual complexity of cultures that had, until then, been deemed heathen and primitive. After all, it was not Egyptians who developed the cult of ancient Egypt that Egyptians are so proud of today. It was European students of antiquities, beginning with those who arrived with Napoleon in 1798, who rediscovered the pharaohs' tombs, established the importance of the pyramids, and figured out how to read hieroglyphs. Similarly, it was Aurel Stein, the Hungarian-born Jewish British explorer of Central Asia who found buried in the sand and neglected by local peoples and governments the Buddhist cave temples now deemed by China to be central to its heritage. The cult of the exotic is more than simply a colonialist impulse; it is one of genuine curiosity, a thirst for knowledge, an element in the exploratory impulse that, strangely, nearly always originated in the West and was directed toward the East and rarely, if ever, operated the other way around. And this impulse to investigate exotic cultures and faraway peoples usually resulted in admiring descriptions of their greatness.

But Said took this mostly progressive tradition and turned it into an instrument of colonialist domination, arguing that Western portrayals of the East—indeed, the very Western attempt to know the East—was a tool of subjugation. In eloquent, erudite, sophisticated paragraphs, Said laid out the view that this scholarship was based not on verifiable facts about the East but on fantasies, clichés, and stereotypes embedded in the Western mind, which never saw the East as it really was but instead saw it as a minor variation on an already-existing image.

Sex plays a role in Said's view. The Western view of sex in the Orient, as reflected in the works of Flaubert, Burton, and Edward William Lane, whose *Account of the Manners and Customs of the Modern Egyptians,* written between 1833 and 1835, was long thought an indispensable compendium, is all part of the reductive and feminizing discourse that was itself part of the imperialist project. Said quoted Lane to the effect that in the view of the West, Eastern sexuality was characterized mainly by a "freedom of intercourse." In fact, any reading of Lane's work would reveal a vastly more nuanced and complex view of Eastern sexuality, one, for example, wherein polygamy is theoretically allowed but not frequently practiced. But never mind. In Said's interpretation, the Western vision of the Orient is a highly eroticized one that arose not from reality but from the need to find in the East what had been planted in the Western mind even before Westerners started going there: "suggestive ruins, forgotten secrets, hidden correspondences, and an almost virtuosic style of being," a place where the Romantic, Byronic wish for exotic adventure could be entirely realized. "So the Orient was a place where one could look for sexual experience unobtainable in Europe," Said wrote. Many writers who treated "the Orient"—and Said mentioned a long list of them, including Flaubert and "Dirty Dick" Burton, along with Herman Melville, André Gide, Joseph Conrad, and Somerset Maugham—were involved in this quest to establish "the association . . . between the Orient and the freedom of licentious sex."

But was there truth to this association? Was sex available to Western men in the East in a way that it was not in the West, or is this notion mere fantasy? Said was actually ambiguous on this question. One problem is that he seemed uninterested in what the Orient really was; he wanted only to show that the images of it presented in the West were mostly variations on earlier images, going back to the fanciful and mostly untrue accounts of John of Mandeville and the like. His constant suggestion was that the "association" between the Orient and sex is imaginary, but he never established what the sexual truth was and where it differed from what was imagined.

"Why the Orient seems still to suggest not only fecundity but sexual promise (and threat), untiring sensuality, unlimited desire, deep generative energies, is something on which one could speculate," he wrote. Said might have contemplated the sculptures of Khajuraho as one starting point for speculation on the origins of this image of the Orient, but he didn't talk about them. He did speculate, however, and what he said was that the eroticized Orient of the Western imagination was a sort of distorted mirror of the increased regimentation and institutionalization of sex in the West, where, especially in the nineteenth century, it had come to entail "a web of legal, moral, even political and economic obligations of a detailed and certainly encumbering sort." And so the Orient came to satisfy the desire for a place "where one could look for sexual experience unobtainable in Europe." If Voltaire saw in the eighteenth-century Chinese emperor Qianlong the philosopher-king he wished for in Europe, nineteenth-century writers like Flaubert and Burton found in the East the zone of enlightened sexuality they longed for in repressed, sexually ignorant Victorian Europe. The European writers were looking, as Said put it, for "a different type of sexuality, perhaps more libertine and less guilt-ridden."

What, then, was the reality of the various countries of the East? Did this different type of sexuality exist or did Western men only imagine that it existed? What about the harem, which certainly did exist in its various forms from the North African lands of the Ottoman Empire all the way to China? What about Vishnu and Lakshmi, Shiva and Parvati, or the pillow books of China? Said didn't say, and neither do his numerous followers who have attempted to illustrate his thesis with examples of the reductive and demeaning "Orientalist" imagination at work. None of them has offered a picture countervailing those offered up by Burton and Flaubert and the others. And why is that? Is it because the East, unlike the West, is unknowable? But if that were the case, these scholars would seem to be engaging in the same acts of demeaning imagination—portraying the Orient as deeply enigmatic, shrouded in an impenetrable fog of exoticism—that they attribute to the Orientalists. Or perhaps it is because what knowledge we have suggests—the inevitable clichés and stereotypes, *The Mikado*s and

*Turandot*s and the like aside—that the eroticized vision of the East carries a hard kernel of truth, which the followers of Said are loath to acknowledge.

IN THE 1980s, Chinese archaeologists working in an ancient ruin in Hunan Province discovered a trove of previously unknown books dating back to the second century B.C. One of them, *Lectures on the Super Dao of the World,* had some very good advice for newly married men. Engage in foreplay with your lady, it says. Be patient, and when you see that her nipples have hardened and beads of sweat have formed on her nose, you will know that she is aroused, in heightened anticipation of pleasure, ready to receive you. And when it comes to inserting your penis, commonly called *yang-ju,* or "sun tool," in Chinese, "you should insert it slowly and be in harmony with your lady." Once it is inside the fabled *yu-men,* or "jade gate," the advice continues, you can thrust vigorously when that gives your lady pleasure, but you should "sometimes keep your penis in her vagina without any movement at all, to wait and let her sexual climax come."

Sex advice is to be had aplenty in China today, but for a good twenty or more years the Chinese government imposed a strict androgynous regime of sexual puritanism with few equals in history. Sex was deemed to be within the national interest and so, therefore, was its strict regulation. Particularly during the ten or so years of the Cultural Revolution—initiated by Mao Zedong to eliminate his rivals in the government and to keep the revolution pure—the pursuit of sexual pleasure itself was branded counterrevolutionary. People caught up in romance and sex, after all, had less time to love Chairman Mao. Men and women dressed alike in shapeless blue costumes. Pigtails were mandatory for girls and women. Love was purged from movies, magazines, newspapers, and the theater. In the 1950s, the new Communist authorities had pursued vigorous campaigns to wipe out prostitution and venereal disease, and in the 1960s one of the country's proudest boasts was that for the first time in Chinese history, both of these scourges had ceased to exist. But these impressive accomplishments were followed by the attempted suppression of sexual desire altogether.

It was as if, in adopting the very Western notions of Marxism for itself, China had also internalized the Western association of sex with sin.

The impression was left during this period, moreover, that China was naturally puritanical and always had been, and, indeed, there is certainly support for this view in the Chinese tradition. Confucianism, the official state doctrine for more than two thousand years, puts a lot more stress on moral propriety than on carnal satisfaction. It condemns debauchery, fosters moderation, and decrees strict rules for relations between the sexes. The *Book of Rites,* which describes the social forms and ceremonies of life in ancient times, holds that except for the performance of conjugal duties in the bedchamber, which are desirable for perpetuating the family line, husbands and wives shouldn't even touch each other, not even to pass a cup of tea.

But China is a universe, and a great deal exists within it, including, as *Lectures on the Super Dao of the World* indicates, an open, lively, and irreverent erotic culture that condemned debauchery but always allowed for male sexual pleasure, a diversity of sex partners, and prostitution—and all that almost from the beginning of recorded Chinese history. The great historian of the Later Han dynasty, a scholar named Ban Gu who lived in the first century A.D., listed eight books on sex within a longer list of the most important works then in existence, among them *Sex Handbook of Master Jung Cheng* and *Recipes for the Bedchamber.* While Ban Gu's list has survived, none of the sex books on it have. A poem of the second century B.C., however, describes a bride talking to her husband on their wedding night in a manner that seems to show evidence of Ban Gu's influence. She says that she'll take instruction from one of the very manuals named by Ban Gu "so that we can practice all the various positions," and she predicts, "Nothing shall equal the delights of this first night."

Another text of the time describes the wonders of dancing girls, an early proof that there were dancing girls. "Their bodies are beautiful, supple like grass moving in the wind, they put forth all their charms so that one forgets life and death."

China, at least according to some scholars, had the first-ever sex-education manuals, dating back well over two millennia, and a rich erotic literature to go with them. A Chinese medical doctor and sex researcher named Ruan Fang Fu (who dissented from what he regarded as the repressive sexual policies of the Communist government and eventually immigrated to the United States) wrote about a two-year period he spent reading otherwise banned books in a special collection in Beijing that is closed to the general public. Ruan reported that the historical erotic literature covers every conceivable practice and position. A favorite in the literature is the irreverent depiction of the sexual activities of Buddhist and Daoist monks and nuns, who are supposed to remain chaste. Incest, pedophilia, and orgies are to be found in abundance in the literature, along with a full range of sexual techniques, such as masturbation and oral and anal stimulation, including the mutual simultaneous stimulation colloquially known as 69. Also to be found in the rich erotic Chinese literature: male and female homosexual relationships "in full and sympathetic detail," transvestism, exhibitionism, voyeurism, sadism and masochism, dominance, submission, necrophilia, urophilia, and rape.

Ruan's list was aimed at demonstrating his thesis, which is that contrary to the conventional image of China as sexually repressed and conservative, the Chinese tradition demonstrates remarkable openness to sexual pleasure and exhibits very little of the sin and guilt that are associated with it in Christianity. Like other scholars, most notably the great Dutch Sinologist Robert Hans van Gulik, the first Western writer to seriously examine the sexual history of China, Ruan has shown a great deal of poetic appreciation of the erotic arts. These are reflected in the metaphors used in China—like "sun tool" and "jade gate," "crossing the snowy mountains" (caressing a woman's breasts), "catching the fire across the mountain" (rear entry), "opening the peony" (when a man performs oral sex on a woman) and "moistening the inverted candle" (woman on top).

Sex is deeply embedded in basic Confucian cosmology, the relations between man (yang) and woman (yin) mirroring the relations between heaven and earth, sun and moon, fire and water. The Daoists, who as dissenters from the Confucian orthodoxy, were researchers into alchemy and believers in the possibility of immortality, were freer spirits than the Confucians. They elaborated theories of eroticism that sound an awful lot like justifications for a polygamous and kinky licentiousness.

According to Daoist theory, the yin essence of woman invigorates the yang essence of man, which, translated into practice, means that men should soak up as much yin from as many women as possible, and soaking up yin happens during sex. "Changing partners can lead to longevity and immortality," reads a Daoist text on polygamy from the sixth century A.D. titled *On Delaying Destiny by Nourishing the Natural Forces*. Its author continues: "If a man unites with one woman only, the *Yin qi* [female vital energy] is feeble and the benefit small. For the *Tao* of the *Yang* is modeled on Fire, that of the *Yin* on Water, and Water can subdue Fire. . . . But if a man can couple with 20 women and yet have no emission, he will be fit and of perfect complexion when in old age."

Lest anyone think that a man should never release his semen, lest he have wrinkly skin in old age, other texts warn that while disciplining one's impulses is good, going too far is unhealthy. If a man tries never to ejaculate, "his urine will become putrid, and he will suffer from the illness of haunting by incubi and succubi." The basic Daoist doctrine, which some scholars attribute to the early Chinese sex manuals, holds that multiple partners and very young partners make all the difference. Female sex partners were called *ding* in Daoist literature, a *ding* being a bronze pot with three legs of the sort that can be seen in any museum show of ancient Chinese bronzes. It was used in alchemy, which established a connection between the search for elixirs that will bring health and longevity and the sexual means of achieving those goals. The ideal female *ding* is 5,048 days old, Daoist doctrine holds. That's a girl of about fourteen years. Needless to say, it is important that she be a virgin so that none of her yin energy will have been depleted. The same logic applies to multiple partners and explains the advantage of always finding fresh partners whose yin is yet untapped.

China went through phases, with sexual openness sometimes seemingly ascendant, sometimes repressed. The famous erotic novel *Jou Pu Tuan* (*The Prayer Mat of Flesh*), written in the late years of the Ming dynasty, illustrates both attitudes. It is essentially the story of a young scholar whose prudish wife rejects his desire for sexual pleasure. He shows her an album of erotic paintings, *Spring Reigns in All the Thirty-six Palaces*, each palace representing a different conjugal position, and she lets loose her inhibitions. In an eerily similar way, van Gulik's inves-

An erotic color print from the Ming dynasty, published 1624,
showing a monk on the verge of "opening the peony" with a
woman disguised as an itinerant nun, accompanied by her maid.
Koninklijke Brill N.V.

tigation of China's sexual history began when he discovered a set of
Ming-dynasty pornographic paintings in a Beijing curio shop. Van
Gulik is best known and loved for a series of mystery stories he wrote
over the years, in which a certain Judge Dee, who is based on a historic
Ming-dynasty magistrate, solves various crimes. But to scholars of
China, van Gulik's greatest contribution is his classic book *Sexual Life
in Ancient China*.

Van Gulik argued that China remained open and open-minded in
sexual matters for at least two millennia but then veered toward repression during the Mongol dynasty, which lasted from 1206 to 1368,
because the Mongols were foreigners and barbarians, and Chinese men
developed the custom of hiding their wives and daughters lest they be
abused by the conqueror. As Chinese authoritarianism became stricter
in later dynasties, control over sex became ever more a device of dictatorship. The official neo-Confucian philosophy of the Ming dynasty

reinvigorated the prudish aspects of China's official doctrine, which had always specified clear rules of sexual propriety.

But despite official Ming prudishness, the Chinese erotic tradition, in van Gulik's description, was rich and varied, with pornographic novels, treatises on sexual pleasure, popular novels about courtesans and concubines, and Daoist practices persisting through the entire long stretch of Chinese history. Even in the Mongol and later dynasties, both erotic literature and erotic arts continued to be produced. A popular literature featuring stories about prostitutes and courtesans stretches from the Tang dynasty (the seventh through tenth centuries) into the twentieth century. One Mongol-dynasty chronicle, called *Records of the Green Bowers,* contains biographies of seventy courtesans of the time, many of them famous as singers and actresses. In short, China's erotic culture, unstifled by Christianity's conflation of pleasure and sin and unburdened by the threat of everlasting torment in the afterlife, always seems to have survived attempts to repress it, whether by neo-Confucian strictures or, centuries later, Socialist morality.

And then there was prostitution, which was banned in China for the first time ever when the Communists came to power, in 1949. References to "camp harlots," prostitutes organized to service imperial soldiers, date from the second century B.C. Prostitution always flourished, and like concubinage, it was always seen in China as a natural and inevitable phenomenon, to be regulated by the state but never prohibited. Late in the thirteenth century, when the Mongols were in power, Marco Polo estimated there to be twenty thousand prostitutes in Beijing and an uncountable number in Hangzhou, the Mongols' southern capital. One nineteenth-century document, *Memoirs of the Plum Blossom Cottage,* written by the pseudonymous Master of Plum Blossoms, includes practical advice to prostitutes on pleasing their customers, instructing that "your job is to satisfy their desires, not yours" and, if necessary, "fake orgasm even with a man who discharges the moment he enters you." The acceptance of prostitution never changed even after the overthrow of the last dynasty by modern-minded nationalist revolutionaries led by Sun Yat-sen. In 1929, there were 332 registered brothels in Beijing, 3,752 registered prostitutes, and many thousands more unregistered. In 1920 in Shanghai, there were 60,141 registered prostitutes.

Finally, also illustrating a devotion to a strange, even unique form of eroticism, there was the custom of binding the feet of girls in order to make them more attractive as wives or as the concubines of the wealthy and powerful. The practice seems to have begun in the tenth century and continued for the next thousand years, until, finally, it was proscribed during the Republican period. Girls starting at the age of six would have their feet bound in cloth so that the feet wouldn't grow; instead, the bones would break and the foot would curve inward. It is, to say the least, a practice of inconceivable cruelty and stupidity by today's standards, but it was deemed for a millennium to be intensely erotic and desirable—not only the foot itself, but the way a woman with bound feet was forced to sway delicately as she walked. The fragile, tiny foot aroused feelings of "both pity and lust," the main Western student of this practice has written. Men "longed to touch it, and being allowed to do so meant that the woman was his." The practice "created a whole repertoire of sexual gestures, including kissing, sucking and inserting the foot in the mouth, adoringly placing it against one's cheeks, chest, knees, or virile member." The academic left of today may wish to believe that all sexualized images of the East are products of pure Western male phantasm, but foot binding was no phantasm, and it is unmistakable evidence, first, of the subordination of the female body to an unbridled and undisguised male eroticism and, second, of the existence of a sexual culture with practices and attitudes very different from those of the West.

Even Confucianism, with its stress on propriety, its condemnation of debauchery and license and even boasting about the beauty of one's women, never held sex to be sinful or immoral. A husband's sexual duties to his wife never ceased, and the wife was entitled to sexual enjoyment, so that a man could have several wives and concubines but was required to copulate with each concubine once every five days until she reached the age of fifty.

MORE IMPORTANT FOR OUR PURPOSES, entirely unlike Christianity, even official Confucianism never upheld monogamy as a value. Like most of the cultures from the Ottoman Empire eastward, China was officially polygamous, and it was polygamous for thirty-five hundred years, beginning with the first dynasty, the Zhou, which corresponds to the time of the kings in ancient Israel. Van Gulik attributes this tradition to the ancient practice by which Chinese males were required to make sacrifices to their ancestors, which led to the perceived anticipation among the living of one day themselves being dead ancestors in need of male descendants to make those sacrifices on their behalf. For if the sacrifices ceased, van Gulik wrote, "the ancestors would diminish and they would become either malevolent ghosts or sink into limbo, with disastrous results for their living offspring." That made it a man's sacred duty to spawn male children, and the best guarantee of being able to do that is to have more than one female partner available for procreation.

Or maybe polygamy was just more fun for the men. Certainly, the culture of the harem has always been designed by and for men, while all that Daoist philosophy of the yin and the yang was directed toward male, not female, well-being. The East, sexually speaking, has always been a good place to be male, and that's one of the reasons when the East became accessible, many Western men went there—and continue to go there.

This does not mean that Asian societies were sexually liberated in the Western sense of that phrase, whereby autonomous individuals were no longer subject to political controls or religious strictures and were free to express themselves as they wished. The East has never been such a place. Women in particular—whether the "good" daughters of respectable families who maintain their virginity until marriage or that class of women designated to spend their lives in the erotic service of powerful men, never to marry—have always been under the tight control of men.

But the harem culture made the East different from the West—perhaps not different in the way of the most common and simplified stereotypes, but different in many ways and, therefore, in Western eyes, exotic. Again, the historical record indicates that this is no phantasm. The harem, whether in Constantinople or Beijing or the court of the Mughals in Delhi, was huge and central, an institution that spawned its own lore, customs, and intrigue and inspired a culture, both visual and literary. It was a political instrument. When Muhammad Sultan, the imprisoned first son of the seventeenth-century Mughal emperor

Aurangzeb, was brought back to court to receive the suddenly restored favor of his father, his rehabilitation was signaled by an expansion of his harem, including the addition of three wives, two of them the daughters of Hindu chieftains with whom the Mughal court wished to maintain good relations. In China, a general or a minister could be rewarded with a gift of an imperial concubine, this granting of the sexual favors of a woman in exchange for meritorious service not a common practice in the West. Certainly in the West, power translated into sex, but it is only in the East that loyalty to the ruler provided an avenue to enhanced erotic pleasure.

And speaking of the harem, it gave birth to the eunuch, a human type that, except for the Italian operatic castrato, was also unknown in the West and entailed a large and pungent subcultural repertoire. A French physician of the late nineteenth century, a certain Dr. Matignon, observed operations performed in Beijing around 1890, usually on young boys who had been brought to the surgeon to be made ready for a career in the imperial household. According to Matignon, the operation, performed by a member of the castrating profession, which was hereditary, "was a crude one, both penis and scrotum being removed in one cut with a sharp knife." We've seen Richard Burton's somewhat more graphic description of castration in the Arab world of the Middle East, where eunuchs also were created to serve in harems. According to both Matignon and Burton, a majority of the boys subjected to the knife survived, though Matignon says 3 percent to 6 percent of them did not.

And, of course, the harem produced a particularly Eastern variation on the universal theme of competition and the struggle for power, both within the imperial harem itself and within the family. Chinese literature is full of such stories, often involving an emperor who falls so thoroughly for a concubine that she emerges as the master of the realm. "The Song of Everlasting Sorrow," the epic poem by Bai Juyi and one of China's greatest literary classics, is a story of obsessive love, treason, and death centering on Yang Guifei, consort of the eighth-century emperor Xuanzong. Yang so captured the heart of the emperor that he neglected his duties, precipitating one of China's most famous rebellions, led by a brilliant obese general named An Lushan. Yang, who was nothing but a pretty peasant girl, became so powerful that generals bribed her sisters in order to gain the favor of the emperor and seven hundred seamstresses were assigned to make her clothing. She was, it should be remembered, not the emperor's wife but his concubine. When the rebellion of An Lushan failed, the belief that Yang Guifei had been to blame was so strong that the emperor had no choice but to have her strangled. "The Song of Everlasting Sorrow" is, as they say in Hollywood, based on a true story.

IN THE 1990S, a debate took place among anthropologists about the British explorer Captain Cook, who discovered New Zealand, Australia, and New Guinea, mapped the South Pacific, and was killed by Hawaiian Islanders in 1779. The standard belief had always been that Cook was taken by the Hawaiians to be a god—specifically, the fertility god Lono—and was deified on his first voyage, which took place during the Hawaiians' season of peace. But when he returned to the islands during the season of war, the Hawaiians' came into conflict with him and his crew, and he was stabbed to death in a skirmish.

The great debate in anthropology was whether the Hawaiians really did believe that Cook was a god. The notion is nonsense, says the main challenger of the standard narrative, a Sri Lankan–born scholar at Princeton University named Gananath Obeyesekere who argued in his book *The Apotheosis of Captain Cook* that the Hawaiians' "practical rationality" would have prevented them from thinking that a ruddy-faced Englishman was Lono. On the contrary, the deification of Cook is part of a Western myth whose underlying purpose is to belittle and infantilize the natives and therefore justify imperial conquest.

Enter Marshall Sahlins, a University of Chicago anthropologist who, in *How "Natives" Think: About Captain Cook, for Example,* retorted that Obeyesekere's notion of practical reality in this instance is a Western imposition, a refusal to accept that cultures do vary widely and that some people do think and behave differently from others. Indeed, Sahlins said, even the supposedly rational West can fall down in the area of practical rationality, as the widespread belief in ghosts, mediums, psychics, and extraterrestrials would seem to indicate. To deny the beliefs of eighteenth-century Hawaiians "without taking the trouble of an ethnographic investigation" is to "endow . . . them with the highest Western bourgeois values," taking away the spirit-saturated world in which they believed they lived. It is also to impose a kind of political vision on another people, to want to make them, for political reasons, like us.

Other peoples aren't like us, not in religion and not in matters of sex. The East is a broad category, too broad in many ways, and in the past, as now, different Eastern zones were different from one another. But most of them had in common that they were collectively different from the West. The erotic world that Western men discovered in the swath of territory from Morocco to Shanghai, passing by India, the Middle East, and Southeast Asia, was really different from the sexual world they knew back home. They may have entertained fantasies and stereotypes about it, but it was also real, and their experiences were real. To assume otherwise, to attribute everything to fantasy without, as Sahlins put it, an ethnographic investigation, isn't much more than an ideological gesture.

CHAPTER NINE

What Happened to the Harem?

T HE LOVE OF THE MUGHAL EMPEROR Shah Jahan for his third wife, the poetically named Mumtaz Mahal (meaning "Beloved Ornament of the Palace"), is no doubt India's most celebrated tale of love and fidelity and the one with the most beautiful enduring monument. Shah Jahan built the Taj Mahal to serve as a tomb for his favorite, the mother of fourteen children. Not far away is a pavilion of the Red Fort, the imperial residence of the Mughals, where, for the final eight years of his life, the emperor was imprisoned by his own son, Aurangzeb, who usurped his power. And there, under a stone cupola, Shah Jahan—or so the legend goes—spent his hours gazing through a latticed balustrade at Mumtaz's tomb.

It is fitting in its way that Aurangzeb is seen by some historians as standing at the beginning of the transformation of India from erotic openness to erotic inhibition. Aurangzeb ruled from 1658 to 1707, coming to power after killing all three of his brothers (and some of his brothers' sons) in a struggle for power that came with the physical decline of Shah Jahan. Though the son of the gentle Mumtaz and the romantic Shah Jahan, he was a warlike Sunni fundamentalist who differed from the previous Mughal rulers in his devotion to a strict and exclusive interpretation of Islamic law. Just how ruthless he was in persecuting Hindus is a matter of dispute. Hindu historians are persuaded that he set out to destroy everything he deemed to be non-Muslim, while their Muslim counterparts are equally persuaded that he attacked Hindu institutions only when they threatened his political supremacy.

He indisputably did destroy several important Hindu temples and shrines, including the twelfth-century temple of Somnath and temples in Benares and Mathura, the birthplace of Krishna, who was, from Aurangzeb's point of view, one of the false gods of Hinduism. Then he changed the name of Mathura to Islamabad (it was subsequently changed back). All the old mosques and monasteries that had become ruins because of the neglect of his predecessors were ordered "made as new," and salaried imams were appointed to supervise them. In Delhi alone, six hundred mosques were maintained out of the state treasury. Aurangzeb created a new censor of morals to enforce strict observance of Muslim law among ordinary people, so that, in the words of one contemporary chronicler, "the innovators, atheists, heretics who had deviated from the straight path of Islam, infidels, hypocrites, and the spiritually indifferent who had spread over India were chastised and forced to give up their wicked ways." Among the activities to be punished were drinking distilled spirits, gambling, and "illicit commerce of the sexes." In the eleventh year of his reign, music was banned at the court, and the nobility was enjoined from listening to songs. Two carved stone elephants (forbidden graven images) were removed from the gates of the Red Fort in Agra. Anything that smacked of Hinduism at court was abolished, even the common Hindu gesture of salutation (raising the hand to the head).

Islam in general, which had come to India with the Mughal conquest, was of course much closer to Christianity in its view of sexuality than it was to Hinduism, especially the Hinduism of Chola sculpture and the sensual representations of the gods. The Muslims in general tended to celebrate renunciation far more than uninhibited sexuality. Still, Hindu life continued under the Mughals, especially in the Indian south, where Islamic writ was either weak or nonexistent, and even in the lands directly under the control of the Mughals most Hindu temples remained standing, so it can be said that there was no wholesale destruction of Hindu institutions. In many ways what happened to the British later happened to the Muslims then: they took on the trappings of the maharajas. At the courts of Delhi and Agra and, as we will see shortly, in other great centers of the Mughal Empire, the successors to Aurangzeb had many wives and concubines, and so did the various nawabs, maharajas, and zamindars, who grew wealthy through their control of villages and rural estates. One of the grandsons of the abstemious Aurangzeb commissioned miniatures of himself in the act with his concubines.

Courtesans, dancing girls, and concubines, the essential dramatis personae of the harem culture, were an ever-present aspect of Indian society, both Muslim and Hindu.

But the climate changed with Aurangzeb. The trend was toward a more austere and exclusive version of Islam, a foreshadowing of the Wahhabi puritanism that would emerge in the deserts of Arabia later, and away from the more insouciant sensualism of Indian tradition. Aurangzeb rejected the relaxed eclecticism of predecessors like Akbar, the first of the great Mughals to be born in India and a man with an appreciation for what we would today call diversity. Akbar celebrated Hindu festivals, took Hindu wives, and inducted Hindu allies into the Mughal ranks as emirs, or nobles. Aurangzeb was, by contrast, harsh, intolerant, and ascetic. He saw pleasure as vain and deluding. His appointment of a kind of morality police anticipated what would happen in the twentieth century when the mullahs took over in Iran and, for a time, Afghanistan. And Aurangzeb was the last of the great, all-powerful Mughals. Slowly, after his death, the empire built by Persian-speaking warlords who came initially from Afghanistan would be absorbed piece by piece as Britain followed its practice of slow aggrandizement. And in the British and the other Victorians who came in their wake—the prim administrators, the missionaries, the social reformers who sought to liberate Indian women from the chains of a kind of medieval servitude—India's sexual culture would meet its greatest challenge.

IN 1870, Isabella Thoburn, an eager, deeply religious, and enterprising Methodist missionary from St. Clairsville, Ohio, arrived in the former Mughal cultural and artistic center of Lucknow and immediately set about to rescue it from perdition. Thoburn, thirty years old and unmarried, wasn't the first Protestant missionary to arrive in Lucknow, though no missionaries had been permitted to proselytize in India before the early years of the nineteenth century; the British authorities worried until then about offending the sensibilities of Hindus and Muslims alike. But in 1813, the British had opened India's doors to missionaries, acceding to the pressure of evangelical groups whose sentiment, as William Wilberforce, the great parliamentary anti-slavery

crusader, had put it, was that "our religion is sublime, pure, and benefi-
cent; theirs is mean, licentious, and cruel." That word *licentious* is
important to bear in mind as the British implemented what was, more
for India itself perhaps than for the British, a historic decision, one that
signaled a new era in the British attitude toward India, which had once
encompassed a kind of hands-off policy with regard to the local culture
and now turned intolerant and disrespectful. India became a field not
just for missionaries but for all sorts of moral crusaders and social do-
gooders to carry out a British version of the civilizing mission. "Am I
the keeper of the Hindu, the Indian, the Hottentot?" the Anglican
bishop of Oxford, who happened to be William Wilberforce's son,
asked rhetorically, giving an answer that, by today's standards, reeks of
smugness and condescension: "If all have sprung from the same parents
then the wild wanderer, the painted barbarian, is thy brother." Among
the consequences of this new crusading attitude was a new restrictiveness on sexual contact between the colonizers and the colonized, even
though, as Burton's case proves, it hardly stopped altogether. Another,
far more important consequence was the proliferation of missionary
schools for Indian children, who were subject to what the historian
Lawrence James has called "the crassest propaganda."

Crucial in this, the missionary schools, reflecting the prestige of the
colonial power, were popular among upwardly mobile Indians even
though the Indians themselves never converted to Christianity in large
numbers. A new elite, nourished on Protestantism and Western sexual
morality, was formed as a result, not only in the formally Christian
schools but in the English educational system in general. Most of the
leaders of India's independence movement, including Gandhi himself
(University College London) and Jawaharlal Nehru, India's first prime
minister (Harrow and then Cambridge), were the products of Western
education, out of which they fashioned a hybrid culture. Gandhi and
his friend Motilal Nehru, Jawaharlal's father, both of whom adopted
Indian dress, were not brown Englishmen by any standard; yet over
the years, the prestige accorded to Western education furthered the
change begun with Aurangzeb, even if Aurangzeb's model was certainly
not Christian Europe. It was all a big change with many consequences,
one of which was to hasten the demise of a sexual culture that had
endured for many centuries. And the decline of India's sexual culture

represents an extraordinary global phenomenon. Not long before Isabella Thoburn arrived in Lucknow, most of the world still subscribed to what I have been calling the harem culture, and in only the few countries of the West, the small peninsular domain of Christendom, did a different attitude prevail. By the time Thoburn had passed from the scene at the start of the twentieth century, the Western ideal of monogamy had become the global norm. This enormous social and moral transformation was partly a result of a change in British attitudes. At one time, the English in India had seen the country as a gorgeous pageant fit to be imitated in the cushioned homes of British nabobs. In the nineteenth century, many Brits, especially those looking at India from the vantage point of the Victorian homeland, deemed it a backward and abominable place requiring reform. Simultaneously the colonized Indians, a bit like the middle classes of England, internalized Victorian sexual morality as their own, in part out of a sort of snobbish identification with the conqueror. Then, decades later, as Britain and the rest of the West learned to celebrate an almost pagan and certainly very non-Victorian sexuality themselves—one in which, paradoxically, the old Indian erotic culture was revalued—the nineteenth-century erotic conservatism that the Indians had adopted as their own endured.

LUCKNOW, AS ONE OF THE MAJOR CITIES of northern India, was a natural target of missionary endeavor, and it was the American Methodists who seem to have had the biggest impact there. In 1862, a Methodist by the name of J. H. Messmore had founded what was to become the Lucknow Christian College, which is still among the city's major educational institutions. Churches had existed in Lucknow for a long time because Europeans had lived and prospered there as early as the second half of the eighteenth century. The missionaries already working in the city, who included Isabella's older brother and biographer, James Thoburn, had won a few converts there and in surrounding villages, so a small native Christian community was in place. Indeed, it was brother James who wrote to Isabella back in St. Clairsville, asking her to come to India to do what the male missionaries had been unable to do. Kept by Muslim practice apart from virtually any contact with women—except to talk to what he called "invisible persons" sitting behind a screen—James understood that only a female missionary would be able to undertake the grand task of educating and Christianizing Indian women, and that is what he proposed that Isabella do.

She took on that task with enormous enthusiasm and what became the dedication of a lifetime. Sponsored by the newly formed Woman's Foreign Missionary Society of the Methodist Episcopal Church, she sailed from New York on November 3, 1869, and arrived roughly three months later in Lucknow after a journey that had taken place partly on a bullock cart. Her immediate challenge, as she saw it, was to teach Indian girls to read, which she knew would be the key not just to their salvation but also to their ability later to become what were called native missionaries, spreading the "Good News" to every corner of India. It must be said of Thoburn that she had a strong this-worldly practical streak in her, a desire to improve the lives of women in the here and now, which mingled with an abiding sense that, ultimately, her purpose was to save souls in a society tragically devoid of spiritual grace.

She was tremendously successful. A few months after her arrival, she began a school for girls in a single mud-walled room in the city's noisy bazaar. At first only six (some sources say seven) students, children of Indian Christians, were in attendance, but the school gained a reputation for academic excellence, and it grew quickly, taking Christian and non-Christian girls alike. Only one year after its founding, it became a boarding school, and its staff could thus keep its students "cut off from the demoralization of heathenism." Thoburn had a gift for raising money, and six years after she founded her school, with $7,000 of donated money she was able to buy the Lal Bagh, a handsome villa that had belonged to the treasurer of the last nawab of Lucknow. A Mughal mansion, in other words, was converted into a place of Christian learning, a sign of the coming new order. In 1888, persuaded by Thoburn's argument that Indian women needed to be trained to "come up and out into a busy world's work," American Methodists donated the funds needed to create Lucknow Christian College, whose name was changed to Isabella Thoburn College in 1902, soon after Isabella herself succumbed to cholera in Lucknow at the age of sixty-one.

Isabella Thoburn College is still in business, with more than one thousand students, young men and women, housed in an imposing neoclassical building at the intersection of University and Faizabad roads, one of several institutions that were merged a few years ago to form Lucknow University. It is said to be especially patronized by "middle and upper class, urban Indian families, who desired their daughters to obtain an English education." Many of the teachers in the Indian state of Uttar Pradesh are graduates.

In 1900, while on her final furlough in the United States to raise funds for her missionary activities, Thoburn presented one of her star Indian students, Lilavati Singh, to demonstrate the tremendous promise of Indian education for women. Singh, dressed in an Indian costume, dignified and unpretentious, made something of a sensation as she called on her audience to support the cause of Christian education for Indian women. Hearing her in New York, none other than Benjamin Harrison, the former president exclaimed, "If I had given a million dollars to foreign missions, I should count it wisely invested if it had led only to the conversion of that one woman." Elaborating on the civilizing mission of Thoburn, Singh said that six hundred graduates of the college had gone into "Christian work" all over India. Her peroration was one that no doubt thrilled her audience with the prospect of a glorious future. "No one, I say, but Jesus ever deserved this precious diadem India," she cried, "and Jesus shall have it!"

WELL, JESUS DIDN'T GET INDIA, which remains overwhelmingly Hindu and Muslim, with Christian conversion, when it has taken place at all, occurring not among the elite but among the poor and the dispossessed. And yet it was a strikingly apt sign of the times that Isabella Thoburn would have been sent to Lucknow, which only a few short decades before she arrived was widely viewed, as one local chronicler put it, as "the last example of the old pomp and refinement of Hindustan, and the memento of earlier times."

Lucknow, on the north Indian plain, an overnight train ride from New Delhi, is in this sense a particularly sharp illustration of the transformation of India during the latter decades of colonialism. Today the city is decayed and poor, its many crumbling sandstone edifices sad reminders of its grand Mughal past. At the end of the eighteenth century, however, Lucknow was a great cosmopolitan world-class capital, a place of both commercial vigor and a cultivated hedonism. As the British historian of India John Keay put this, it was a city that "had come to combine the monumental magnificence of Shah Jahan's Delhi with the scented allure of Scheherazade's Baghdad." A late-eighteenth-century visitor described it as "a vision of palaces, minarets, domes azure and golden, cupolas, colonnades, long façades of fair perspective in pillar and column, terraced roofs." In Lucknow, it was said, even the courtesans could recite Urdu love poetry by heart. It was a place where, as Keay has put it, "a swarm of eunuchs, courtesans, concubines and catamites" surrounded the local nawab. "In short, to the best of their limited abilities," Keay concluded, "the last nawabs fulfilled to the bejewelled hilt their role as the dissipated Oriental despots of European imagining."

Lucknow was given its identity by a succession of minor Mughals, officials who built the city in the wake of Aurangzeb's death, when the once-great empire was breaking up and central authority was vanishing. Its first Mughal ruler was Saadat Khan, a Persian-born official who had been appointed nawab of Oudh, a former province that is now part of Uttar Pradesh, by the emperor in Delhi but who proceeded to make the whole province effectively independent. His grandson, Shuja ud-Daula, nawab as of 1754, worked to transform Lucknow into a rich cosmopolitan center and gave it much of its personality as a place where money and pleasure were pursued with equal avidity.

In fact, Shuja had been defeated in battle by the British, who in the second half of the eighteenth century continued to rule India largely through native maharajas, nawabs, and the Mughal court in Delhi, which was still theoretically in charge of most of northern India. The British set Shuja up as a puppet ruler of Oudh, taking payments from him for both the costs of the war it took to defeat him and the cost of keeping the British troops who were then stationed in Oudh to "protect" it. British and other merchants moved to Lucknow, including a Frenchman named Claude Martin, who was reputedly the richest man in town and built several European-style mansions (one of which later housed La Martinière School for Girls). This was the swashbuckling time of Warren Hastings and the British nabobs so reviled by Edmund

Burke, when ordinary soldiers or company factors set themselves up in business, squeezed local princes for loot, and established their own imitation Mughal lives. One Englishman with the Dickensian name Felix Rotton, born in 1795, served the nawab in several military capacities, got rich, married several Indian women, and had twenty-two children by them. The only thing Rotton did not do in following the classic nabob model was return home, buy a rotten borough, and become a member of Parliament.

Lucknow's last Mughal ruler, Wajid Ali Shah, came to power in 1848 and was removed from office by the British in 1856, with the city being annexed to the ever-larger portion of India administered directly by the British. Shortly after Wajid's involuntary exile to Calcutta came the anti-British uprising known as the Sepoy Mutiny, during which the siege of Lucknow's foreign community by rebel troops and its relief by a column of British army regulars became an iconic episode of that terrible war. All of this happened only a bit more than a decade before Isabella Thoburn arrived from Ohio to instruct the Indians in the proper way to live. In other words, the gloriously decadent ways of Lucknow under the last nawab were then very recent.

A good deal of what we know about Lucknow before and after the British annexation comes from a local journalist and novelist named Abdul Halim Sharar, a devotee of Urdu poetry who, starting in 1913, wrote a long series of articles describing a way of life that was already disappearing. The pattern described by Sharar is this: the British and their garrisons controlled the city even as they encouraged its nominal rulers to live lives of a nonthreatening sort of hedonism and dissipation, with the lures of the harem seldom resisted. Shuja ud-Daula, he wrote, "was by nature attracted to beautiful women and was fond of dancing and singing. For this reason there was such a multitude of bazaar beauties and dancers in the town that no lane or alley was without them. Because of the Nawab's rewards and favors they were in such easy circumstances and so wealthy that most of the courtesans had abodes with two or three sumptuous tents attached to them."

These were the last days of the Indian harem culture. When the nawab traveled, Sharar said, these courtesan tents "would be loaded with stately grandeur on to bullock carts . . . and guarded by a party of ten or twelve soldiers. And, as this was the practice of their ruler, all the rich men and chieftains openly adopted it, and courtesans would accompany them on their travels."

And so it was with Shuja's successors. His son, Asaf ud-Daula, was, Sharar reported, mainly interested in his pleasures, and the British gave him money to encourage him in this. Among Asaf's pleasures was spending money on "the embellishments and comforts of the town" to help him "in satisfying his desire for voluptuous living." The last ruler, Wajid Ali Shah, started out by trying to restore some independent military power, and he would spend hours sitting on his horse in the sun commanding his soldiers' drills. But a clue to his real interest lay in his creation of what Sharar called "a small army of beautiful girls" who drilled in the same manner as the men.

In less than a year, Wajid became tired of military matters and began to consort more and more with "beautiful and dissolute women, and soon dancers and singers became the pillars of state and favorites of the realm." Wajid wrote poems about his own love affairs and the amorous escapades of his youth, leading Sharar to observe that while "few ministers and nobles in their early youth have not given full rein to their sexual desires," it was only Wajid Ali Shah who "has made public his sensuous transgressions." He fell in love with "female palanquin-bearers, courtesans, domestic servants, and women who came in and out of the palace, in short with hundreds of women, and because he was heir to the throne, he had great success with his love affairs." Once a year, he organized theatrical evenings devoted to the very un-Islamic Krishna's amorous affairs. Wajid played Krishna, and "decorous and virtuous ladies of the palace acted as *bopis,* milkmaid loves of Krishna."

This portrait of Wajid and his immediate ancestors marks a natural history of the decay of the Oriental despot. The vigor and power of figures like Akbar and Aurangzeb may long before have disappeared, but the decadence of the harem culture remained. It wasn't only sex that characterized the life of the Lucknow court and nobility in those years; it was an entire connoisseurship of refined pleasure. Storytellers were hugely popular, and, Sharar said, there was hardly a rich man in Lucknow who did not have one as part of his entourage. Urdu love poetry flourished, including poetry that "stirred the souls of the sensually inclined and the King." A particular poetic form that Sharar called *vasokht* was developed in Lucknow: in six-line verses, the poet proclaims his beloved, describing her charms and bemoaning the nonreciprocation of his ardor. Then he invents a fictitious other love, telling his true love that he has become enamored of somebody else, whose beauty and charm he also describes, until the pride and resistance of the first woman are broken and the two are reconciled. The dance, as always in Mughal culture, was everywhere. Animal fighting and bird fighting of all sorts, from elephants to cocks, were favorite pastimes.

And at the heart of it all were the courtesans, who were often highly skilled in dance and could recite long poems from memory. It turns out that "dancing and singing girls," the British administrative category for courtesans, were in the highest tax bracket. After the British broke the siege of Lucknow in 1858, many of the courtesans were accused of having helped the rebels, and their property was confiscated. This, according to the municipal records, included houses, orchards, factories, and retail stores selling food and luxury items. The British also recorded the items seized from the three hundred consorts who lived in Wajid Ali Shah's harem, including "gold and silver ornaments studded with precious stones, embroidered cashmere wool and brocade shawls, bejeweled caps and shoes, silver-, gold-, jade-, and amber-handled fly whisks, silver cutlery, jade goblets, plates, spittoons, hookahs, and silver utensils for serving and storing food and drink, and valuable furnishings," the whole haul worth an estimated $2 million at the 1857 value of the dollar.

Sharar confirmed the privileged place of the courtesans in disapproving fashion, our Urdu poet having, it seems, adopted a bit of Victorian morality as his own. "Association with courtesans started during the reign of Shuja ud daula," he wrote. "It became fashionable for noblemen to associate with some bazaar beauty, either for pleasure or social distinction . . . these absurdities went so far that it was said that until a person had an association with courtesans, he was not a polished man. This led the way to a deterioration of morals in Lucknow. At the present time there are still some courtesans with whom it is not considered reprehensible to associate, and whose houses one can enter openly and unabashed."

But what remained of the old lifestyle was just a shadow of what had come before. True, perhaps for some wealthy men in Lucknow even in the early years of the twentieth century, female entertainment was still a central element of life, but there couldn't have been very many such men, and this was not only because of the pressure brought to bear by missionaries. The British, who had once been content not to meddle in the social affairs of the "natives," not only confiscated the wealth of the courtesans but, perhaps worse, also transformed them into common prostitutes. With thousands of British soldiers stationed in Lucknow, especially after the suppression of the Sepoy Mutiny, the colonial administration did what it did elsewhere in India—set up lock hospitals for prostitutes found to have venereal disease and *lal bazaars* for the troops. Devoid of royal patronage when Lucknow was annexed by the British and the nawab removed, many former courtesans were compelled to serve the British stationed in their city, who, needless to say, were uninterested in the finer points of the nautch, the Indian dance, or in Urdu love songs. "The imposition of the contagious diseases regulations and heavy fines and penalties on the courtesans for their role in the rebellion signaled the gradual debasement of an esteemed cultural institution into common prostitution," a contemporary British historian has written. "Women who had once consorted with kings and courtiers, enjoyed a fabulously opulent living, manipulated men and means for their own social and political ends, been the custodians of culture and the setters of fashion trends, were left in an extremely dubious and vulnerable position under the British."

In particular, the women, cultivated as they were, now had to submit to mandatory inspections of their bodies in order to be deemed fit to be paid for sex with British soldiers, while around them Lucknow declined into just another impoverished northern Indian city.

IT'S NOT CLEAR whether Isabella Thoburn was aware that what she witnessed of the old culture in Lucknow was a residue of a world already vanishing or that one ironic consequence of colonialism in the Victorian era was the replacement of a refined sexual culture with an exploitative and unrefined one. Certainly what she saw and recorded disturbed her deeply and gave her the motivation to undertake what became her life's work. She did not, as she set about to do this, make the mistake of underestimating the power of the hybrid Muslim-Hindu culture that had brought about what she could see only as a lamentable spiritual condition. She found Lucknow dazzling in its way, "worthy of the Oriental romances," she wrote in an article in the official journal of the Woman's Foreign Missionary Society, a publication produced for much of the second half of the nineteenth century under a title that today seems like a parody of itself: *Heathen Women's Friend.* But, Thoburn quickly added, Lucknow was corrupt, and not only corrupt but "a dark home for many a sin-darkened soul." She heard a beggar calling, "Pity me for Allah's sake," and she was horrified by the attractions of a false religion. She saw a funeral procession on the way to the burning ghat, where Hindu cremations were performed, and everything disgusted her, from the chants of "Ram, Ram" to "the sickening smell" of the flowers. "Heathenism is never so revolting as in death," she wrote. Floating down to the street from some unseen "upper room comes the weird, monotonous singing of a band of dancing girls," and that to Isabella Thoburn was a sign not of people engaged in the pleasures of music and movement but of "the sin and misery that darken this fair Eastern city."

As Thoburn saw it, the women of India were effectively prisoners in their own houses, kept there by domineering husbands. But, afflicted by what Karl Marx might have called a false consciousness, they remained unaware of their own imprisonment. Thoburn, no fool, understood what she called the "charms" of social position, "which few women seem able to resist," and she saw that many of the Indian women, even those whose lives were spent in what she called "jewel-bedecked idleness," had exactly that.

"The system is thoroughly bad, but it is deeply rooted in the most ancient traditions of the Oriental world," her admiring brother wrote, describing her introduction to Lucknow's society, "and can not be uprooted and cast away in a day, or a year, or a generation. But light can be made to penetrate its inmost recesses, and in God's own good time the unnatural system must give way, and the Oriental harem be supplanted by the Christian home."

The point, of course, is that Britain and the West created two morally opposed ways of life in India. Some, like Richard Burton, wished to take advantage of India erotically and to learn from it. Others, like Isabella Thoburn, wanted to wipe its moral slate clean. Where Burton saw opportunities for a plenitude of existence and a greater richness of experience, Thoburn and her like in the missionary crusade saw sin and the need to eradicate it. Needless to say, India would have changed even if there had been no missionaries. In the twentieth century, most Eastern cultures (Japan, India, China, and the countries of Southeast Asia) officially adopted monogamy and banned concubinage, and even where they didn't—in parts of the Muslim world, for example—it was only the very wealthy who continued to enjoy the harem.

But if it was the West, through thousands of individual actors like Isabella Thoburn, that advanced new, foreign principles for private life, it was the East that acceded to them. Burton exported Indian ways to the West before they died out in their native place; Thoburn imported Western ways to India even as sexual prudishness back home was losing its grip. Both of them were elements of the West's encounter with the different sexual culture of the East, even if one valued it and the other sought to stamp it out, and both of them owed their success to their association with imperial power. In a way, the eventual and perhaps inevitable ascendancy of Victorian mores in India represented a comeback for the sexual and moral culture of Christendom. For decades, India had prevailed in the encounter of the Eastern and Western sexual cultures, turning supercilious and racist European traders and soldiers into little sultans. But by the late nineteenth century, even as Burton was creating a sensation back home by publishing the *Kama Sutra* for the sexually repressed British, what one European writer has called "the long night of Victorian morality" was descending on Lucknow and the rest of India itself.

The question of whether it was indeed a long night is a complicated one. Certainly the implantation of Western morality coincided with Lucknow's loss of both commercial and cultural vitality, and the city today is no doubt a good deal less fun than it was two hundred years ago. But then there is the matter of women's equality and liberation from a way of life wherein a woman's highest possible attainment was either to enjoy her "jewel-bedecked idleness" or to serve as a courtesan, both alternatives centering on the view that the chief role of a woman is to give pleasure and service to men. That was an attitude that would have had little staying power in the twentieth century, and certainly Thoburn deserves credit for the part she played in speeding it along its road to oblivion—or at least partial oblivion. There were other progressive aspects to her work as well. She created one of the few institutions in India in the nineteenth century where Europeans and Indians mixed as equals. "Lal Bagh became a place where racial prejudice was almost completely unknown," one student of Thoburn's wrote. Among the graduates of the school were the first Muslim female doctor in India and the first female dentist. Thoburn wanted to turn girls into native missionaries as part of a long-term project to Christianize India, and in that effort she taught her girls English, geography, and physiology and sent them out to villages in the Lucknow vicinity as assistants to European missionaries and Bible readers. But you never know what literacy will produce.

In the case of Isabella Thoburn College, it produced major contributions to a woman's literature in India that powerfully transgressed both Eastern and Western traditions. Among the college's graduates, for example, was Ismat Chughtai, whose short story "Lihaf" ("The Quilt"), published in 1942, has been proclaimed by feminists today as an illustration of lesbianism as resistance. "Lihaf" is about a young bride "installed . . . in the house" of her aristocratic husband "with the rest of his furniture." The husband, whose interest is in beautiful young men, neglects her, and she finds fulfillment and solace in an erotic relationship with a maid.

Isabella Thoburn, who most likely died a virgin, would probably not have approved of the theme (and neither did the British authorities, who tried, unsuccessfully, to prosecute Chughtai for obscenity after the publication of "Lihaf"), but in the twentieth century the college that bears Thoburn's name allowed girls to read not just the Bible but Freud and Darwin and the great British novels of the nineteenth century as well. Thoburn herself—again using money she cajoled from supporters in America—founded in the 1880s what seems to have been the first magazine in India written for and, more important, by women. Called *The Woman's Friend,* it was published bimonthly in Hindi and Urdu and was free of charge to those who wanted to receive it. Thoburn had in mind what she called Christian literature—Bible and family stories and the like—and she herself contributed a regular column. In the context of late-nineteenth-century India, a magazine written by women in association with a school for girls was nothing short of revolutionary. "The women's colleges promoted something radically new, at a time when only men were exposed to western education," one current-day scholar has written. "Only the Christian schools educated women for public employment, rather than to be wives and mothers."

Part of the college's appeal was that it had the prestige of the Western label. Women who went there had a better chance of attracting Western-educated Indian men as husbands, and more and more Indian men of the elite class were Western educated. "Education is looked on as a passport to marriage," the British principal of a Christian school in Lahore said. But in Lucknow in the twentieth century, Isabella Thoburn College was more than an adornment for prospective wives. It was part of the ferment of the moment when many traditions, including the tradition of British rule, were being questioned. Lucknow was the place where the anthology *Angare* (*Embers*) was published, an attack on traditional Muslim ways that so outraged the Muslim establishment that local imams issued fatwas calling for the death by stoning of its four authors.

Another alumna of Isabella Thoburn College was Attia Hosain, whose father, educated at Cambridge University, was a friend of Nehru's father. Hosain, who died in 1998, was best known as the author of the novel *Sunlight on a Broken Column,* another literary landmark in India representing a break with the old order. It is the story of a girl who rejects the main lesson inculcated in her by her traditional family, which is that a woman must learn to accept unhappiness as her unavoidable fate.

IN THE LATE 1990s, the British journalist and historian William Dalrymple visited Lucknow precisely to record the destruction of its old Hindu-Muslim culture. The final blow to the city's grandeur had come with the partition of the former empire of India into India and Pakistan, leading many of the city's Muslims to leave. "What was left of the old Lucknow, with its courtly graces and refinement, quickly went into headlong decline," Dalrymple wrote. "The roads stopped being sprinkled at sunset, the buildings ceased to receive their annual whitewash, the gardens decayed, and litter and dirt began to pile up unswept on the pavements."

Dalrymple spoke to people who could remember a few vestiges of the city's greatness, and they described the process by which power in Lucknow, once in the hands of cultivated if decadent princes, "has passed to the illiterate." Corruption had become rampant. The descendants of nawabs pull rickshaws or work as common prostitutes, servicing their customers in Clarks Hotel for five hundred rupees. Let's be clear: it's not the fault of Isabella Thoburn, whose eponymous college still does the job of educating Lucknow's women, and far better to have that institution than not. Lucknow's decline can't be separated from the poverty of India in general, and that is a complicated product of a corrupt and ineffectual political leadership, the country's long pursuit of a sort of socialist autarky, its fragmented and class-bound social structure, and its failure to universalize education and health care (in contrast, for example, with China).

Still, Isabella Thoburn, with her certainty that her way ought to be India's way, is a sort of milestone on the way to the disappearance of a remarkable hybrid culture, one that we most likely will never see again.

CHAPTER TEN

The Inescapable Courtesy of Japan

VERY SOON AFTER HE ARRIVED in Japan during the U.S. occupation of that country, Martin Arnold got his first, unforgettable lesson in the historical relationship between Western power and Eastern sex. It was 1947, a year and a half or so after the Japanese surrender, and Arnold, whom I spoke to in 2007 in New York, was assigned to work at a prison and psychiatric hospital run by the army in Tokyo. He was put on the penicillin team, and on his rounds he ran into another soldier he knew from high school back home.

"He says, 'Come on, I'll take you out tonight,'" Arnold remembered.

"We get on a train," he said. "We go out to the suburbs. We get off the train and go to a little house, and there were Papa-san, Mama-san, and two daughters-san. Papa-san and Mama-san disappear into a room, and we get it on with the daughters-san.

"And the other guy was reading a fucking newspaper and smoking a cigar while doing it," he said.

Money probably changed hands, though Arnold didn't remember that part of the transaction. He did remember that a lot of sex in Japan in those days was exchanged for things like soap and candy bars, almost impossible for ordinary Japanese to get but easily available to American soldiers at the PX.

"We then get back on the train," Arnold continued. "We go to the engine door, which is stenciled 'Off-Limits to Allied Personnel.' The other guy opens the door, picks up the engineer by the shoulders and puts him in a corner, grabs the throttle, and off we go back to Tokyo. We went through all the stops. Nobody could get off or on the train.

He pulls into our station, opens the door, and says, 'Run!' " And run they did, military police whistles blowing, back to the hospital.

BY THE TIME the United States became what it seems accurate to call the neocolonial power of Asia, the British and the French empires had come to an end, and therefore so had the large-scale erotic activities of the British and French in India, North Africa, and Indochina. The Americans more than picked up the slack. They turned the East-West erotic relationship from a sort of private and relatively discreet matter into something very American—commercialized, democratized, and mass in scale. Wherever Americans were stationed in Asia—Okinawa, Clark Air Base in the Philippines, Udon Thani in Thailand (site of a B-52 base from which North Vietnam was bombed during the Vietnam War), or Cam Ranh Bay in Vietnam—the same scene inevitably followed: the transformation of certain streets into sprawling entertainment areas, whose neon signs advertised places with names like Honolulu Bar, Suzie Wong's, or the Pussy Cat Club; the thousands of girls with brown skin, skimpy outfits, and enlarged breasts bantering in a kind of universalized pidgin ("Hey, Cheap Charlie, why you no buy me drink?"); the spawning of out-of-wedlock fatherless children, and the spread of venereal disease.

In Japan in 1945, for the price of a bar of soap and a candy bar, you could screw the daughters of a defeated and humiliated Japanese couple. You could, if you were so inclined, even read the newspaper and smoke a cigar as you coupled, to display your utter mastery over the defeated nation, your insouciant use of the subjugated other for your own pleasure, and then, to demonstrate that to a wider audience, you could turn the train to Tokyo into your private limousine. As the historian John Dower has noted, one consequence of this phenomenon was an enduring transformation of the image of Japan in American eyes, from "a menacing, masculine threat . . . into a compliant, feminine body on which the white victors could impose their will." The cost on an individual basis was virtually nothing. During the early years of the occupation of Japan, a short visit to a prostitute cost fifteen yen, or a dollar, while cigarettes on the tight post-war Japanese market cost thirty yen.

The occupation itself ended in 1952, but Japan remained a place of easy, cheap sex for the American troops at bases in the country into the 1970s, when the booming economy eventually put sex for purchase largely out of the reach of ordinary GIs and tourists. But until that time, Japan was a sexual free-fire zone, especially on the island of Okinawa (returned to Japanese administration only in 1972), the place with the most U.S. troops.

In his lacerating memoir of Vietnam, *A Rumor of War,* Philip Caputo told of one sergeant who missed the convoy as the first combat troops to be dispatched to Vietnam headed for the airport on Okinawa, where they had been stationed until then. His name was Colby and he showed up "wearing a sport shirt and a silly grin" just as his buddies were leaving.

"Just gettin' me a little poontang, lieutenant," Colby told Caputo, explaining his afternoon absence. (*Poontang* seems to have derived from the French *putain,* or "prostitute.")

WHILE SEX IN POST-WAR ASIA was different in scale (greater) and style (more vulgar) than the earlier Western experiences, it followed the same basic pattern. Like the British in India before them, the Americans in post–World War II Japan, Korea, and Vietnam took advantage of their power, their wealth, and the existing sexual culture to acquire erotic advantages. In the East, power and money always conferred a sexual advantage, and the GIs who were there had plenty of power and money to spare, and so did the journalists, contractors, diplomats, spies, pilots, and others who made up the full American complement, especially when the scene moved to Indochina in the early- to mid-1960s.

The contrast between the two defeated powers of World War II is telling in this sense. Germany and Japan were similar in so many ways. Both had been fascist, militaristic, and aggressive, cruel in victory, responsible for some of the most terrible destruction in human history. Both countries also, once defeated, accepted occupation without protest or resistance, and both also cooperated in the American-inspired conversion into genuine, durable democracies, though in the German case, of course, this conversion took hold at first only in the western half of the divided country. Both, by virtue of wartime exhaustion, invasion, occupation, and retaliation by former enemies, also suffered terrible privation and abuse, the Germans in particular victimized by Soviet troops who raped an uncountable number of German girls and women as they pursued the fleeing German army from the Polish border to Berlin. During the years of occupation, both countries essentially had no sovereign power; they were governed not by themselves but by the occupying powers, four of them in Germany, one in Japan.

But the two countries differed greatly in the matter of sex. In Germany, once the military conflict was over and the four-power occupation had begun, there was no official effort to make sexual services available to the occupiers. Whatever happened between the victors and defeated women—and a great deal did happen—happened privately, whether by consent or not. In Japan, by contrast, the government resorted to a very Asian solution, one derived from the harem culture, to deal with the expected sexual consequences of having a quarter of a million American soldiers stationed on Japanese soil. In part, the Japanese were motivated by the knowledge that if they had been victorious and the United States had been defeated, their soldiers would have raped that defeated country's women in much the same way Soviet soldiers did Germany's and Japanese soldiers did in what is rightly called the rape of Nanjing, the Nationalist Chinese capital that was occupied and pillaged by Japan during the war.

Indeed, as is well-known, the Japanese forced thousands of women in the countries they conquered to serve in brothels organized to satisfy the sexual needs of their troops. These *ianfu,* or "comfort women"— Koreans, Chinese, Filipinas, and others—were themselves a distorted and criminalized expression of an Asian harem culture. The phenomenon arose out of the expectation that there should always be a class of women whose purpose is to satisfy the sexual desires of men, in part so that the prized virginity of "good" women from the same society could be preserved, the forced promiscuity of some women protecting the virtuousness of others.

With the Americans due to arrive, the Japanese were thus fearful that the occupier would do to their women what their soldiers had done to the women they conquered during the war. As Dower has put this in his study of post-war Japan, "The sexual implications of having to accommodate hundreds of thousands of Allied servicemen had been terrifying, especially to those who were aware of the rapacity their own forces had exhibited elsewhere." And so the government sent instructions to police departments across the country to prepare "comfort facilities" for the occupation, and this duly was done.

The Japanese had a well-known historical precedent and heroic point of reference for the women who served in what became known as recreation and amusement centers. A few years after Commodore Matthew Perry had arrived in his famed "black ships" in Tokyo Bay in 1854, forcing Japan to open its doors to trade with the West and to residency for large numbers of Westerners, the first U.S. consul general, Townsend Harris, arrived in Tokyo. According to Japanese records, Harris demanded that the local authorities provide him with a female companion, to act as both maid and bedmate, or else, he warned, treaty negotiations would be halted. Harris made no mention of this request in his own diaries, published in two volumes. Indeed, in an early example of the sort of hypocrisy that the Christian value of chastity and celibacy often created, Harris publicly expressed distaste for what he called "the lubricity of these people," even expressing moral contempt for a Japanese vice governor who, he said, offered to supply him with any woman he fancied.

Still, Japanese internal communications indicate that Harris wanted a woman, and the Japanese authorities, though reluctant in this matter, provided him with a certain Kichi (known with the Japanese honorific as Okichi), the daughter of an impoverished widow. It was not a happy relationship. Harris employed (if that's the word) Okichi for only two brief periods before turning her loose, replacing her later on with two other mistresses. Still, Harris would not have demanded a woman from his official diplomatic counterpart if he had been carrying out a negotiation in, say, Spain, France, or Brazil. But evidently he knew enough about the local sexual culture and the history of foreign men in Japan to demand one there, treating himself to the same sexual advantages that any Japanese feudal lord or wealthy merchant would have considered his due.

Okichi herself subsequently acquired the status of a tragic heroine among her countrymen and countrywomen. Though the analogy may have been strained, the women assembled by the private entrepreneurs designated by the Japanese government to create post–World War II "comfort" facilities were called *showa no tojin Okichi,* "the Okichis of the present era."

"We are not compromising our integrity or selling our souls," this first contingent of Japanese comfort women declared in an oath they read as part of their induction into this strange institution. The oath defined sleeping with the former enemy not as prostitution but as an act of patriotic duty. "We are paying an inescapable courtesy, and serving to fulfill one part of our obligations and to contribute to the security of our society."

Not that this declaration successfully disguised for a young Japanese woman the inherent ugliness of having to have intercourse with up to sixty foreign soldiers a day. Dower reported that when the first recreation and amusement centers opened in Tokyo's Omori district, the local police chief wept at the sight of it. One nineteen-year-old woman who had been a typist before her recruitment to this new patriotic duty committed suicide right away. A few months later, in January 1946, reacting not on moral grounds but to the wildfire spread of venereal disease among the troops and the women, the occupation authorities banned public prostitution, though, needless to say, prostitution continued unabated, even giving rise to a new social category in Japan, the *panpan,* as women of the night came to be called.

A certain glamour attached to them, as well as a certain shame. "The panpan arm in arm with her GI companion, or riding gaily in his jeep, constituted a piercing wound to national pride in general and masculine pride in particular," Dower said, prefiguring what would happen in other countries later. Indeed, more than fifty years later, speaking to a reporter for *The New York Times,* the famous Vietnamese singer Trinh Cong Son acknowledged that the image from the Vietnam War that most haunted him and reminded him of his country's poverty and moral degradation was "the rich American man walking down the street hand in hand with the beautiful Vietnamese woman."

But the relationships that grew out of the contact between the Americans and local women were complicated, and certainly many of them had nothing to do with prostitution. Trinh Cong Son allowed that there were genuine feelings involved, including love, mutually experienced.

What marred the more general picture, of course, was the material differential, the impossibility of disentangling, especially in the minds of the women in question, the lure and the necessity of money from the authenticity of their affections. For surely glamour attached to being the representative of the most powerful nation on earth, and a representative with PX privileges to boot, the source of otherwise unattainable liquor and cigarettes for one's family, perfume and a motorbike for oneself. And a certain glamour accrued also to the display itself, vulgar though it may have been, of nice dresses and Revlon lipstick and money of one's own to spend on what one wanted.

But we were talking here about the contrast between occupied Japan and occupied Germany. In Japan, brothels were created for the occupying forces; in Germany, they weren't. It is not that there was no prostitution in Germany at that time or isn't any now. In the immediate post-war months and years in Germany, the same economic desperation experienced by Japan pushed many young women to engage in sexual relations with soldiers of the occupying armies. There was a great deal of prostitution in Germany. Indeed, even today prostitution is legal and regulated in Germany, and in European countries where it is not legal it is common and obvious, and it thrives in particular on the demarcation lines between rich countries and poor ones. Drive over the border today from Germany to the Czech Republic or Poland, or from Romania to Bulgaria for that matter, and there they will be: the women showing their legs, beckoning to motorists looking for sex at prices far cheaper than they will find on their own side of the border. And these prostitutes, driven in many instances by the new opportunity and the economic dislocation that accompanied the downfall of the Communist regimes of Eastern Europe, are no doubt paying a portion of their take to local police—otherwise how could their blatant, undisguised, and technically illegal trade, plied within a stone's throw of the immigration post, be explained?

Prostitution in these territories, in other words, has a sort of official sanction, even if a corrupt one. Beyond that there is the vastly uglier criminal trafficking in women and children that has also been on the rise since Communism and tight social control came to an end in Eastern Europe, where gangsters have filled the vacuum, finding ways to cater to the illicit and perverted desires of men.

But what happened in post-war Asia, starting with Japan, is not that, though certainly, along with "normal" prostitution, there has been, and still is, plenty of the nasty and criminal sort, including the trafficking and sexual exploitation of children, widespread in places like the Philippines and Cambodia. This has nothing to do with Western desire meeting the Eastern sexual culture because there is nothing particularly Asian about sex with children. That takes place in every country where the forces of law, order, and civil society are too weak or too corrupt to prevent it.

Still, desperate, ruined, and poverty-stricken as it was, Germany after the war did not recruit women to provide sexual services to foreign occupying troops, and it would have been culturally unimaginable for it to have done so. The Japanese response to the U.S. occupation was built on centuries of a sexual culture that was always different from that of the West. It isn't that the Japanese saw promiscuity as permissible. If anything, the Japanese were and are more prudish and more conservative in sexual matters than Germans or any other Westerners. Fathers and mothers expected their daughters to be innocent and virginal until marriage, an expectation that explains why the humiliation of that couple with the two "daughters-san" outside Tokyo must have been very great. And yet Japan exhibited the paradox of most harem cultures, which, fed by male desire and male power, are sexually prudish on one level and unrestrained and licentious on another. The harem culture is both more realistic about male sexual desire than the Western culture of chastity and monogamy and less sentimental about it. Japan was always a place of pleasure quarters, and after its defeat in the war it was deemed that there was no choice but to extend the traditional pleasure quarter to the occupier.

INDEED, THE FIRST KNOWN ACT of sexual intimacy between a European man and a Japanese woman accompanied the very first known appearance of Europeans on Japanese soil. In 1543, two Portuguese men sailing off course on a Chinese junk arrived on the island of Tanegashima, off the coast of southern Kyushu. Impressed by the harquebuses found in the Portuguese men's luggage, the lord of the island, Tanegashima Tokitaka, ordered his chief sword smith, a man named Kiyosada, to copy them. Unable to do so, Kiyosada offered his daughter to one of the Portuguese in exchange for technical assistance. Kiyosada expected his daughter to remain with the foreigner for only a short time, but the two fell in love and got married, the daughter eventually sailing away with the foreigner, though the couple later returned to Tanegashima with a Portuguese gunsmith in tow, and Kiyosada acquired the technical knowledge that he had exchanged his daughter for in the first place.

That first arrival in Japan followed the great exploits of Portuguese maritime exploration, when figures like Vasco da Gama discovered the far side of Africa and the Malabar Coast of India. The Portuguese led the way to the commercial penetration of East Asia, setting up a trading post at Macau on the South China Sea and then sailing on to Japan. In both China and Japan, these early traders discovered what must have seemed, coming as they did from a strictly Catholic country, an amazing and thrilling opportunity. "As soon as ever these Portuguese arrive and disembark," an Italian trader named Francesco Carletti wrote following a visit to Japan in the 1590s,

> the pimps who control this traffic in women call on them in the houses where they are quartered for the time of their stay, and enquire whether they would like to purchase, or acquire in any other method they please, a girl, for the period of their sojourn, or to keep her for so many months, or for a day, or for an hour, a contract being first made with these brokers, or an agreement entered into with the girl's relations, and the money paid down. . . . And it so often happens that they [these Portuguese] will get hold of a pretty little girl of fourteen or fifteen years of age, for three or four *scudi,* or a little more or less, according to the time at which they wish to have her at their disposal, with no other responsibility beyond that of sending her back home when done with.

The foreigners had an unusual and precarious situation in Japan, with the local authorities never sure whether they wanted contact with them at all, much less sexual contact. In the early decades of the seventeenth century, the Japanese gradually implemented a policy of seclusion, banning trade with countries that practiced Christian prose-lytism, and imposing ever greater restrictions on Japanese-foreigner contact—including a prohibition on Japanese travel beyond Korea or Okinawa. Still, Portuguese, Spanish, and British merchants were allowed to settle in Kyushu, and even though the English and the Spaniards gave up the Japan trade in 1624 and 1625 respectively, a strong Christian subculture formed among tens of thousands of Japanese, their Christian identity leading the shogun to suspect their loyalty. In the 1630s, Japanese Christians, frustrated by their exclusion and believing that God would come to their aid, rebelled, and in what must have been one of the great mass murders of the seventeenth century, some thirty-seven thousand of them were slaughtered at the castle of Shimabara, near Nagasaki. Suspecting that the rebels had been incited by foreign Catholics, the shogun expelled the Portuguese, leaving the Protestant Dutch as the only European traders allowed in Japan. And although they remained, the Dutch, whose trading network extended from New Amsterdam in North America to the Moluccan archipelago in what is now Indonesia, were confined to the small island of Deshima in Nagasaki Harbor.

Meanwhile, in an act of racial nationalism, the shogun expelled mixed-blood children along with the Catholics. "[We] Japanese desire no such intermixture of races, and will not incur the danger that, in course of time, any one of such descent will rule over [us]," decreed the Great Elders, speaking on behalf of Shogun Tokugawa Iemitsu.

All of these actions against foreigners were part of the policy of *sakoku,* by which Japan as of 1641 was closed to contact with the outside world, except for the few Dutch allowed to stay on Deshima, until Perry made his naval show of force in Tokyo Bay more than two centuries later. But even during the period when foreigners were kept off all of Japan except that one small, isolated island, they could enjoy the privileges of the harem culture recognized as a man's due. Starting around the middle of the seventeenth century, the Dutch on Deshima were allowed visits by courtesans from the famous brothels of the Maruyama pleasure quarter of Nagasaki. Indeed, a sign placed on the bridge that connected the mainland to the island suggestively read: "Whores only, but no other women shall be suffer'd to go in." Occasionally, the Dutch were allowed onto the mainland to visit the

Maruyama pleasure quarter itself, though always with a Japanese escort. Imagine a delegation of Japanese traders in France being escorted by Louis XIV's police to an elegant Parisian brothel. It wouldn't have happened even if there had been Japanese traders residing in Europe at that time, which, of course, there weren't.

Whether by intention or not, in allowing the Dutch into Maruyama, the Japanese were introducing them to an erotic pageant, even a kind of erotic connoisseurship, that must have seemed wondrous to men whose frame of reference was the austere Holland of the seventeenth century. Japanese sexuality was a world apart from the sexual culture of Europe. It was a gorgeous and refined demimonde, many of whose details are known to us through Japanese literature and woodblock prints, in which the pursuit of sensual pleasure, far from being condemned as vain, deluding, and sinful, was esteemed as a form of art. And the moral—or immoral—principle on which the demimonde was based was that men were entitled to refined sexual pleasure outside the home much in the same manner as they might have felt entitled to a refined cuisine that their wives were unable to produce, and it was naturally engraved in the order of things that there should be a class of women—not their daughters, but the daughters of other men—kept and trained to provide it.

The pleasure quarter of Maruyama was itself a tightly controlled district within the larger tightly controlled world of Tokugawa Japan, presided over by the shogun, whose chief political goal, aside from remaining in power, was to prevent a recurrence of the civil war and disorder that had prevailed in Japan before the Tokugawa clan came to power. The first pleasure quarter in Japan is supposed to have been created early in the seventeenth century, when Toyotomi Hideyoshi, the most powerful of Japan's feudal lords, allowed a favored servitor to establish a brothel, known as Yanagimachi, or "Willow Town," not far from the shogun's palace. At the same time, largely through the influence of a kimono-clad troupe of female erotic dancers led by one Izumo no Okuni, a legendary figure of Japanese cultural history, Kabuki theater came into being along the banks of the Kamo River in Kyoto.

Eventually, in order to keep the temptations of the pleasure quarter distant from the capital itself, the district of brothels, teahouses, and theaters was moved farther south, to what became the famed Shimabara pleasure quarter, which was in turn a model for the Maruyama pleasure quarter of Nagasaki familiar to the Dutch. In 1661, a writer named Asai Ryoi gave the whole establishment the name by which it has been known ever since, *ukiyo,* or "floating world," the idea being that since life is transient and fleeting, it ought to be spent in refined hedonism. That the Dutch were enthusiastic participants in this floating world, which was entirely absent from their native country, is well established. Evidence includes a Dutch-Japanese phrase book from about 1770, compiled for the owner of the Ebi-ya, an inn in Kyoto where the Dutch delegation stayed on its annual pilgrimage from Nagasaki to that city, seat of the shogunate. Eight of the book's eighty short phrases have to do with hiring the services of women, as in this exchange:

> Do you like that girl?
>   Yes, I like her a great deal.
> Would you like me to make appropriate arrangements?
>   Yes, please do.
> Understood.

Dutch pleasure seeking was itself a matter of some titillation for local people, who are depicted in any number of Japanese woodblock prints of the eighteenth and nineteenth centuries flocking to get a glimpse of the strange foreigners on one of their excursions to the Maruyama brothels. A print from the 1790s by the celebrated artist Chokosai Eisho depicts a Dutchman, recognizable by his black triangular hat and curly muttonchops and beard, with his penis well inserted into the vagina of a Maruyama courtesan. The inscription has the courtesan complaining that she doesn't understand a word of what the Dutchman is saying, even as she instructs him to "push—do it harder!" An incense burner in the background has been interpreted to mean that the Dutchman had a rancid odor that needed to be covered up.

Such scenes, whether accurately depicted or not, were repeated over the next two hundred years as the Dutch maintained their Japanese trading monopoly, with various expressions of astonishment and, from

Japanese woodblock prints showing Dutchmen in the pleasure quarter of Maruyama.

Victoria and Albert Museum

time to time, disapproval amply scattered throughout the record. Japan, said the Italian trader Carletti, is "more plentifully supplied than any other with these sorts of means of gratifying the passion for sexual indulgence, just as it abounds in every other sort of vice." By every other sort of vice, Carletti seems to have had homosexuality in mind, widely practiced and generally tolerated in Japan, to the consternation of the prim and repressed Europeans.

In the mid-seventeenth century, Iemitsu banned public performances by women, whereby Kabuki was taken over mostly by teenage boys, who not only played the female roles but also dressed and lived as women offstage and earned money as homosexual prostitutes. Buddhist monks, forbidden sexual relations with women, were among their clients, as were many samurai, for whom *nanshoku,* or male sex, was the purest form of love. As early as the late sixteenth century, Alessandro Valignano, a Jesuit missionary who lived in Japan before the expulsion of the Catholics, wrote of the "great dissipation" of the Japanese "in the sin that does not bear mentioning." Not only was homosexuality not seen as a mortal sin by the Japanese, the offended Valignano complained, but "it is even something quite natural and virtuous."

THERE WERE, of course, brothels and prostitutes in Holland, but the pictorial and literary record shows nothing to match the sumptuousness and the erotic cultivation that had been part of Japanese culture for hundreds of years, certainly since the early eleventh century, when Lady Murasaki wrote the immortal *Tale of Genji,* whose underlying subject is erotic obsession. It would be easy to idealize the world of erotic refinement that emerged in the great era of peace and prosperity following the establishment of the Tokugawa shogunate in the seventeenth century. Historical descriptions of Japan convey the impression that the entire country glittered with lacquer, smelled of incense, and vibrated to the sound of the samisen.

In fact, of course, the whole edifice depended on desperate rural poverty in much the same way that the sex trade of post-war Japan depended on desperation during the American occupation in the 1940s. The women of the pleasure quarters of Shimabara or Maruyama started out as girls turned over to the brothels by their poor rural parents, who felt that they were improving their daughters' prospects, ensuring that they would eat well, wear rich clothing, and spend their days and nights amid the splendor of the city rather than in backbreaking labor in the fields. There is an eerie similarity between that situation and the circumstances today that propel young Thai women to work in massage parlors and go-go bars in Bangkok. Northeastern Thailand serves the same function today that rural Japan once did, and it serves that function for, among others, Japanese men, who, because they pay the highest prices, are said to have at their disposal the most beautiful women of the night in Bangkok today. There is, in this regard, nothing new under the sun.

And then as now, what the pleasure quarters provided, with their geishas and teahouses, lacquered chambers, silk bedclothes, hot sake, and artfully arranged flowers, was a dreamworld that paralleled the everyday world of the commerce, affairs, and hard labor of most men, as well as an escape from the tedium and responsibilities of the family. Typically, Japanese men didn't expect to find sexual fulfillment with their wives, or to provide it. They expected to find sex and pleasure outside the home, with women who, for the well-off, were highly trained specialists in the erotic arts. The pleasure quarters were the ultimate expressions of Japanese artifice, like the courtesans themselves, who, as one writer has said of the geisha (who was not a prostitute in the ordinary sense), bore the same relation to a natural woman as a bonsai tree does to a natural tree. They were extraordinary visions, made for the night, "shamanesses who could transport men into another world, a world of dreams."

Not every Dutchman, it can be assumed, was a connoisseur of sensuality, as that print by Eisho suggests. But surely the Dutch enjoyed access to Japan's luxuriant floating world, just as others from Europe and America had access to it after Perry's ships arrived in Tokyo Bay. The symbolism of Japan being forced open to trade is irresistible; its women were forced open to Western men as well. "By the mid-nineteenth century," the historian Gary Leupp has written of Europe, "sex devoid of love, commitment, and responsibility was considered more shameful than ever. Yet it was available in Japan, provided cheerfully and without judgment, as it had been from the beginnings of western contact." It is no wonder that Townsend Harris insisted on his share of the fun. After the 1854 Treaty of Kanagawa, forced on Japan by Perry, set up the first treaty ports, in Shimoda and Hakodate, Japanese entrepreneurs, in the spirit of their sixteenth-century forebears, began procuring Japanese prostitutes for foreign visitors. Already on Perry's second voyage to Tokyo Bay, Lieutenant George Henry Preble noted from the deck of the ship *Macedonian,* "The inhabitants crowded the hills, and beckoned us on shore, and by most unmistakable signs invited our intercourse with their women." By 1857, under American pressure, the Japanese government had built what were called rest houses in Shimoda, where ten to twenty women catered to hundreds of foreign men.

"There was a fair sprinkling of men," wrote Ernest Mason Satow, a British diplomat in Japan at the very end of the nineteenth century, "who, suddenly relieved from the restraints which social opinion places upon their class at home, and exposed to the temptations of Eastern life, did not conduct themselves with the strict propriety of students at a theological college." (Satow himself had two sons by his common-law Japanese wife.) By the 1860s, there were fifteen teahouses serving foreigners in Yokohama, the largest of them, called Gankiro, a place of lacquered carvings and delicate paintings, was connected to the docks of the city by a long wooden bridge. Gankiro consisted of three long halls divided into "stables," each occupied by a girl, who, if not employed, would lean forward and show her face when a customer arrived, in the hope of gaining a client.

"Anyone, married or single, who can afford the expense, is at liberty to keep a mistress without loss of respectability," wrote William Willis, a British physician who lived in Japan from 1862 to 1877. In *Madama Butterfly,* it is a Japanese broker who is shown providing the foreigner with both his house and his mistress—and those two services were commonly provided by a single entrepreneur in late-nineteenth-century Yokohama.

In other words, the sad story of Okichi—who is said to have run a brothel herself and died of syphilis after her unhappy encounter with Harris—was hardly unique. Thousands of young Japanese women in dozens of Japanese brothels serviced foreign visitors, who often became bored with them and dismissed them after a time. But when the Japanese lost the war in the Pacific in 1945, the stage had already been set for the occupying troops to enjoy what foreign men had been enjoying in Japan for centuries, if on a scale and a level of commercialism unknown before.

. . .

THEN, TWENTY OR SO YEARS LATER, the scene shifted to Indochina, where the sexual possibilities and the openness of it all were perhaps even greater. In Vietnam, as in Japan, the Americans followed precedents that had been established centuries before. During the era of French colonialism and in the early days of Vietnamese independence, the corrupt and venal emperor Bao Dai gave a criminal secret society known as Binh Xuyen, which controlled Vietnam's police, a monopoly on both gambling and prostitution, with, needless to say, a rake-off going to the emperor. Prostitution was deeply entrenched during the era of French colonialism. And so when the Americans arrived in large numbers, they perpetuated the established pattern, thereby unwittingly lending credence to the image of them as a new generation of Western colonialists.

In Vietnam, the perversely glamorous *panpan* of Japan yielded to the bar girl of Saigon, whose glamour came from the same source—the American PX, which furnished the whole Vietnamese black market with items like underarm deodorant and Revlon lipstick. In Japan, the authorities reluctantly found it necessary to grant imperial privileges to masses of Americans. In Vietnam, more corrupt and uncontrolled than Japan, it was the system of criminal gangs and government protection that offered up sex for sale to the foreigners. Add to that the severe dislocation caused by the war itself, the tens of thousands of rural families uprooted from their villages with no source of income other than that provided by the daughters who became prostitutes. Throw in the immense material lure represented by more than half a million American men with money to burn, and all the ingredients were present for a wartime erotic circus of historic proportions.

The Butterfly Complex

"I COULD HAVE WRITTEN Puccini's libretto," Pascal "Ron" Politano told me, referring to *Madama Butterfly*, and he could have by virtue of literary aptitude and life experience. Politano, a former Green Beret who saw duty in Vietnam, also served in all of the Asian arenas where U.S. troops were sent after World War II. Now he lives in retirement in a rustic house in upstate New York. His back window looks out on verdant hills sweeping up to the Adirondacks. He lives among books and bottles of good wine, and he writes poems, stories, and novels, most of which he has published privately. He has had an adventurous life and a stormy personal one that included a suicidal wife with severe emotional problems who left four children in his care even as he was based in Japan, Korea, Okinawa, Thailand, and Vietnam, as well as various locations in Europe.

Once, in Vietnam, Politano intercepted an army truck loaded incongruously with mountain (cold-weather) sleeping bags, useless and destined for incineration. By amazing coincidence, he had earlier that day visited a Catholic orphanage, where the kids were sleeping on bamboo slats, sharing the few blankets in the good sisters' possession, and so the fortuitous discovery of a mountain of sleeping bags seemed like an act of God.

"We backed that deuce and a half up, lowered the tailgate, and started unloading," Politano said. " 'Do you know what these are?' I said to the mother superior. She said, 'I don't know, but I think we can use them.'

"In a place like Vietnam, with all those staff officers in their air-conditioned offices with their TV sets and ice buckets—and these kids sleeping on slats," Politano said. "I have to say, that made me feel pretty good. Those bags provided bedding for more than two hundred children."

Politano, like a lot of men in post–World War II Asia, also dallied with the girls, and not only in Vietnam but also in Thailand and before that in Korea and before that in Japan. In Vietnam, he heard the story of a lieutenant who was fragged (intentionally killed by fellow soldiers) by his sergeant because the lieutenant had been sleeping with the sergeant's Vietnamese girlfriend. He knew that in Seoul, which was still recovering from the ravages of the Korean War when he was there, the place to find girls was at what was called the water point, a central location where the troops drew potable water. In Japan, where he worked for military intelligence in 1958, he had an apartment in Shibuya-ku, one of Tokyo's central neighborhoods, and he spent a lot of time in Shinjuku, for years the city's main entertainment district.

"Saturday seemed to be the day for the big wheels," Politano said. "You'd see a big black limousine with four stars, and you'd know that General Lemnitzer was in the bathhouse. It was almost a ritual. In Shinjuku on Saturday, Lemnitzer and the subheads would be there with the Japanese girls bowing and scraping."

But Ron Politano's most poignant memory is his *Madama Butterfly* incident in Japan, poignant in part because it attaches him both to a long history, with roots in the real-world Nagasaki of the nineteenth century, and to a famous story, familiar to several generations of operagoers. Many critics have noted the implausibility of the opera's main theme—namely, that a fifteen-year-old Japanese girl would find her American husband so desirable that she would continue to love him even when he betrays her and would then destroy herself out of a sense of her lost honor. The more radical critics have dismissed Puccini's libretto as a Western male-power fantasy, the Japanese woman's submission and compliance to the point of self-sacrifice as a kind of feminine ideal. Indeed, you don't have to be a radical feminist to note that the object of Cio-Cio-San's true love is an unworthy Westerner rather than Prince Yamadori, her Japanese suitor, and that detail illustrates the fantasy, going back to Ludovico de Varthema, by which the superior Western man serves as the romantic *beau idéal* of the Oriental woman.

For decades, until modern feminist sensibility caught up with him,

Puccini got away with what many have seen as an assault on credibility. The biggest moment in this sense came in 1988, with the appearance of the Broadway play (and later movie) *M Butterfly* by David Henry Hwang, in which *Madama Butterfly* is subjected to witty and ruthless examination. Hwang's key line comes in the first act, when a French diplomat who has just seen a performance of the opera in Beijing tells the Chinese singer who performed the role of Cio-Cio-San how "beautiful" he felt the story was.

"That's because you're a Westerner," the singer sourly retorts, and she continues with an enlightening hypothetical: Imagine a "blond homecoming queen" cutting her throat because of her unrequited love for a "short Japanese businessman who treats her shabbily," she says. "I believe that you would consider this girl to be a deranged idiot, but because . . . [Cio-Cio-San] is an Oriental who kills herself for a Westerner, ah, you find it 'beautiful.'"

Hwang's play, which received glowing reviews and occasioned much academic discussion, was inspired not only by Puccini's opera but also by a weird episode of sexual concealment and deceit that, in Hwang's mind, represented an inversion of the *Madama Butterfly* story. A French diplomat in Beijing, given the name Gallimard by Hwang, did indeed fall in love with a Chinese opera singer, called Song Liling in Hwang's play. Gallimard's real-life counterpart, a minor French functionary named Bernard Boursicot—believed that his paramour was a woman when, in fact, she was a cross-dressing man who sang female roles in Chinese opera (where all roles until recently had been performed by men). In order to continue seeing her, Boursicot passed French diplomatic secrets to the Chinese authorities, and for that he was convicted of treason and sent to prison in France. *M Butterfly* follows the same plot, and Gallimard is the narrator of the play, telling its sad story while sitting in prison. The allegory that Hwang cleverly fashions out of the two stories has to do with the long-held Western dream of a feminine Asia submissive and compliant to its wishes, a dream that turns into a nightmare with Gallimard's discovery that the Asian girl is actually a man. Hwang, taking poetic license, makes Gallimard an architect of Western policy in Vietnam, suggesting that the racism and sexism inherent in the Western fantasy of Asian women extended to entire Asian countries, which were expected to be as submissive to

Western demands as their women were to Western men, though in fact Boursicot actually played no role in formulating any policy whatever.

M Butterfly's inversion of Puccini's opera to expose it as a colonialist male fantasy is brilliantly entertaining and thought provoking. Moreover, who can deny the truth of that observation by Song Liling that if a Western woman did for an Asian man what Cio-Cio-San did for her American lover, Western audiences would howl in derision. The experience of the West in Asia has indeed made it seem not just plausible but also deeply moving that Cio-Cio-San would do what no semi-sane Western woman ever would.

But is that all there is to it? In its assumption that the *Madama Butterfly* story is sheer racist and sexist fantasy, *M Butterfly* imposes a late-twentieth-century politically liberal judgment on a late-nineteenth-century view of the East and West, a view that was uninformed by Harvard-Berkeley post-1960s convictions about sexual equality. In this sense, Hwang's play enacts the Orientalist fallacy, by which no research into the real, historical world is required. But the fact is that, just as the strange story of Boursicot and his Chinese lover was true, so are the stories that Western men actually lived in Asia. Ron Politano's experience in Japan was real. And so, it turns out, was the story that inspired Puccini's opera. It was based on an event of love, abandonment, and attempted suicide in Nagasaki, the Japanese port that was a great romantic and sexual mixing ground for European men and Japanese women in the late nineteenth century.

Indeed, in the case of *Madama Butterfly,* the real and the made-up are so intertwined that it's hard to disentangle them. But to dismiss the opera as pure, ungrounded, and ridiculous fantasy is to neglect any consideration of the idea that the Asian sexual culture was genuinely different from that of the West. It is, similarly, to dismiss the historical details of the fictional Cio-Cio-San's fateful meeting with her American husband, among them the psychological implications of Western technological prowess, which had at the time forced Japan to submit to foreign demands, including the demand that its women serve the sexual needs of visiting Western men. The assumption of the Orientalist critique is that a fifteen-year-old Japanese girl in Nagasaki in the nineteenth century would behave with a Western-style late-twentieth-century feminist-inspired self-interested rationality, when, in truth, fifteen-year-olds don't live up to much of a standard of rational self-interest at any time or in any place.

Were Japanese girls and women different from Western girls and women one hundred or more years ago? The evidence is that, under the powerful sway of Japanese Confucian values, they were, or certainly knowledgeable observers of the time thought they were. Lafcadio Hearn, the most celebrated Western commentator on Japan in the nineteenth century and a man thoroughly enamored of Japanese women, talked about "the childish confiding, sweet Japanese girl" as compared with "the calculating, penetrating Circe of our more artificial society." The Japanese girl portrayed by Western culture may even be a believable product of a culture whose chief values were obedience to authority, devotion to duty, and reverence for hierarchy, particularly the Confucian hierarchy, in which the godlike emperor stands at the apex of the nation and the revered father and husband at the apex of the family. Sir Edwin Arnold, an English journalist and poet whose wife was Japanese, marveled at the "gracious sweetness and bright serenity" of Japanese women, who, he wrote, were "the most graceful for deference and attention, and the most attached and faithful in return for affection." Alice Mabel Bacon of New Haven, who visited Japan in the late nineteenth century and founded an English-language college for women there, also noted the "unselfish devotion" of Japanese women, who, she said, internalized the values of duty and sacrifice early in life.

To be sure, Japanese audiences themselves have seldom shown much enthusiasm for *Madama Butterfly*, and Cio-Cio-San is not deemed a persuasive tragic heroine in Japan. The problem for the Japanese is that the real Cio-Cio-San would have to have been unimaginably naïve not to have known that in late-nineteenth-century Nagasaki, most marriages between Japanese pleasure girls and Western men were paid for by the men, were temporary, and were intended to be so from the start. Moreover, she would have known that in patriarchal Japan, women had few rights and that if she had a child, the child would belong to its father. In hoping for something different— particularly for the sake of a callow rascal like Pinkerton—the fictional Cio-Cio-San appears less a tragic heroine than a very foolish girl.

In other words, the view of current-day Japanese and that of David

Henry Hwang are very similar. But there are other reasons why Japanese audiences wouldn't be very fond of *Madama Butterfly.* The opera, after all, depicts a Japan that was truly at the mercy of militarily superior Western countries, and it was a Japan that, as a consequence of its weakness, did make its women easily available to Western men—and neither of these depictions is likely to go over well with contemporary audiences in Tokyo or, for that matter, Nagasaki. The question isn't whether Cio-Cio-San was foolish; it is self-evident that she was. The question is whether the story embodies something accurate about the state of personal and national relations in the last quarter of the nineteenth century, and the answer is that it did. Of course *Madama Butterfly* is an operatic melodrama, not a historical document. And yet it does a pretty good job of exposing both the casual attitudes of Western men toward their temporary Japanese spouses and the deeply patriarchal nature of Japanese society at the time, when women were indeed expected to be submissive and compliant to the point of self-sacrifice. What *Madama Butterfly* illustrates is not a male-power fantasy but, more simply, male power.

The opera in this sense might well illustrate the foolishness of a love-struck fifteen-year-old, but it also portrays the cavalier attitude of Pinkerton, his shallowness and his deceitfulness. As the opera opens, Pinkerton, waiting in his leased house for his betrothed to arrive, unabashedly admits that for him, Cio-Cio-San is just someone to be used for his pleasure. The American consul, Sharpless, is there to witness the wedding, and he warns Pinkerton that it would be a grave moral crime to harm a girl as delicate and innocent as Cio-Cio-San, but to Pinkerton the whole thing is a game. The Yankee travels the world for business and pleasure, he tells Sharpless. "Life is not worth living if he can't win the best and fairest of each country, the heart of each fair maid." As for Cio-Cio-San, he says, she is ravishing, a "pretty little plaything." Once Cio-Cio-San has arrived and the marriage has taken place, she indicates to Pinkerton that she is not playing games. She has abandoned her family and her religion, she tells him, and has adopted his as her own.

A terrible irony forms the crux of the tragedy. Cio-Cio-San has adopted the monogamous ways of Christendom, Pinkerton's religion, even as Pinkerton, liberated by Asia from the trammels of Western sexual morality, has gleefully relinquished them. Like the British nabobs of a century earlier, Pinkerton goes native, sexually speaking, but he does so in selective fashion, enjoying the pleasures that accrue to a Japanese gentleman but assuming none of the responsibility. The paradox is that in the harem culture, monogamy is repudiated but duty is not. Mistresses may be acquired, but the honorable man does not abandon his wife. The woman may be a plaything, but she is not to be harmed. "Nobody is, indeed, ever brutal to a woman in Japan, as in Europe," Edwin Arnold wrote. "She has nowhere and never to fear cruelty, violence, or even harsh words. But her status is traditionally inferior." This is what accounts for one of the most remarkable aspects of Japanese society, which is wives' loyalty and devotion to husbands who, as one writer has put it, "saw philandering as their God-given right." In the late nineteenth century, the Japanese husband experienced no social censure for his incorrigible sexual straying but was looked down on if he neglected or insulted his wife.

Cio-Cio-San, being Japanese, ought perhaps to understand the rules of the game—namely, that the temporary wives of foreigners in Nagasaki were at best genteel courtesans whose duty was to serve the demands of male imperial entitlement. But she is to be forgiven nonetheless for thinking that in marrying Pinkerton, she has become an American. She's had, after all, to forsake her family and her religion, and this act has given her both a new identity and an escape from the traditional Japanese rules. This idea is explicit in Puccini's libretto. At one point she tells the importuning Prince Yamadori that he has many wives, so, she asks, why would she want to be yet another of them? (To which Yamadori replies that he'll give up all the others.) Cio-Cio-San believes that Pinkerton has freed her from the second-class status accorded women in a culture of multiple sexual partners. When Sharpless, in trying to persuade her to accept Yamadori, tells her that Pinkerton's long absence legally constitutes a divorce, Cio-Cio-San's reply is that that may be the case in Japan, "but not in my country, America." Her love has sadly blinded her to the plain facts of her situation, most important of which is that she has not become an American and has gained no protection from the monogamous assurances of Christendom. And so in the end, when she sees Pinkerton's American wife standing outside her house waiting to take Pinkerton's child away, Cio-

Cio-San understands that she has gotten the worst of both worlds: Pinkerton's temporary and opportunistic adoption of Japanese polygamy enabled him to treat her as a plaything even as the requirement of monogamy in connection with his "real" American wife meant that there was no more room in his life for Cio-Cio-San, and having renounced her Japaneseness, she has no place in Japan either. Her only recourse is to bring her life to an end, which she does in a resigned return to Japanese custom—by piercing her throat with the very sword that her father, who was also disgraced, had used to kill himself many years before. In the standard view, *Madama Butterfly* is about the self-sacrificing devotion of an Eastern woman for a Western man, and it is. But the opera is also a dark image of the opportunistic and duplicitous West reflected in the mirror of the betrayed Cio-Cio-San's eyes.

AT THE TIME Puccini wrote *Madama Butterfly*, the spectacle of a Japanese woman dying for the sake of the conviction that death is preferable to a dishonorable life was well-known in Europe. Not long after Perry's voyages suddenly made Japan a real place for Americans and Europeans, a tremendous vogue for what writers call Japonisme (the French spelling is generally used for this concept) swept the West. Monet, Degas, Manet, and other artists fell in love with Japanese woodblock prints, which depict the "floating world" of pleasure and frivolity that would soon come to be associated with Japan. In actual fact, Japan, far from being the quaint, dollhouselike country of the Western imagination, was in the course of becoming a great military and commercial power. In 1905, with its stunningly decisive victory over Russia in the Russo-Japanese War (which gave Japan control over Korea and the Liaodong Peninsula in Chinese Manchuria), Japan became the first Asian country to defeat a European country in battle. The sword was replacing the chrysanthemum as the West's chief image of Japan.

But until then, it was the "flowery beauty" of Japan that fascinated and intrigued Westerners. In 1862 in Paris and in 1875 in London, galleries specializing in Japanese prints and objets d'art opened their doors and were patronized by a sort of Who's Who of writers and artists. For the Universal Exhibition in Paris in 1867, the Japanese government put on display one hundred *ukiyo* prints, which were later sold to the public. The image of Japan that was presented could be entirely satirical, zany, and ridiculous, as it was in Gilbert and Sullivan's *Mikado*, which opened in 1885 in London and stayed open for 672 performances, presenting a charmingly outlandish and exotic Japan—the Lord High Executioner and the Lord High Everything Else, and so on. But the fascination with Japan was also respectful and even gripping. In Paris, the art critic and painter Zacharie Astruc, forgotten now but well-known in his time (a great portrait of him by Manet hangs in the Kunsthalle in Bremen, Germany), formed a secret society whose members met to talk about Japanese art while wearing kimonos, drinking sake, and eating with chopsticks.

And then there was the sensational Sadayakko Kawakami, a real Japanese geisha who performed to great acclaim in the United States, England, France, and Italy between 1900 and 1902 and was widely known as the Japanese Sarah Bernhardt. Sadayakko was married to an entrepreneurial and adventurous Kabuki actor, Otojiro Kawakami, and the two of them, having run into hard times at home, went to America (where she was on the cover of *Harper's Bazaar*) and then to Europe to make their fortune.

Even before Sadayakko's arrival on the European scene at the very beginning of the new century, the Japanese geisha was well-known in Europe, and so was onstage suicide as an act to which geishas were prone—to preserve their honor or put an end to some inconsolable grief. This was due to a series of popular, mostly English melodramas set in Japan with titles like *The Geisha* and *The Little Japanese Girl*. Sadayakko performed in real Kabuki-inspired dramas with her husband, often as the dying geisha onstage—which means, of course, that the Japanese girl dying onstage is not a Western racist invention. In 1902, Puccini, who had already embarked on the composition of *Madama Butterfly*, saw Sadayakko do one of her signature performances in *The Geisha and the Knight* in Milan. It's the story of a geisha who rejects one suitor in favor of her true love but then commits hara-kiri when she learns that the true love, not so true after all, is betrothed to another woman. One critic wrote that the action of the play had "that type of insane and uncontrollable intoxication characteristic of primitive peoples," though, in fact, there was nothing primitive about either Japan or Sadayakko. In any case, Puccini was entranced by her. The two met and talked. Sadayakko, her biographer has written, "provided him with a model for a flesh-and-blood Japanese woman to give reality to his imagined Madame Butterfly."

The story of the opera came from several sources and real events stretching through much of the nineteenth century. Early in the century, many Europeans knew of the experience of a German doctor and Japanologist named Phillip Franz von Siebold, who had entered into a temporary marriage with a pleasure girl of the Maruyama district named Kusumoto Taki, who bore him a daughter. Siebold left Japan after seven years, acquired a "real" wife in Germany, and then, twenty-nine years later, returned to Japan, where he met both his Japanese wife and his daughter, now thirty-two years old and, after medical studies arranged for her by her father, became the first female physician in Japan. Siebold's story contains some of the elements of *Madama Butterfly*—the temporary wife, the child, the "real" marriage in Europe, the return to Japan, and the reunion with the temporary Japanese wife—though not its searingly tragic aspect. In contrast to the Pinkerton of Puccini's script, Siebold was not absolutely cavalier in his treatment of his Japanese wife.

Siebold's story was followed a couple of decades later by that of Louis-Marie-Julien Viaud, known by the pen name Pierre Loti, who, as a French naval officer, lived in Nagasaki in 1885 and "temporarily" married a seventeen-year-old Japanese girl named Kane. A photograph survives showing Loti and a friend standing, with Kane, in a kimono, seated in front of them.

Loti wrote a novel, *Madame Chrysanthème*, based on a diary that he kept of his time in Nagasaki. The novel's narrator relates how, as he arrived in Nagasaki, he told a friend about his determination to marry "a little yellow-skinned woman with black hair and cat's eyes," and to live with her in "a little paper house." He then realizes his fantasy by going to a broker, who arranges both his bride and the rental of a house overlooking Nagasaki Harbor. For a fee of one hundred yen a month, he has the live-in company of a girl called Kiku. *Madame Chrysanthème* enjoyed a huge success in Europe, going into twenty-five editions after its initial publication in 1887.

Loti's book, more than Siebold's story, illustrates the lighthearted attitudes of Western men toward their temporary Japanese spouses, a theme that is even more conspicuous in what was Puccini's most immediate inspiration. This was a short story titled "Madame Butterfly" by an American lawyer and writer from Philadelphia, John Luther Long. It was Long who created the characters of Cio-Cio-San and Pinkerton—though they seem to have been modeled closely on Loti and Kiku—and outlined the story later used by Puccini's librettists.

The evidence is powerful that Long's story was based on a real event, told to him by his sister Sarah Jane—the wife of a Methodist missionary who lived with her husband in Nagasaki for five years in the 1890s—while visiting him in Philadelphia in 1897. One close student of the origins of *Madama Butterfly* and its real-life roots has persuasively argued that Sarah Jane told Long the story of three brothers from Scotland named Glover who lived in the foreign concession of Nagasaki. One of the brothers, though which one is not certain, had a relationship with a Japanese woman named Kaga Maki, who almost certainly worked in Nagasaki's Maruyama pleasure quarter. Kaga Maki bore Glover's child in 1870, and when Glover married another woman, also Japanese, Kaga Maki was forced to turn the child over to the new bride (though whether Kaga Maki, who lived until 1906, attempted suicide is not certain).

In fact, given the time that has elapsed, it is impossible to prove that it was one of the brothers Glover who was Cio-Cio-San's unfaithful husband. Another researcher looking into the origins of *Madama Butterfly*, Arthur Groos, believes that the real Pinkerton was an American naval ensign named William B. Franklin. But there is no doubt that Puccini's story is based on something that Long's sister Sarah Jane knew about, either through her own experience or through the gossip mill in late-nineteenth-century Nagasaki. There is also no doubt that it was common for foreign men to engage in temporary marriages with Nagasaki's women of the pleasure quarter and that not a small number of children were produced in those marriages. *Madama Butterfly* may contain elements of fancy, including, perhaps, male-power fantasy, but for the most part it seems a plausible tale, something that could actually have happened.

AND THAT BRINGS US BACK to Pascal Politano, who during the time that he lived in Tokyo in 1958 met a Japanese woman at Suehiro, a famous downtown restaurant.

"A Japanese friend introduced us," he said. "She wasn't a streetwalker. She came from a good family."

They kept company and enjoyed intimate relations for a brief time, and then Politano had to return to the United States. Unlike Pinkerton, he made no promises about returning to Japan, but he did give his girlfriend the address of an aunt of his in New Jersey, whom he knew he would be visiting on his trip back home.

"When I returned," he said, "my aunt said, 'You know, there's a letter for you.' I walked around for a long time without opening it because I was afraid of what might be in it. Asian women are not my cup of tea somehow. They have some fine qualities. I treated [my Japanese girlfriend] like a lady. I didn't treat her any differently than I treated any lady; except for the fact that I abandoned her, I treated her the same as my wife. I opened the door for her, stuff like that. This girl had tremendous self-respect, a serene dignity. She had integrity, Goddamn it, I find myself wishing that I had been more attracted. I would have been proud to have her on my arm in any environment."

Politano hesitated for a second as he told his story in his rural cabin, and his eyes misted slightly. He is both a literary man and a moral one, and he understands the resonance of his story, its primordial quality and its sadness.

"She only hinted at the child," he said. "That's the kind of woman she was. Somebody else would have written, 'Goddamn you, I'm having a child.' But she said, 'I honor you.' "

" 'I honor you,' " Politano repeated. "I destroyed the letter. I just couldn't keep it."

CHAPTER ELEVEN

"I Souvenir. You Boom-Boom."

T HE FIRST MARINES officially assigned to combat duty in
Vietnam waded onto the beach in Danang on March 8, 1965,
thereby beginning the process by which the war turned from a
mostly Vietnamese matter into an almost entirely American one. Until
units of the Ninth Marine Expeditionary Brigade appeared on that
muggy afternoon, the U.S. military advisers, by then twenty-three
thousand of them, had theoretically only advised the South Vietnamese military as it strove to deal with a growing North Vietnam–
supported Communist insurgency. But to the teeth-gnashing
frustration of the Americans, the South Vietnamese had been fighting
badly, often refusing to fight altogether, and by the year of that first
marine landing in Danang, eighty thousand Vietcong regulars controlled some 40 percent of South Vietnam.

Later studies of the war have shown that the South Vietnamese
leadership, under the American-installed president Ngo Dinh Diem,
hadn't wanted to risk casualties by attacking the Vietcong insurgents, who were skilled and aggressive. Instead, Diem's government
wanted to use its loyal forces to quell other opponents of this capricious
dictatorship—Buddhists demonstrating against their tyrannical ways,
for example—and to deter would-be plotters of coups among rival
South Vietnamese cliques. Diem and his various secretive, duplicitous,
and dictatorial relatives figured in any case that the Americans would
eventually get directly into the fight against the Vietcong and take care
of the Communist insurgency for them. In the early years of the war,
until 1965, as the number of U.S. advisers increased, Americans did fire
their guns at Vietcong forces—and in February 1965 fighter jets based

on offshore carriers had bombed Vietcong positions. When the Ninth Marines arrived in Danang and the Americans embarked on an open, direct, and ever-escalating war, Diem and his supporters had already been overthrown by exactly the sort of coup they had feared; still, in a way, they had posthumously gotten their wish.

The move did not go unnoticed by the enemy, of course, whose propaganda machinery quickly leaped into action to brandish reports of the havoc and suffering that, the insurgents said, American combat troops were causing. There were land appropriations, house evictions, and the theft of food from ordinary people, the Vietcong's Liberation Radio informed its listeners. The American troops were "exterminating our compatriots in a very cruel way." And along with the indiscriminate bombings and the killing of civilians that were laid at the feet of the United States, the propaganda soon began stressing another element in the picture. As a clandestine broadcast in November 1965, monitored by American intelligence, put it, "The depraved, obscene U.S. cowboy culture has spread widely, poisoning the minds of our youths. Prostitution has become a humiliating scourge. Cases of vagrancy and rape have taken place in Saigon daily. The U.S. aggressors have seriously upset our good customs and have trampled on our national traditional morality and on our human dignity."

It was a theme that the North Vietnamese would harp on continuously during the war and afterward, with the Communists' triumph in 1975, as well. "It was the U.S. puppet clique's joint policy of promoting prostitution that forced numerous innocent and chaste women to become prostitutes," Radio Hanoi said in July 1975. "Prostitution became the Saigon puppet cliques' open business from which it made huge profits every year."

The toll was enormous, Hanoi claimed: half a million mixed-blood children, the offspring of American fathers and Vietnamese prostitute mothers, some 3 million cases of syphilis in South Vietnam, 130,000 drug addicts, and associated problems of "robbery, theft, blackmailing and other evils left behind by the U.S. puppet clique."

Very likely that figure of 3 million syphilitics in a total population of 50 million in 1975 is exaggerated (the disease that seems to have rampaged through the American ranks, in any case, was gonorrhea, not syphilis). Moreover, the argument here is not that Vietnamese propaganda had a serious effect on South Vietnamese public opinion. Indeed, there are no clear signs that the alleged depravity of the Americans and their "puppets," as Hanoi put it, particularly bothered a substantial part of the local population.

Still, the propaganda machinery was certainly right on its main point: those hundreds of thousands of American troops and other Americans did produce an explosion of prostitution in South Vietnam. And that suggests in turn the way in which the Vietnam War was not just a tragic misadventure but also a weird misadventure. It was weird in the way innocence and corruption were inherent in the relationship between half a million Americans, most of them young and inexperienced, and the Vietnamese, whose ancient culture the Americans experienced mostly through their interactions with bar girls, mistresses, and the purveyors of sex. If the war was weird in the contrast it presented between a sort of heedless American do-goodism and the shadowy, corrupt, and ruthless world of Vietnamese politics, that weirdness presented itself to the ordinary GI as an intermingling of mortal danger and erotic pleasure.

For the American troops who were in noncombat roles—the clerks, the supply officers, the members of medical teams and intelligence groups, the technicians, motor pool drivers, the truck and helicopter repairmen—as well as the thousands of civilian contractors who built the barracks, the bases, and the airfields, the mortal-danger half of that equation was diminished and the erotic-pleasure half was more accessible and of a higher quality than each half was for the combat troops. "American men in South Vietnam became sexually privileged males," wrote Neil Sheehan, who was a young reporter there in the early 1960s. "Claiming that a mistress was a housekeeper . . . or bringing a woman to one's quarters in the evening, or carrying on after hours with the Vietnamese secretaries from the office (the women had no choice but to submit it they wished to retain their jobs), was considered perfectly normal." But even for the men who patrolled in Vietnam's mountains, jungles, and paddy fields, the sexual possibilities were everywhere. As the authors of one book highly critical of U.S. policy put this phenomenon, service in Vietnam might have cost many American mothers sleepless nights of worry, but for the young soldiers who went there, a hitch in the army was "a chance for protracted debauchery."

"There's a lot of plain and fancy screwing going on around here, but I suppose it's all in the interest of the war effort," the U.S. ambassador in Saigon, Ellsworth Bunker, said at one point in the conflict, thereby adding his confirmation to the Communists' propaganda claim. David Lamb, a veteran American journalist at the *Los Angeles Times* who was in Vietnam from 1968 to 1970, said in an interview: "Half the American servicemen of that young age must have lost their virginity in Vietnam."

Sex and combat, like rape and pillage, have always accompanied each other in war—or, as *Time* magazine put it in 1966 in an article aimed at downplaying the importance of sex in Vietnam, "Strumpets trailed the trumpets of Joshua at Jericho." That's probably true, and yet it was the sheer scale of sexual opportunity and the frequency with which it was exploited—and the fact that it came in the twentieth century A.D., not the twelfth century B.C.—that made the Vietnam War different. Never before had wartime sex been so much a part of the scene. It was there in Saigon, it was there in the field, even in dangerous combat zones, where the girls on motorbikes beckoned to GIs from just beyond the perimeter, and it was there in the several Asian destinations—Thailand, Taiwan, the Philippines—where troops were sent for "rest and recreation" ("gin and sin," as the GIs themselves called it). Of course, not every soldier, diplomat, and journalist indulged; none of them went to Vietnam for the purpose of engaging in "debauchery," but for an extremely large number of Americans who served in Indochina (including Laos), sex was a standard part of life, like eating in the mess hall or drinking a few beers in the NCO club.

The rate of venereal disease provides proof of this assertion. In no other U.S. conflict did VD reach anywhere near the levels recorded in Vietnam. According to army statistics, in World War II there were 82 cases of venereal disease per year for every 1,000 men. In Korea, the rate went up to 146. In Vietnam, it was 325 cases per 1,000 men. It's worth dwelling on that number: it means that in any given year, one third of the American forces who served in Vietnam contracted a sexually transmitted disease. And if one third of the military personnel got the clap or something else, the percentage of American soldiers visiting prostitutes must have been higher, since, obviously, many men who saw prostitutes and actually obeyed the widespread injunction to use condoms, or who were lucky enough to have relations with uninfected prostitutes, did not come down with any infection.

According to the Department of Defense, 2,719,908 American soldiers served in Vietnam, which means that some 900,000 of them contracted a sexually transmitted disease at one time or another during the war. A lot of plain and fancy screwing is right, a phenomenon that was inscribed in GI jargon. American soldiers talked about their "pussy cutoff date," or PCOD, meaning the last day on which a soldier whose tour of duty was coming to an end could have sex with a local girl (or, in the common parlance, an LBFM, a little brown fucking machine) and still have time to be treated for VD before his return home. And, for those willing to live dangerously, there was the more risky APCOD—absolute pussy cutoff date.

"Because you were on your way home and didn't want to catch anything you couldn't get rid of," explained Frank Maguire, who served three tours of duty in Vietnam, mostly as an adviser to the Army of the Republic of Vietnam (ARVN), the South Vietnamese army. But not everybody met the PCOD, Maguire, who was interviewed at his home in Connecticut, added: "One of the marines who was on our team in 1965 was a good soldier, an absolute straight arrow. I don't know if he got it on R and R or if they took him to Saigon because he needed to relax and he had a girl, but he got himself a case of gonorrhea that was almost incurable. And he was supposed to be going to Honolulu to meet his wife. I think his CO [commanding officer] wrote a message saying that his presence was required here."

IN INDOCHINA MORE THAN ANY OTHER PLACE in the East where thousands of U.S. and other soldiers were stationed between the end of World War II and the end of the Vietnam War, casual, or not so casual, relations with local women were an element of a larger culture, a louche exotic, and intensified version of what became the sex, drugs, and rock and roll culture back home, which, paradoxically, accompanied the anti-war movement. So many soldiers in Vietnam were nineteen or twenty years old. Sex was cheap and easy. Drugs were everywhere. There was an attitude of moral distance from official policy, a skepticism about the supposed purpose of this risky, life-threatening gesture that intensified among the troops as the years of costly and indeterminate conflict passed by and that was intimately related to the moral dissolution represented by the sex and the drugs. You carried a rifle and, if you were in combat, you used it to kill the enemy, and you could be killed; or you jumped from a helicopter into a jungle clearing, taking deadly fire from guerrillas hidden in the nearby tree line, and then you were evacuated to base camp, just outside of which you could go for a little boom-boom, as the bar girls put it, some weed, maybe even a visit to a full-fledged, traditional Asian opium den. It was as detached as life can get from the strictures and prohibitions of home without leading to arrest.

"Asia was very romantic, and Indochina was the most romantic place in Asia," said Richard C. Holbrooke, who served in Vietnam as a young foreign service officer from 1963 to 1965, before going on to a brilliant and distinguished career in diplomacy and finance. "The place was absolute heaven. It was a world of war, drama, politics, and sex. What could be better?"

Holbrooke, speaking in an interview was, of course, being partly tongue in cheek about Vietnam, but only partly. The exotic adventure that was Vietnam for many American men, the way of life that became possible during the war, Vietnam's status as a scene of youthful wild times—all of those elements retained a hold on the minds of many veterans.

One aspect of recreational sex and romance in Vietnam was that it took place throughout the ranks. The grunts got theirs in the field or found girls in the bars on Tu Do Street or got fellated at one of the many massage parlor steam baths that catered to foreign soldiers, which they called blow-bath steam-job places. For a time, the Diem government had tried to impose a regime of sexual puritanism on Vietnam, going so far as to ban social dancing, though it didn't seem to have had much effect on relations between soldiers and bar girls. Still, out of deference to Diem's sensibilities, the commanding U.S. general, Paul D. Harkins, forbade soldiers to kiss their Vietnamese girlfriends good-bye at the airport.

But there were different social levels. The grunts were mostly limited to the Tu Do Street bar girls. Officers, diplomats, journalists, and civilian contractors often found steady girlfriends from good families,

young women of the sort who wouldn't have been caught dead anywhere near Tu Do, though the higher-ranking, more upper-class American men in Vietnam went to the bars and massage parlors also. A lot of
the men in this latter category, men for whom Vietnam was a stage in a
promising career in diplomacy or business, lived in colonial-style villas
that might once have belonged to a French planter or a senior adminis-
trator, with a car, a driver, servants, and a local girlfriend to keep them
company.

It wasn't just the girls that made Vietnam special, important as they
were as a sort of lifestyle accessory; it was the whole somewhat decadent
and even luxuriant atmosphere, especially in the first few years, when
Saigon was a pretty safe place. You could have your morning café au lait
with croissants as good as you'd get in Paris while poring over your
Saigon Post in the garden of the Hotel Continental and watching pea-
cocks wandering among the tables. In the afternoon, you might play
tennis at the Cercle Sportif, another leftover from the days of the
French. And then you could wind up the day collecting gossip and
drinking French wine at La Cigale in the Cholon district or perhaps at
the Tu Do Day and Night Club, which advertised "captivating starlets"
in the very *Saigon Post* you'd read in the morning.

The story is told that when David Halberstam, the famed *New York
Times* reporter, first arrived in Saigon, in 1962, when the war was still
young and the total U.S. troop commitment was about ten thousand
or so advisers to the ARVN, one of the first things he noted was that a
beautiful Vietnamese woman accompanied almost every American
journalist. Halberstam, as it turned out, arrived just in time for the
going-away party for François Sully, the French correspondent for
Newsweek, whom the Diem government had ordered to leave the country. The beautiful Vietnamese women Halberstam saw that night were
very far from bar girls, most of whom came from Vietnam's poor countryside, had little education, and certainly no social standing. The
women who accompanied the reporters, as well as the diplomats and
higher-station personnel in Vietnam, were middle-class women
attracted to the glamour and adventure of dating a smart and swanky
young American.

Vietnam in this sense illustrated the status often enjoyed by foreigners in Asia merely by dint of being foreign. Saigon, in particular, had

only recently emerged from French colonial rule, one of the characteristics of which was a good deal of mingling at the upper social reaches.
Now, as the French were leaving and the Americans were taking over,
almost everything associated with the United States glowed with a special excitement—the money, the cosmetics from the PX, the fast and
exciting life, the Kennedys, the power, and the fearless young men in
khaki safari suits who covered the war during the day and went to fashionable clubs and restaurants at night.

"All the Young Turks had beautiful Vietnamese girlfriends," wrote
William Prochnau, who chronicled the lives and adventures of the
band of American reporters who covered Vietnam in the early stages of
the war. The reporter who was to become Halberstam's closest friend in
Saigon, Neil Sheehan, then a handsome Harvard graduate working for
United Press International, was famously attached to a fashionable
young woman known as Blue Lotus, "a stunning *Saigonnaisse* whose
every curve seemed to have been sewn tightly into an expensive
Parisian party dress," as Prochnau described her. Blue Lotus was soon
to introduce Halberstam to one Ricki, an already-married school-
teacher whom Halberstam dated for a year or so, risking the rage of her
jealous and sometimes gun-toting husband. "You vill love zis place,
David. It iss VUN-derful!" Horst Faas, a German photographer, said to
Halberstam at Sully's going-away party, nodding in Blue Lotus's direction. Sheehan's main professional rival, Malcolm Browne, the Associated Press bureau chief, was about the only reporter at the party not
accompanied by a local woman, but that was only because his girlfriend, Le Lieu, who had quit her job as deputy director of information
in the South Vietnamese government in order to be with him, was temporarily out of town. Browne and Le Lieu married—and remain married, living in New York, to this day.

All the reporters were in a way outdone by the swashbuckling
American soldier who turned out to be their best source. This was
Lieutenant Colonel John Paul Vann, the legendary military adviser to
the ARVN Seventh Division, who used to talk late into the night at his
headquarters in the Mekong Delta, telling Sheehan and Halberstam
that the Vietcong were gaining the upper hand over the corrupt South
Vietnamese, who were often unwilling to fight. Vann was a man of
medium physical stature but larger-than-life character, and he had

utterly prodigious sexual appetites. He had a wife and family back home, two steady and serious girlfriends in Saigon, each set up by him in their own house and each ignorant of the existence of the other. Vann went through a marriage ceremony of sorts with each of them, largely to satisfy their families. But they weren't enough for him. According to Sheehan, who wrote a book on Vann, it was not unusual for him to have sex with both of his kept women and one or two bar girls on Tu Do Street all on the same day.

Certainly such a life would have been impossible back home. On a visit to Saigon in 2002, by which time many American ex-servicemen had returned to the country to work or just to visit, I met one veteran who boasted that he'd had two wives living with him in the same house, sleeping with him in the same bed. He was proud that when the evacuation came, on the eve of the Communist victory in 1975, he was able to get both his "wives" on military airplanes leaving the country and that he had continued to live with them in the United States, having children—all of whom he sent to college—with both of them.

Vann was different from most, not only in the clarity of his analysis of the shortcomings of the Saigon regime but also in his awareness of the impression—and it was not a good one—that such "fraternization" made on the Vietnamese. He told Halberstam that whenever he visited one of the district chiefs in the area patrolled by the Seventh Division, he would be offered a woman for the night. It was just standard Asian hospitality. But, Vann said, he always turned down the offer. "It lowers our prestige in their eyes," he said. "They're trying to get something they can hold over you. Too damn many Americans in this country are sleeping with Vietnamese women. It's bad for our image. The Vietnamese don't like it. It arouses their resentment." And, of course, it created a sense of corruptibility, putting the Americans in the same category as many of the very corrupt Vietnamese officers, where they didn't want to be.

Clearly Vann's opinion on this matter is remarkable given that he slept with innumerable Vietnamese women, though apparently not in the districts where he worked and built his relationships with local people. Vann was one of the few to see that the South Vietnamese government, with so many corrupt officials looking out above all for their own interests, was going to be no match for its hard, clean, and dedicated enemy. "We're going to lose because of the moral degeneration in South Vietnam coupled with the excellent discipline of the VC," he wrote to a friend back home. And part of that moral degeneration was sexual. Vann learned of one American aid official who had allowed a Vietnamese contractor to steal U.S. Operations Mission building materials in exchange for women, one of whom was the contractor's wife. Sex didn't cause South Vietnam and the United States to lose the war, but it was nonetheless symptomatic of the larger demoralization of the society that the Americans were fighting to save. It's hard to win a very tough war and be devoted to erotic entertainment at the same time.

"Just next to the UPI office was the Melody Bar, which became kind of a journalist hangout," recalled David Lamb. He was speaking of a later time in the war, after the departure of Sheehan and Halberstam, when the number of troops and reporters had skyrocketed, and, therefore, so had the amount of plain and fancy screwing. "A lot of the guys from UPI had steady girlfriends from the bar that they lived with. When I called sometimes, the phone would ring and ring and ring because they were all next door with the ladies.

"There was no place in America where you could get a girl as easily," Lamb continued. "It was exciting living in another landscape that you didn't know existed."

"It was a very sad experience, but for me it was wonderful," Frank Maguire said, explaining the reason somebody like him, a bachelor in his thirties at the time, would want to do three tours of duty in a war that was nonetheless a tragedy for the United States and Vietnam both. "I sometimes get a guilty conscience because I enjoyed it so much. People laugh when I say I kept going back because of the girls and the food, but that's not too much of a lie."

THE ACTION TOOK PLACE at China Beach, the real China Beach, where American soldiers and others went for some seaside relaxation during the Vietnam War, but it wasn't the sort of action likely to make it into the later television series of that name. Eliseo Perez-Montalvo, an air force sergeant who conducted technical debriefings with pilots at

Danang Air Base, remembered one scene that sheds light on several aspects of the Vietnam sex circus.

"Over at China Beach, there was a serpentine wire that separated our beach from a Vietnamese beach," he said. "And there were some scraggly pine trees that grew higher up above the water line." Perez-Montalvo was speaking in 2003 to an interviewer for the Oral History Project at the Vietnam Center and Archive at Texas Tech University. "And what the Vietnamese ladies would do, I guess the GIs, the Marines, this is an R and R center for the Marines. They would go there and rent a cot, a bunk, and they could buy a beer. They had a little PX there for them.

"And the enterprising Vietnam ladies would take sheets that the GIs would bring them from the barracks and tie them like a little barrier about three or four [feet] high from the pine trees that formed a little quadrangle and this was their house.

"And you would see the Marines, they wouldn't even take their boots off or their pants off all the way. You'd see their feet sticking out from underneath the sheets."

So far, it is a scene that illustrates nothing more than young men willing to take their pleasure where and under what conditions it is offered, and in Vietnam pleasure was offered under many different conditions. It was what happened after the sex in Perez-Montalvo's account that evokes the poignancy of the situation for the Vietnamese.

"Then they would throw the condoms away," he said, "and you would see small Vietnamese boys, they would pick up the condoms and take them to the ocean and rinse them in seawater and roll them up again and insert them in the little containers and try to resell them."

The interviewer asked if anybody bought them, unlikely as that seemed, given how cheap they were and how easy it was for GIs to get them at the PX. You would think that marines who had the forethought to bring sheets with them to the beach would also bring condoms, but maybe some of them would forget that little necessity and, rather than postpone their joust with the lady, would take what the Vietnamese boys provided.

"I imagine so," Perez-Montalvo said. "I imagine they did. I don't know. The Marines were crazy. I don't blame them. They had a very tough job, a lot tougher than ours. And when they came back to town, they enjoyed themselves as much as possible because they had no assurance of what it was going to be like tomorrow."

I don't blame them either. I was young once, and I understand the power of the urge. The globe didn't acquire its more than 6 billion inhabitants via caution, restraint, and morality-induced abstinence. It produced them in the same way that the Vietnam War produced those half a million mixed-blood children spoken of by the Communist propaganda machine. The theoretical position of the U.S. Army and the American government on this matter was to discourage what it rather insipidly called fraternization, which normally translated to sex with prostitutes. The rules were not much enforced.

"The town was off-limits to us but nobody checked," Perez-Montalvo said. "It was easy. You just walk out the gate. Our PX was outside the gate. So you just go [to] the PX and then keep going, get lost in the crowd, hitch a ride."

Once, he remembered, he was in Danang. Near the market, he saw a television crew from one of the news services, its camera running, and he turned away until it had passed.

"I didn't want to get in trouble," he said. "We'd then go to the Da Nang Hotel where they had a massage parlor and a steam bath and I would take a steam bath and afterwards I would have mamason rub me and do fellatio on me for money"—about $4 or $5, as he remembered it. Once, he said, he came down with a venereal disease from an encounter at the same hotel and had to lie about where he'd caught it so as not to admit he'd been in town. He told the NCO orderly who treated him (who "wanted to hang me") that his exposure had taken place in one of the bunkers of the enlisted-men's club with one of the girls who worked there, and the the story's credence is a sign of how ubiquitous the sexual opportunities were.

Many other stories from the front lines of Vietnam confirm this. One of the best-known places in war-era Vietnam was one that GIs called Sin City, a circle of bars in the town of An Khe, in Binh Dinh Province, the nearest town to the sprawling Camp Radcliff, home to a rotating group of military units, including the celebrated First Cavalry Division, the 173rd Airborne Brigade, and the First Battalion of the Fiftieth Infantry (Mechanized). In 1966, *Time* reported on Sin City in an article called "Disneyland East." Initially, after the First Cavalry had moved into Camp Radcliff, what *Time* called "the uncontrolled squalor and rapacity of the riffraff" was hurting the American soldiers, mainly by causing a rapid increase in venereal disease. So the First Cavalry's commanding officer, General Harry W. O. Kinnard, declared An Khe off-limits. Not surprisingly, the troops were unhappy. They were fighting bloody battles in the jungle for weeks at a time, and when they got back to their base, they "had little to come home to." A group of Vietnamese elders then approached Kinnard with a solution: the army would build a brothel quarter to be staffed by Vietnamese women—they were given the euphemistic official designation "entertainers" and had a card identifying them as such—who were required to get preventive penicillin shots and weekly exams.

Eventually some forty concrete blocks surrounded by concertina wire, known to the GIs as boom-boom parlors, were built in a rough circle, in the middle of which was a clinic. The blocks were owned by Vietnamese or people from other countries—one GI I spoke to remembered an Indian owning at least one of them—and each had a bar and eight small cubicles in the back, where the carnal hospitality took place. They had names like Caravelle, Paradise, Golden Hind, Hill Billy, and the Moderate Tearoom. The price per girl was $2.50 to

Western man with a Vietnamese bar girl in Saigon, 1966.
Marilyn Silverstone, Magnum Press Images

$5, depending on demand, though *Time* quoted one unnamed GI complaining that the $5 price was exorbitant, a rip-off, an outrageous instance of someone taking advantage of a monopolistic situation, and he suggested that Kinnard set a uniform price of $3 per session. Immediately the incidence of VD plummeted, however, a good result, though American officers still felt morally ambivalent about what they had wrought. "Forced to choose between morality and the morale of their men, the division's officers are clearly troubled by Disneyland," *Time* reported. Not so the men.

"Sin Cities were whorehouses sanctioned by the army," one veteran wrote in an online memoir. "The military police would be stationed outside during the day, and they made sure that you were gone before nightfall. GI's would go there to have a little fun and blow off some stream with the mama-sans. You could buy a beer for around 50 piastres and sex for 300 piastres. The mama-san would say, 'You number 1 GI,' which meant great, number 10 meant you suck, and sex was 'boom boom,' and that usually happened in a small room behind the bar."

An Khe itself was, as Frank Maguire, the ARVN adviser, put it to me, "typical of a small town in the highlands." It was a strip of houses and stores along a winding highway. "Sin City was an appendix stuck on it a little behind everything. It might have been ten, maybe twenty little bars in a circle with places in the back where the girls would go.

"I thought it was a damn good idea," Maguire said. "Young men out in the jungle, three or four days, sometimes longer, and sometimes you're scared out of your wits, and they had no idea where they were. They came back, and they could relieve themselves. It was under government control, with a medic assigned to it, so girls could be checked."

Maguire also remembered what might have been the most attractive aspect of it, which is that, somehow, the women who worked there didn't seem quite like prostitutes. This viewpoint is in contrast to *Time's* assumption that it was mostly the "rapacity of the riffraff" in Vietnam that created places like Sin City. It seems more than a little high-handed to condemn poor people for doing what they can to get some money from rich outsiders, and even at $2.50 to $5 a shot it's hard to imagine the women in question getting rich, at least by American standards. In any case, some of the men who experienced Sin City don't remember it as a place of riffraff at all, but one of rather charming women who had genuine feelings for the GIs they got to know.

This is a common observation about the sex trade in Asia. The women seem nicer, fresher, more eager to please, than their Western counterparts. They are more affectionate and don't fit the image of the hardened and cynical purveyors of their own bodies that you would find in, say New York or on the rue Saint-Denis in Paris. They are poor girls with dreams for themselves and sometimes a vulnerable attachment to the American men they meet. In Vietnam, relationships were formed; marriages took place—and often came to an end after the couple moved back to America.

"I never thought of them as prostitutes," Maguire said. "They weren't on the clock, put it that way. You know, 'Okay, that's it, next!' "

Is this merely Western sentimentality, the transposition of the old saw about the whore with the heart of gold to rural Vietnam? There is no doubt some of that at play. It is a quality of young men in general, and American young men in particular, to want to be liked. Either way, there is a real poignancy to Sin City, stemming less from the fact of prostitution itself and more from the transience of the relations formed, the melancholy inherent in the meeting of young men with money to spend and homes to go back to and poor women whose homes were being wrecked by war.

" 'You no have wife-san,' " Maguire remembered one woman telling a soldier in an attempt at persuading him to marry her. " 'You no have baby-san. Who cry for you when you die?' "

"I had the feeling that the Americans didn't look down on the prostitutes," said Nguyen Ngoc Luong, who was a translator and reporter for *The New York Times* Saigon bureau during the final years of the war. "Because you lived far away from home without your family, so you need them. And they are very gentle, and they don't cost you too much."

Luong, whom I interviewed in 2008 in Ho Chi Minh City, used to go with Gloria Emerson, one of several *Times* correspondents he worked for, to the Tan Son Nhat airport to see the GIs boarding flights for the trip home, many of them taking their Vietnamese wives along. The American consulate in those days did a brisk business in visas for new spouses.

"In Japan, there were few marriages," Luong said, meaning few marriages between U.S. soldiers and their Japanese girlfriends. "In Vietnam, there were many. Why? I don't know."

Perhaps it was because by the time of the Vietnam War, interracial marriage was more acceptable back home than it had been during the occupation of Japan, a generation earlier. Perhaps it had to do with the greater willingness of the Vietnamese to leave their country. Japan had already been defeated and was rebuilding itself, whereas Vietnam, which was poorer than Japan, faced the real possibility of a Communist takeover. Japan had also been an enemy country, whereas South Vietnam was supposedly a friend. In any case, while there was a great deal of raw, vulgar prostitution in Vietnam, deep and even lasting relationships were formed. "I don't think many of the girls became prostitutes in a strict sense," Luong told another interviewer, "but most of them had a small room somewhere nearby where everything was paid for by one specific GI. They had a GI boyfriend and when he died or went home they would have another. They liked the GIs very much. Most American soldiers were very good with girls. Very amiable. You'd have to be there to see it. The girls behaved very warmly with the GIs and the GIs were like children with them. Like babies. The girls took care of them."

MAGUIRE AGREED, though he has a somewhat darker view of the consequences of relationships bound to be temporary. "The girls were nice," he said in my interview with him. "They were dramatic, and they would get involved." Those who want to dismiss the narrative of the whore with the heart of gold need to hear the tale of one woman who worked in a Sin City bar.

"She developed a passion for my executive officer," Maguire said. "She was a very nice girl. Her name was Jackie. I think I have a picture someplace. And we had a party, and I think he was getting ready to go home, and she came to the party, and she said, 'You know how much I love you? I love you this much'—and she took a knife and cut off this digit." Maguire pointed to the first joint of his little finger.

"She said, 'I'd cut off my shoulder for you,' and she meant it."

Sad to say, Maguire's executive officer left on schedule, and Jackie remained in Vietnam. When the Communists took over the south in 1975, one of the first things they did was send thousands of former prostitutes to reeducation camps, where, though the women were treated as victims of the imperialist Americans and their lackeys, discipline was harsh and the stay lasted several months. In 1978, three full years after the end of the war, I was taken on a guided tour of such a center in Ho Chi Minh City, where I saw hundreds of young women sitting on the floor learning crafts like weaving and embroidery. We visitors were not given an opportunity to speak with any of the camp's residents. In any case, I didn't know at the time to look for a woman missing part of her small finger, but it is likely Jackie and the other entertainers of Sin City were there, or in places like it elsewhere in Vietnam.

AROUND THE TIME that *Time* disclosed to its millions of readers the existence of official Vietnamese brothels for American troops, there was a short-lived controversy in the United States about the sexual morality of the war. In a speech at the School of Advanced International Studies at Johns Hopkins University, William J. Fulbright, who as chairman of the Senate Foreign Relations Committee was emerging as a leading critic of the administration's policy in Vietnam, famously charged that the "arrogance of power" had led the United States into a war beyond both its capabilities and its interests. One of the elements in the American effort to "create stability where there is chaos . . . and honest government where corruption is almost a way of life" was the moral transformation of Vietnam. But the American presence was in itself a cause of a new sort of immorality.

"Both literally and figuratively," Fulbright said, "Saigon has become an American brothel." Fulbright didn't attribute any of this to Vietnamese culture, in which prostitution and second wives had always been part of the scene, but he attributed it entirely to Vietnamese poverty and the economic distortions caused by the American presence. The wives and daughters of economically displaced Vietnamese families were willingly peddled to U.S. soldiers to serve as mistresses, to the great shame and humiliation of those families. "It is not unusual to hear a report that a Vietnamese soldier has committed suicide out of shame because his wife has been working as a bar girl," he said.

Fulbright's accusation was cited in articles in the American press, and it drew rebuttals from an embarrassed Johnson administration. A couple of weeks after his Johns Hopkins speech, Fulbright held Senate hearings on Vietnam, during which he asked Secretary of Defense Robert McNamara what he thought of the brothel charge. "I have not been to Saigon since November 30. It was not a brothel then and I do not believe it is today," McNamara replied.

"You do not agree?" Fulbright persisted.

McNamara said, "I think we do a disservice to the Vietnamese and to our own men when we characterize it as such. I do not mean to say there are not prostitutes in Saigon. There are in Washington, and I do not mean to say that civilian and military personnel of our country are not patronizing them. They do."

That indeed was generally the tone of the response to those trying to fend off criticism that the war aimed at saving Vietnam from Communism was destroying it in other ways. Mrs. Oswald B. Lord, an occasional United Nations emissary of President Johnson's, happened to be at the end of a long State Department–sponsored tour of Asia when Fulbright made his comments, and she forthrightly declared that, yes, "some of this goes on," but she quickly added that "it goes on right here in Washington." In any case, mostly American GIs "are not in town with the bar girls," she said. They are doing other things, like helping with orphanages and rehabilitation centers—"that's the way they spend their days off."

The notion that Saigon was no different from anyplace else was a theme developed by *Time* as well in its defense of both American behavior and the war itself. "Not everyone in Fulbright's own Arkansas cities of Little Rock and Hot Springs patronizes prostitutes either," it declared, "though there is an abundance of whores, ranging from massage-parlor employees ($5) to $200-a-night hotel call girls." The article included the phone number (FRANKLIN 4-2181) that airmen stationed at Little Rock Air Force Base could call to "find out if 'the ice is on.' The price of ice starts at $15 a dish."

Still, to dismiss Fulbright's brothel charge with the argument that Vietnam is no different from Hot Springs is truly to miss the point. To be sure, when American troops invaded France, Germany, and Italy in World War II, there were prostitutes available to them, but nowhere do we find the construction of brothels exclusively for the use of U.S. soldiers, nor were entire central stretches of Paris or Berlin transformed, as veterans often described Saigon's Tu Do Street, into a district of wall-to-wall brothels. More than one GI reflecting in later years on the sexual opportunities of Vietnam used a simple analogy to describe the scene.

"It's like a kid in a candy shop; you just walk in and you can eat anything you want," Michael Harris, a radioman on a river patrol boat, said in an interview for the Vietnam Center and Archive. "Most of us were lured or subjected to that to the point where we got involved, and I admire guys that didn't who were married or had religious beliefs that they didn't become involved. But, the majority did and I believe like myself many came away with sexually transmitted diseases."

The sexual temptation was so widespread even in combat zones that platoon commanders had to decide on a policy to implement. Phil Price, an advertising executive from Lubbock, Texas, remembered how, during his first few days as an infantry platoon leader near Pleiku, his men told him they wanted him to meet somebody. "Her name was Kim," he said, "and she had on black pajamas, and [was] really built well, and she opened it up and said, 'I souvenir. You boom-boom, you let me boom-boom GI's.'" Price told Kim to leave. As he put it, "I would not let my guys do that. Some of the officers when they went in would buy rubbers for their guys and what have you; I didn't. I didn't allow them to fraternize. We just didn't do that. It wasn't a moral issue, it was more of a safety. I figured they [the prostitutes] already knew where all my machine guns were at night and everything else so we just didn't need any more of that. There were a couple of times I would throw smoke grenades to get them out from around us."

Another former officer told me that he noticed his men seemed to be taking his battalion's jeeps to be washed more often than seemed reasonable, so once he went to the car wash to find out why. He learned that the women who worked there were doing boom-boom with the men. In the Vietnam Center and Archive at Texas Tech, there is a color snapshot of a woman labeled "Viet Nam carwash girl." There is no explanation, no indication of where it was taken or why, only that it comes from the Army Special Photographic Office. In any case, car wash girls weren't the only ones who freelanced as prostitutes when the occasion presented itself.

"My experience was almost exclusively with girls working in the laundries," said another veteran, Eric Larsen, who runs a local Veterans of Foreign Wars post in a bar he owns in Pattaya, Thailand. Larsen, whom I interviewed in Pattaya, was talking about his time in Vietnam, when he was part of an engineering detachment near Chu Lai. "You'd go into the city of Chu Lai, where there were laundries, shacks with corrugated aluminum roofs, and that's where the women were, add-ons to clean clothes."

Another former soldier, Wayne Smith, a combat medic who served with the Ninth Infantry Division, told an interviewer that sex was held up indirectly as an inducement to kill the enemy. "In our unit, guys who got confirmed kills would get a three-day in-country R and R," he said. "Those guys got sent to the beach at Vung Tao," he added, referring to a coastal town north of Saigon that was a center for steam baths, bars, and brothels.

Don Halsey, who did counterintelligence work at Thai Ninh in the Mekong Delta in 1970 and 1971, is one of many Americans who understood the economics of the situation: women from families that earned a few dollars a month would not normally have been prostitutes but did not resist the temptation to make unimaginable sums selling their bodies to the hordes of GIs.

"You'd walk around in Saigon and they'd grab you in an alley," Halsey remembered. "I went into a department store in Saigon, and a prostitute [said], 'Hey GI,' and pulls her dress up. This right in the middle of a department store. In the Vietnamese villages that we were in, we'd be right out in the middle of a jungle and hear this purring, and we'd look and here comes some Honda motor scooters with these ARVNs with a girl on the back trying to sell those girls right out in the field. It was really sad, what you saw in the movie, *Full Metal Jacket,* with ARVN and the girl, it's real typical of it."

The reference is to the film directed by Stanley Kubrick, which depicts a marine platoon's entire experience of the war from their brutal training in America to deadly combat in Vietnam; in one scene, while the American soldiers are resting near some bomb-ruined buildings, a girl is brought to them on the back of a motorcycle, and they take turns going into a rubble-strewn room to have sex with her.

Wayne Smith remembered the "steam bath" right at the division headquarters in Tan An. "It was a whorehouse, in effect," he said. "These pretty young Vietnamese teenagers were being fucked by American soldiers. At the time I rationalized it by thinking, well, once we kill off the enemy, the Vietnamese will be able to be fully free and there won't be any more prostitution. But this was clearly just exploitation."

On the subject of steam baths, Ron Politano remembered in his interview with me meeting a Korean woman known as Missy Kim who, he said, ran a whole chain of them. Politano hit it off with her, partly because he knew a few words of Korean. Once he visited her in Saigon, and she introduced him to a Vietnamese man whom Politano took to be the boss. The man invited him to lunch.

"There was something about this guy, the way he was looking at me," Politano recalled years afterward. "He asked me if I'd like to see his office. We go in. 'You live in Hawaii,' he says. 'We've only just met, but I like your looks. I'm going to take you into my confidence.' "

The man opened an office safe—"big, like in one of those old Wells Fargo movies, with brass handles and two doors"—in which was stored what Politano took to be the accumulated proceeds of the blow-bath steam-job places. "The door was closed. Missy Kim was out of the picture. And inside the safe were bundles of money—piastres, French francs, Dutch guldens. I saw lots of U.S. dollars. The bundles were literally falling out of the safe. I don't know the exact figure, but he quoted something in the millions."

Politano soon got the drift. The man asked him how many footlockers he would take back home with him when he returned to Hawaii. " 'The Americans are losing the war,' he said. 'Do you know what will happen to me if the big boys come down from Hanoi?' So this guy was going to be hanging from a lamppost if they caught him with all that money.

" 'Let me ask you the obvious question,' " Politano said to him. " 'Why am I doing this?'

" 'You're doing this for half a million dollars,' " the man said.

" 'But then down the road if I get caught, I'd lose everything,' " Politano said. "So I left. Thanks a lot. No hard feelings. I never saw him again, but I do sometimes wonder what happened to all that money."

RELATIONS WITH LOCAL WOMEN became so commonplace that few Americans at any level in Vietnam seem to have bothered to wonder what sort of an effect this aspect of the war would have on Vietnamese attitudes. The matter seems rarely to have climbed the chain of command, though it did, on certain rare occasions, as when Fulbright spoke at Johns Hopkins and *Time* reported on Sin City, enter into the public discourse. In July 1965, a generally upbeat cable from the embassy in Saigon to the secretary of state mentioned "some resentment" at the growing American presence, which was causing higher rents for local people and a scarcity of goods. Also, the cable said, a series of newspaper articles in *Chinh Luan,* a Saigon daily, reprinted in the *Saigon Daily News,* "complained that wide circulation of dollars in Da Nang has debased the piastre, barter of gasoline for local purchases has created serious fire hazards, prostitution, and bars flourishing, etc. All these conditions are ascribed to presence of US personnel." But despite this, the cable continued, "behavior of US personnel appears correct and disciplined to Vietnamese observers."

This rare mention of bars and prostitution came just four months after those first marines landed in Danang, but the issue produced no deep discussion in Washington or at the Pentagon, in part because the increase in prostitution occasioned only the rarest protest in Vietnam itself. Early on, in 1964, the commander of South Vietnamese forces in Danang, Brigadier General Nguyen Chanh Thi, wrote to *The Saigon Post* to say that he'd received three hundred letters from parents complaining of the proximity of bars on Doc Lap Boulevard to schools throughout that area of the city. Nine bars were closed, he said.

And that was that. "We thought it was natural," Nguyen Ngoc Luong said when I asked him what the Vietnamese in Saigon thought of the pursuit of local women by American men. To be sure, the prostitutes were looked down on, but they had been there under the French and were there still under the Americans. Moreover, Vietnamese men behaved no differently than the foreigners, though the places they went for their pleasure were less conspicuous than those patronized by Americans. The Communist propaganda made a fuss about it, but the South Vietnamese didn't, and in the absence of local complaints the American authorities only warned men about the danger of venereal disease, taking no steps to stop them from "fraternizing."

There was nonetheless a kind of moral corruption in the laissez-faire attitude of the American command. I interviewed one veteran, a marine who had seen action in the deadly battles in the A Shau Valley, which was a major staging area for North Vietnamese forces moving south. "It was bad," he said. "You can't even make people understand, it was that bad." He told me he never took the R&R leaves he was entitled to because he was afraid they would affect his concentration when he had to go back on patrol. "I know guys who got killed because they were dreaming about pussy in Bangkok, weren't paying proper attention," he said.

In fact, it would be hard to argue that dreams about Bangkok massage parlors had a serious military effect in Vietnam. Still, while sex during the Vietnam War was a sidelight of the conflict, it was also reflective of the lavish way in which Americans went to war, with all the advanced heavy military equipment that money can buy and a concerted effort to provide the material comforts and luxuries of the American way of life—overstuffed bureaucracies, massive staffs of non-combat personnel, air-conditioned quarters, Walmart-like PXs, turkeys for Thanksgiving, Bob Hope and Raquel Welch for entertainment, officers' and enlisted-men's clubs, and all-expense-paid vacations for GIs to various "gin & sin" destinations in Southeast Asia. The argument here is not that this was wrong but to point up the tremendous contrast with the way the enemy waged war, fiercely but economically, with ever-more-sophisticated weaponry (much of it captured from the ineffectual ARVN), but with no air power at all, with black pajamas for uniforms and sandals cut from old tires for shoes, and with no brothels, beer, ice buckets, massage parlors, go-go bars, or R&R junkets to Bangkok or Sydney or Kuala Lumpur; with no bedsheet shelters amid pine trees for getting laid on the beach with their boots still on; with no noontime hotel-room trysts with Vietnamese secretaries and no local women kept in small apartments around town by men whose wives were waiting in Bangkok or Stateside for their husbands' brief visits. The routine of the other side in Vietnam did not include sexual adventures with women. Sex wasn't the reason we lost the war in Vietnam; still, it was part of the way we went to war.

During one of his tours, Frank Maguire was seconded to the State Department to work in JUSPAO, the Joint United States Public Affairs Office, in the Mekong Delta region. Every once in a while, he had to go to Saigon on business, and he always stayed at the same hotel, which was under contract with the State Department. Every time he went, he told me, a Vietnamese woman came with the room, for his pleasure. He didn't ask for a woman; she was just there.

"I was sent there, and all the people in it were State Department people, and for whatever reason I always got the same girl," Maguire said. "She was very sweet. She gave me a chain with a cross on it. She was just one of the amenities. I can't remember if I ever gave her any money. I must have, but it just didn't seem like it was that kind of a proposition."

PETE (AS I CALL HIM; he prefers to remain anonymous) was a pilot during a long career in Indochina, going back to 1956, when he flew C-124 transport planes from Saigon to New Delhi, with stops in Bangkok and Calcutta. After that, he flew planes for Air America, the airline of the CIA during the war in Indochina. He remembered his introduction to the sexual possibilities of Southeast Asia on an early overnight stopover in Bangkok. "The air force rep, who lived in a business hotel that no longer exists, took us out to a place with all these girls behind a glass door, with a number pinned on. They were knitting, because there was no TV." It was an eye-opener, and it was more than that. It was a vision of an alternative erotic world. "It was all so totally different from anything I'd ever seen, being born and raised in Pennsylvania, sex being so open and so readily available."

Pete was a risk taker; his reputation among other veterans is that of a very brave man. He flew spotter planes in Vietnam, sometimes drawing fire in order to locate the enemy in preparation for retaliatory air strikes. He remembered the early days in Saigon. Tu Do Street was already "wall-to-wall bars" in the 1960s, "though there weren't any touts outside the expat bars trying to get you in. The girls didn't hustle you for drinks in those days.

"I had a couple of girls move in," he said, "since going downtown was getting a little tired. It was cheaper than going downtown every night," he said, "and I was cheap. The first girl I paid $50 a month and had to buy a carton of Winstons for her mother. If things got too serious, I'd just send them on their way, but they were willing to do that," he said.

"I was in Laos in 1970 and 1971," he continued. "It cost the price of a 150-cc Honda motorbike to get rid of a girl you didn't want anymore. I knew one guy who had five Hondas running around Vientiane, and that started the practice for the rest of us. We were making plenty of money. I only had to buy one girl a motorbike."

Pete told his stories of Indochina honestly and frankly, describing his experience of being young with money to burn while living in places where poor village women had survived for centuries selling their charms and their bodies to men. It would be easy to judge his behavior, and that of thousands of others who behaved similarly, as wicked and depraved, but the question of economic and psychological realism has to be factored in to that judgment. What would have been more moral for a pretty young woman from a war-torn village in Vietnam or Laos, where, as a matter of fact, every village had its brothel: to labor in the rice fields, married to a rough peasant man who beat her, got drunk, gambled, and visited the aforementioned brothel, or to have sex for money with men in the city who treated her decently, even giving her money to replace the family's dead water buffalo or to pay her kid brother's school fees? And from the standpoint of your average twenty-two-year-old man with nothing to do of an evening? To be sure, it would have been more moral for him to have stayed in his hooch or his hotel at night reading the New Testament, refusing to go down to Tu Do Street for a couple of beers rather than open the door when he knew that the person knocking on it had long silky hair, smooth nut-brown skin, and a perfume of orange and spice on her breath. How many young men with nothing else to do would have resisted the temptation?

Pete didn't resist. "There were these parties in Vientiane at a hotel, they were called tea dances, on Saturday afternoons," he said. "Young girls would be there. They weren't in the trade, but if one of them caught your eye, she would be perfectly happy to go off with you. These were girls from the best families in Vientiane.

"And then there was a bar in Vientiane," he said. "The oldest girl in the place was maybe fifteen years old. I don't know how old the youngest one was. It was across the street from the guesthouse where I used to stay.

"A friend and I went in one time. There was just one girl by herself. She got between us and grabbed two handfuls of crotch and said, 'Who's first?' She told me she was eleven years old, and she looked it."

I asked Pete how he felt about that—eleven years old and looking it.

He didn't hesitate to answer. "It didn't bother me," he said. "I knew guys who were shacked up with eleven-year-olds."

A Room of Her Own

IT WAS ABOUT TWO YEARS after arriving with her husband in Singapore that Amy R's marriage broke up, and it did so in the way that not a few marriages of Westerners break up in Asia. Not that it's much consolation for Amy to have company in matters like this, especially after she had given up a perfectly good career in the United States—she had worked in publishing for thirteen years, including four as the marketing and sales director of a university press—in order to go to Singapore in the first place. Her husband, a Dane, had been sent to Singapore by his employer, a big shipping company, and Amy went with him in 2002.

"In 2004, September, he went on a business trip to Denmark, and he e-mailed me saying basically the marriage was over," she recalled. At the urging of friends, Amy saw a lawyer, who told her that, most likely, her husband was seeing somebody else, but she didn't believe it. Then when her husband came home from his business trip, she saw a digital camera and two airplane tickets on his bed.

"I asked him what they were, but he didn't say anything," she said. "Then I looked at the camera, and there were pictures in a sort of tropical-paradise setting of him and another woman, with the woman's intimate parts in full view. The airplane tickets were to Bali.

"She was Filipina," Amy said of her husband's new paramour. "She was younger, in her thirties, but she had a tough face, figure was not outstanding." Amy found out that her husband's lover wasn't educated either, but evidently there was some attraction between him and what she called "this unlettered woman" that satisfied them both. She saw some e-mail exchanges between them, in which the Filipino woman sent provocative pictures of herself and notes saying, "I love you."

"Part of it, 25 percent, was I was stepmom to his kids," she said, trying to explain her ex's sudden choice to make a life with somebody else. "I didn't adore these girls, but I was okay with them," she said. "I was their friend; I didn't try to be their mom. But the younger daughter was getting on my nerves, and I probably wasn't a very nice person in the last six months."

But the deeper reason, the other 75 percent, she believes, had to do with her husband's susceptibility to the charms of a younger Asian woman, a temptation that has furnished the shoals on which many a Western marriage in Singapore and Bangkok and Beijing has foundered.

"Part of it, too, was the aging process," Amy continued. "Western women and Western men—we tend to get hip heavy; men get bellies. Then the men come to Asia, and they're in their midlife, and because it's a man's world here, a chubby Western woman isn't going to do anything, but an overweight Western man who drinks a lot of beer, he's going to have lots of women after him.

"He has his choice, one-from-column-A, one-from-column-B sort of thing," she continued. "Western women, we're fleshier than the Asians, there's more boob to drop. The Asian women age better, and Western men love smaller women, and that's just the way it is."

THE BREAKUP WAS DEVASTATING to Amy, though she recovered emotionally after a while with the help of a couple of girlfriends, got work and a residency permit, and stayed in Singapore. Knowing that what happened to her has happened to quite a few other Western women who went to Asia with their husbands did not make Amy's breakup feel any less devastating. The unadorned truth would seem to be that the historical and cultural circumstances that give advantages to European and American men in countries like China and Singapore (where most sexual relations do not involve payment) produce disadvantages for Western women, many of whom, when they are unattached, have a hard time getting dates. The standard line on this, and it is Amy's line also, is that while Asian women and Western men enjoy a powerful sort of mutual attraction, that is less often the case with Asian men and Western women. At least that's what her experience and her six years of observation in Singapore have told her.

"What's happening now," she said, "is a lot of Singaporean women are going after *ang-mo*—the local term for a foreigner—and there are various reasons for it. Anthropologists say that women want men who are above them in status. I think, frankly, a lot of Singaporean women are saying, 'We don't want the mother-in-law thing,' and they have choices. Meanwhile, Singaporean men are marrying women from Vietnam and China."

By the mother-in-law thing, Amy meant the whole set of traditional expectations surrounding Asian women and the enduring, if fading, assumption that they belong to the family of their husband. But why should the *ang-mo* enjoy higher status, especially in a place like advanced, modern Singapore, where many local men are rich?

"I think it's in part because the Asians see anything having to do with Western culture as having more panache, especially in Singapore," Amy said. "American—and Western—culture still has a certain zing that's considered exciting and sexy. Western men are seen as having more money also, even if that's not really the case. We're the hegemonic culture, and how cool is that! Western men are at the top of the heap."

But why doesn't the cultural glow operate for Western women? Would the available Western women whom Amy knows in Singapore be interested in dating Asian men?

"Sure, they'd be interested, but Chinese men are scared of us," Amy said. And in multicultural Singapore, Chinese men are about 90 percent of all men. "We're bigger than them sometimes," she said. "I even talked about this with a Chinese guy. He was my real estate agent, and I asked him why that was. He said, 'We're a little scared of you.' I asked him why. He said, 'You Western women are so expressive. You give your opinion right away, don't mince words, especially American women.'"

In other words, Western women, weaned on the milk of equality, free speech, and self-expression, are hard for many Asian men to handle, accustomed as they are to quieter women. I know that this view edges into the domain of cultural stereotyping, especially in portraying the stereotype of the "more masculine" American woman and the "more feminine," gentler Asian man, and this no doubt does some violence to the complicated truth about the variety of both. Moreover, most Western men do not abandon their Western wives when they move as a couple to Asia, and many single Western women do just fine in Asia, thank you very much.

But Amy says she knows lots of Western women who aren't doing well on the social front, and part of the reason is that there is something to the difference between Americans and Asians. She herself is smart, irreverent, both sassy and saucy. She has a sense of humor and a kind of verbally profuse, sometimes profane frankness to her. She doesn't shy away from words like *shit* and *fuck* when she wants them for emphasis. She says what she thinks and makes no bones about it.

"I have a problem, I'm going to tell you," she said, "and a lot of Chinese men, they can't handle that. They want someone who is less in your face, so it doesn't help that I'm Western, fifty-two years old, and from New York. I'm not going to say yes to a man because he wants to hear yes."

There's no point, moreover, in feeling sorry for her. She has a good job in Singapore, as director of studies and manager of a private English-language school, and she likes the city. Her contract expires in 2009, and she's not at all sure she's going to return to the United States when it does. She's a bit like some of the middle-aged Western men living in Asia, for whom there's a colorfulness, a level of stimulation, that makes home seem humdrum in comparison. The gorgeous East is gorgeous not only because of its women. Not long before I spoke to Amy, she had spent a weekend in Laos, touring Luang Prabang and Vientiane by bus. And she was planning a long weekend trip to Penang, an island off the west coast of Malaysia, where she was going with an Indian man she had started to date. Maybe they would be staying at the Eastern and Oriental Hotel, the old colonial-era hostelry that reeks of a kind of retro charm. They might wander the creepy confines of the Snake Temple, go sailing in the Andaman Sea.

On the subject of Indian men, Amy said that, in contrast with the more timid Chinese, they seem more interested in Western women.

The man she is seeing now is not the first Indian Amy has gone out with. "Indian men are attractive," she said, "and they're much more able to deal with verbal interplay."

Amy is not the only woman for whom Asia has been trying on the social front. She is in a way a representative of a statistic or, perhaps more accurately, an assumed statistic, because it's not clear whether there have been any studies of this subject. But the anecdotal evidence strongly suggests that for every ten or so Western male–Asian female couples, there are at most one or two Western women with Asian men.

The Western men who go to Asia are already a self-selected group. Not all of them are there because they want Asian women and don't want to be limited by obligations to anybody else, but certainly many of them are.

"I've done a bit of looking on the dating Web sites for Singaporeans and Westerners," Amy said. "I've seen a few Western guys, and it never went anywhere, and they never really said why, but often on the Web sites the Western men will say they want Asian women. That's who they're interested in."

Conversely, professional Western women sent to Asia on business are rarely motivated by some special fascination with Asian men, who, in any case, and for the reasons cited by Amy, are often not deemed ideal partners anyway. So, while young and pretty women of any color or creed will do just fine no matter where they are, when they get to be a bit older, Western women in Asia have a particularly hard time finding partners for romance and sex.

"I look forty-two," Amy said. "I have good skin. I'm not gorgeous, but I'm okay. There was a Western man, maybe around seventy-one, very fat, I met in a sushi bar the other day, and I know he wanted to go to bed with me, but he was too old, and I just couldn't. The age thing plus the obesity was a mega-turnoff."

Certainly the institutions in Singapore and other Asian cities that exist to relieve the dark and lonely hours of men are unavailable to women. Amy can't go to a bar and find a man half her age for what Flaubert called a *coup* in a short-time hotel or have him move in with her for a few weeks or months and then, when she wanted to move on to another young man, ease his exit with the gift of a motorbike. And even if she did have such a choice, she would decidedly not find it rewarding. It's not what she's looking for. Her choice is to make the most of life in Singapore and to achieve the wisdom of self-acceptance.

"All I can tell you is the older I get, the less patient I am, and I'm not going to deal with any bullshit," she said. "I know I'm smart. People say I'm too acerbic, too strong a personality, and I say, 'Sorry, I can't help that.' "

CHAPTER TWELVE

Thinking of Nana, or Noi, or Am

IT WAS A FRIDAY AFTERNOON in July 2007, and I was sitting with Pete, the former Air America pilot in the Madrid Bar, a watering hole that has been frequented by foreign men in Bangkok since the Vietnam War. He moved back to the United States after the war, then worked as a pilot in Sudan for a number of years. He was married for some of that time, to a Thai woman, but they were divorced, in large part because she hated living in Sudan. After he retired, he returned to Bangkok, where he married the younger sister of his first wife. It was in a long interview I had with him at the Madrid Bar that Pete told me about the practice of ending relationships with girls in Vientiane by buying them a motorbike. We talked for a long time, sitting on a curved banquette behind a small table and drinking mineral water, neither of us wanting alcohol while it was not yet evening. And then, when our conversation seemed to be winding up, something happened that was as good a demonstration as any of the eternal and enduring fascination that Asia, and Asian women, have always had for Western men.

An unusually comely young woman dressed in a simple blouse and jeans, her features fine and smooth, her hair falling gracefully over the front of her shoulder, appeared and sat next to Pete. The two of them greeted each other with the familiarity of old friends.

"She's just had twins," Pete told me when the young woman went to the back of the bar for a few minutes. "She's twenty-two years old."

"Who's the father of the twins?" I asked, wondering if it might be Pete himself.

"Her Thai boyfriend," Pete replied, clarifying the matter and deepening the mystery at the same time. If she had a Thai boyfriend and was the mother of baby twins, what was she doing resting her head on Pete's shoulder in the Madrid Bar? Of course the answer is that she needs money, and she earns it at the Madrid, and her boyfriend, to whom she is not married, doesn't mind. Pete doesn't mind either.

"Just one more question," I said. It was the sudden appearance of what seemed like a mistress—a *mia noi,* or "small wife," as mistresses are commonly known in Thailand—that prompted me to ask for this additional piece of information, which hadn't seemed all that relevant before. Until then I had assumed that Pete went to the Madrid on Fridays just to shoot the breeze with the boys. Now I realized there was more to it than that.

"What year were you born?" I asked.

"Nineteen thirty-four," he said, getting the point, "I'm seventy-three."

Pete keeps in shape. He's not one of those guys with spindly legs and a belly hanging over his belt like a sack of rice, though there are plenty of guys like that in Bangkok, looking old and pasty and sitting in bars and cafés with conspicuously younger Thai women. Pete is a trim man of medium height, his features round, his complexion florid, his hair thinning, a perfectly ordinary-looking person, but he hasn't led an ordinary life. He's seen war and death, risked his life, lived in Africa and Asia. He's a perfect example of a certain human type, a type of American whose first adventure abroad was often in Southeast Asia during the Vietnam War, a type who can't go home again.

Because, after all, what would he do back home at the age of seventy-three? Would he drink beer and watch *The Sopranos,* go to church socials with couples his age, join a bowling league, hang out at the local tavern, talk about his grandchildren and attend their birthday parties? He could do those things, of course, and many aging men who do them find them rewarding and fulfilling and have no desire to live in some foreign country far from home. They prefer it at home, with wives whom they have been married to for many decades, their love changing and deepening over time, more powerful and more indispensable to them than ever. Most men, including most Vietnam veterans, are not like Pete and his you-can't-go-home-again cohort, clinging to the adventure of their younger years even as their hair turns gray and their girth expands, drinking too much and spending their time in emotionally shallow, eleemosynary associations with girls one third their age. Many men, like many women, manage to age wisely, and devoting themselves to grandchildren, fishing, reading, and the VFW back home is just fine, thank you, exactly what one should want for one's dignified senior years. Not all men, moreover, would find Pete's twenty-two-year-old girlfriend more desirable than the women back home. Some men have a strong, visceral attraction to Asian women and are apt to wax rhapsodic about their charms, but this is not an attraction universally shared. And even among those who do share that attraction, many of them would be put off by the inherent sleaziness of the Bangkok money-for-sex market, its inescapable and juvenile hedonism.

But from Pete's standpoint, with his appealing girlfriend making affectionate gestures next to him, home seems like a tame, parochial, and constricting place. For these men, the swirl and excitement of a place like Bangkok are what has become indispensable.

The Madrid is on Patpong Road, perhaps the most famous street for sexual entertainment in the world. Outside, it was early evening and the preparations for the night were in full swing. The hawkers of knockoff Rolexes and knockoff Fendi wallets, silk pajamas, DVDs, paper lanterns, garlands of jasmine, Swiss Army knives, Thai-government raffle tickets with elephants printed on them, and many other things were setting up their long wooden tables, the metal poles they use to do so making a clangorous racket. The T-shirts on sale at the vendors' stands were testimony to Patpong's reputation, bearing captions like "Pizza Slut" and "No Money, No Honey." One of them, a takeoff on the Nike sports-shoe slogan, reads "Just Did It!" The stalls are covered with yellow canvas awnings to protect the sellers from the monsoon rains that often come in late afternoon, not to mention the droppings from the flocks of black mynah birds that sometimes appear without warning overhead. The city's famous bar girls—some of them fresh and pretty, others coarser, looking like hardened veterans—arrived on the backs of motorbike taxis. Some were already sitting in front of the go-go bars, waiting for the night to begin. Others—it's hard to tell which ones—were not girls at all but some of Thailand's renowned *katoey,* transsexuals. Boys and girls alike ate bowls of noodles with red pepper and fresh mint before their place of work opened for the night. Foreign men sat at open-air bars drinking beer, making attempts at nonchalance as they surveyed the scene before them.

Patpong Road has become a bit *dépassé*, outmoded, in recent years. The cognoscenti, like Pete and his friends, go there for the Madrid, which has an old-fashioned authenticity to it, but it's mostly tourists who go to the go-go bars on the other side of the street or down the narrow neon-lit lane known as Patpong 2, parallel to it. Touts flash pictures of massage parlor girls covered with soap suds. They lead interested parties to a few especially tawdry establishments on Patpong's second level, where the bars specialize in sexual circus sideshows—girls blowing cigarette smoke from their vaginas, playing games with Ping-Pong balls and razor blades. But the Bangkok regulars avoid Patpong. They go elsewhere in Bangkok, to Soi Cowboy or Nana Plaza out on Sukhumvit Road, which are not exactly elegant and discreet, but they have a bit less hustle about them, and you can sit and watch without being constantly importuned for a drink.

It is a mostly ugly place, Patpong, a long strip of bars with names like Safari, Super Pussy, Thigh Bar, and King's Castle. There are cheap short-time hotels, snack bars, open-air beer counters and restaurants along with ordinary retail places—drugstores, money changers, travel agencies, tattoo parlors, two 7-Eleven convenience stores, one at each end of the street. A sign reads

Go-Go Girls
Hot Stuff
For Lovers

A banner advertising Chang drinking water hangs across the northern end of the street. Neon signs for Tiger beer glow in stained windows. Seedy and vulgar as it is, Patpong nonetheless suggests something gorgeous and exotic. There is the surrounding commotion of Bangkok, the roar of motorcycles and automobile traffic on nearby Silom Road, the trishaw drivers resting on their vehicles, the beggars waiting for soft-touch tourists, schoolgirls (shy looking, in sharp contrast to the bar girls) hurrying home in their black-and-white uniforms—though I've been told by people who claim to have seen it that there are rooms nearby where some of these schoolgirls change into adult clothing, work for a few hours in bars and massage parlors, then change back and go home.

The warm, humid, heavy air of July ruffles the leaves of the acacia trees on Silom Road. It's the early evening breeze that usually prefigures a downpour. Nearby, the food-stall entrepreneurs have laid out their offerings—fried squid or chicken on skewers, peanuts and diced lime wrapped in emerald green betel nut leaves, noodles in soup, slices of mango, chunks of pummelo, rambutan, mangosteen, passion fruit, and papaya, little bowls of coconut custard. There are smells in the air—red chili frying in vegetable oil, fish, mint leaves. This teeming, ragged night market has something primitive and phantasmagoric about it. It is a place where the disheveled and disorderly street life of Asia coexists in the same narrow lane with the gilded and mirrored emporiums of pleasure, as if they were holograms projected onto the same space without having anything to do with each other. Patpong is repellent and mesmerizing at the same time, decrepit and sequined, a street where you look past a one-legged beggar sitting on a corroded sidewalk and glimpse through half-opened doors nude girls dancing on mirrored stages, who beckon to you like sirens on the shore.

Back to Pete, who looked at me with his wise eyes as he got ready to leave.

"Do the arithmetic," he said. His gaze was steady and unembarrassed. He's made his choices and sees no reason to apologize for them. "She's fifty-one years younger than me," he said, nodding toward his girlfriend. He let that sink in. "Do you think I could have somebody like her in Pennsylvania?"

PETE IS ONE AMONG THOUSANDS of hearty and vigorous post-middle-aged men—many of them, like him, having experienced Thailand during the Vietnam War—who illustrate what might be called the latest phase in the long erotic adventure of the West in the East. They don't live in Thailand only to pursue Thai women, though they are all well indoctrinated in what might be called the Thai bar-girl culture, which they discuss with a kind of worldly good humor. They are there for the warm weather, the cheap accommodation, the beaches, the good food, the vividness of the colors of Thai life, and, very important, the companionship of other men who have shared their experiences, going back to their days in Vietnam. Some think life back home the essence of a sort of event deprivation; some simply feel they wouldn't fit in.

"If I retired to Kansas, who would I ever see?" asked another veteran, Jim Oden, who is head of the VFW for Thailand (with 961 members in all, as of 2007) and had a solid career working for Northwest Airlines after he'd left the service. I met Oden in the coffee shop of the Federal Hotel in Bangkok, along with a few other men whose first taste of Southeast Asia came during the Vietnam War. He's a dignified, avuncular, thoughtful solid-citizen sort of man, the kind you'd reflexively turn to in a pinch. With his former wife, he raised nine children, five of them adopted. "The most likely to succeed in my high school became a dentist," he said by way of illustrating the difference between here and there. It's not that he has contempt for dentists but that being a dentist seems tame. "It's a world about this big," Oden said, and he held his large hands close together to show the narrowness of the life he'd have as a retiree in the United States.

The consensus around the table—Pete and a few other Vietnam vets were also there—was that the Vietnam War was a sexual awakening for many young American men who came from the puritanical American heartland, where sex was an illicit pleasure, and discovered the guilt-free erotic openness of Southeast Asia—or at least the openness displayed by the women they encountered.

"There was sex in high school," Oden said of his hometown, which is in Kansas. "There was skinny-dipping. But it was in the dark. Girls didn't want you to see their bodies. But the Asian girls were proud of their bodies." Then, switching to the scene in Bangkok decades later, he continued. "The femininity of the Thais and the Vietnamese is completely different. Also, they don't care about the age difference. There's no disgrace here for a girl to be seen with an older guy. They feel that a lot of the young guys can't really take care of them."

Most of the men around the table at the Federal Hotel were married to Thai women, and some of them were on their second or third wives, the first of them Americans whom they'd married decades ago. And what they said is that for men like them, what is easy in Thailand—

finding willing, much-younger women—would be impossible back home. I met one former GI of substantial girth in Pattaya, the beach resort south of Bangkok where enough ex-GIs have settled to form a sizable local VFW post, which meets in the bar owned by the chapter president, Eric Larsen.

"I hit the L.A. airport," the man said of a trip to the United States he made some years ago. "I was going to see my kids. I ended up in a bar at the airport. There were these guys talking about lawn mowers, a new garage. Lawn mowers! 'Okay,' I said, 'get me the fuck out of here.'"

"Happiness," the man then said, "is enough money to go out three times a month with beautiful Thai girls."

They all agree that there's no place quite like Thailand. It is the country where the encounter of the sexual culture of Western Christendom with the harem culture of most of the rest of the world is most actively enacted in a present-day setting. It is also a place where the practices of the past have been most vulgarized, commercialized, and globalized. In the early nineteenth century, soldiers of the East India Company soon learned about the *lal bazaar* and what they could do there, but the *lal bazaar* was a local institution, its existence known in the home country, but in the way the Turkish harem was known— through rumor and written accounts and a certain degree of political debate about the alleged sexual immorality of the empire. Today, by contrast, all you have to do is go online, and, sitting in Boston or Berlin, you can see pictures of the women in the bars whom you might invite to a short-time hotel once you've arrived in Thailand. You can read the blogs of foreign men who maintain running accounts of developments within the sex trade—which bars are hot, where the prettiest girls are to be found, what the difference is between a hot-oil massage and a soapy massage, how to tell a lady boy (a transvestite) from a real girl, and how much you should expect to pay for each. There are dozens of online forums in which male travelers describe their sexual experiences and trade opinions about the advantages of this or that place, and many countries around the world are covered.

That, of course, is for the sex tourists, for whom Thailand is an erotic mecca, but men like those in Eric Larsen's bar and like Larsen himself, a Vietnam veteran and retired police detective from San Diego, are not tourists. They are all men of a certain honesty, trustworthiness, and solidity who could lead perfectly respectable lives back home if they chose to do so. But they choose Thailand instead.

"The vast majority of us are here for financial reasons," Larsen said one afternoon, seated at a table in the place he runs on a Pattaya side street. "You can live comfortably here for my house payments in San Diego alone. I couldn't afford to retire in San Diego."

The bar, Larsen said, started as a sort of hobby, and it was always a money loser until recently, when he decided to make available to his clients, mostly veterans like him, what most men in Pattaya are willing to pay for every once in a while.

"I hired three girls and fixed up some rooms upstairs, and business has picked up since then," he said. The first girl was a friend of his wife's, who is Thai. The others came through connections in the demi-monde of Thai bar girls, who are in Pattaya by the thousands. Larsen estimates that there are about eighty large go-go places with dozens of girls each and another four thousand small drinking bars, all of them with maybe ten hostesses for hire. "They live here, and I take care of them," he said of the women who service customers in his bar. "It's a very safe environment because I know everybody that they go with."

"And the men?" I asked. Are they all potential customers, the trim and muscular ones and the potbellied and slowed-down ones too, or do I overestimate the importance of the sexual dimension of life in Pattaya?

"They must be here for the girls," Larsen said, "because they wouldn't be living in Pattaya if it were only for the money, because they can live upcountry for much less than here."

A couple of other countries rival Thailand for the ease with which sex can be obtained—the Philippines and Cambodia, for example. In the Philippines, as in Thailand, the sexual heritage of the Indochina wars is strong and conspicuous. Many Americans, including many former GIs, now live in Angeles, near the former Clark Air Base, where the bars and clubs that once catered to American soldiers have stayed in business even though the base closed down in 1991. (The area it occupies is now a special economic zone administered by the Philippine government.) I have not been to Cambodia, but the accounts of others indicate that it is a place where the sex trade is even less regulated than in Thailand. And numerous press reports and investigations by nongovernmental organizations have focused on the Philippines and Cambodia as countries where abuse of underage boys and girls by local criminal gangs and Western pedophiles is widespread.

Angeles, which I have also never visited, reportedly has plenty of ordinary prostitution involving adult women and adult men, and the women are said to be eager, the prices cheap, and government regulation virtually nonexistent, though the Philippines, like Thailand, is a country where prostitution is formally banned by law. You can sign up with an online travel agency that will arrange an entire package tour in Angeles—airfare, hotel, and women included. "Recreational sex is the sport of choice," one Web site reassured would-be customers, according to a story in *Time*. "You can get loaded and laid regardless of your age, weight, physical appearance, interpersonal skills, wealth or social class." No risk, no disappointment, satisfaction guaranteed, and you needn't worry that a lack of charm, or physical appeal, or hygiene will harm your chances. The American or German or Japanese men who could sit all night in a singles bar back home and never get a nibble are guaranteed their choice of perfumed and nubile creatures in Angeles or on Patpong Road. At the time of the *Time* article, the sex-guide agencies were offering two weeks in Angeles for $1,700.

Publicity given to pedophile gangs in places like Angeles and Cambodia has reportedly led to some improvement in those countries—at least the risk of the prosecution of men traveling the world in search of sex with children has increased, and some such men are in prison in Vietnam, Cambodia, the Philippines, and Thailand. Still, there is plenty of trafficking in underage boys and girls, who end up imprisoned in brothels in Bangkok or Manila or elsewhere. Many of the customers of these children are local men. Still, this midnight side to the globalization of sex illustrates that Asia continues to offer Western men sexual possibilities that they would have far greater difficulty finding at home. But pedophilia has nothing to do with the culture of the harem. It is simply a product of extreme poverty, police corruption, political indifference, and the willingness of the organizers of the brothels and their customers to arrange for and pay for the sexual exploitation of children.

And that has nothing to do with the lives or activities of the thousands of American and other Western men who have settled in Thailand and make an effort to be responsible local citizens. The chapters of the Veterans of Foreign Wars—and there are several in Thailand, in Nakhon Ratchasima (Korat), Pattaya, Udon Thani, and Bangkok, places where American soldiers were stationed during the Vietnam War—all raise money for local causes, like school uniforms for kids who can't afford them or repairs to the local Buddhist temple. And the veterans take care of one another when they get sick and when they die. It's a community of like-minded men, in other words, though it would be a sentimental mistake to believe, as Larsen readily acknowledges, that sex of a sort that would be an impossible dream back home isn't a big reason for their choice of location.

"You'd be surprised at how quickly you can adapt to having women on call twenty-four hours a day seven days a week," Larsen said. Still, Larsen repeats a bit of lore from Thailand's homegrown harem culture that the smart Americans abide by: Thai men have informal rules governing relations with prostitutes, like never patronizing one in your own neighborhood and—most important—never falling in love with a prostitute. Men like Larsen have a certain worldly-wise, studiously unromantic vision of the relations between Western men and Thai women, who, they say, can act oh so sweetly even as they are cunningly employing an arsenal of tricks to separate the men, who really are oh so sweet, from their money. Many is the *farang*—the Thai word for "foreigner," which foreigners use to refer to themselves—who has fallen for a Thai woman only to find himself saddled with unexpected burdens—constant demands for money for his true love's family, followed by death threats if he stands firm and stops paying or tries to get away.

Bad things happen. I heard from a reliable source about one foreign man who paid so much money to his supposedly faithful bar-girl girlfriend that her real boyfriend (thirty years younger than the *farang*) quit his job and the two of them lived happily and contemptuously on the duped foreigner's largesse. And then there was the Belgian I met in Pattaya whose Thai wife was divorcing him, taking with her the five-bedroom house he had bought (because, by Thai law, it had to be in her name), along with a major part of his savings, which she had procured by stealing his bank card. "She wants everything!" he told me, shaking his head with incredulity at the greed of the woman who had seduced him with her seeming fragility and vulnerability. It's no wonder, as noted earlier, that the bar-girl slang for a foreign man translates as "walking ATM." The Belgian man estimated his loss at 5 million baht, or nearly $170,000.

Even aside from these dangers, many men, perhaps even most men, would find a Pattaya go-go bar more repellent than seductive. "It gets old pretty fast," one longtime Bangkok resident, happily married for thirty years to a local woman, said of the bar scene, and no doubt it gets old quickly for many men. My own feeling in visiting a few bars was a mixture of fascination, arousal, and disgust. To be confronted by the sight of naked girls dancing on a raised platform is inevitably to feel tempted. Visiting a go-go bar with a few American veterans in Pattaya in 2007, one former marine exclaimed, as though he couldn't quite believe his good fortune, "You can have any of these girls, any one you want!"

And, indeed, every once in a while a truly stunning creature materializes before you, one who seems distinct from the others, a bit classier, more tasteful, more refined, sweeter, and when that happens (or even if the woman in question might be less truly stunning in the remorseless light of morning than she was in the torrid glow of night), it is almost impossible not to feel the pull of fantasy. "All of a sudden," John Burdett wrote in his novel *Bangkok 8,* "the prospect of going back to the hotel alone is more appalling—and somehow more immoral, a crime against life, even—than congress with a prostitute." And yet for the most part, a Thai go-go bar is a pretty tawdry place, certainly an unlikely venue for the forging of deep ties with a member of the opposite sex.

There are two kinds of men, a friend told me long ago, the kind who does the same thing with one hundred different women, and the kind who does one hundred different things with one woman, and go-go bars are decidedly for the former type. The middle-aged men who repudiate middle-aged women back home and choose Thailand to provide them with private pleasures can enjoy sex on demand, and for many of them that's more than enough. It's as Woody Allen famously said about sex without love—it's a meaningless experience but pretty damn good as meaningless experiences go. Others would find life with a bar girl exceedingly thin, however. As we will see, there are exceptions, but few bar girls would provide comfort or succor or form deep bonds or be a companion, a soul mate with whom to enjoy that slow and steady accumulation of experience that makes for a shared identity and true intimacy—in short, few would be the worthy, self-possessed, intellectually stimulating, and spiritually sensitive woman that men find in a loving companion. And so the wise men keep their expectations under control.

"If you want perfect breathtaking beauty, you can find it here," Larsen said. "But you really don't want to get involved any more than forty-five minutes upstairs."

ONE NIGHT IN BANGKOK IN 2007, I went with Dean Barrett, another long-term Bangkok resident and the author of several novels and other books set in Asia, to a place called AngelWitch, a bar in Nana Plaza, a three-tiered sexual-entertainment emporium that is one of several places foreigners go to find Thai girls (or boys who look like girls). The women dance on an elevated platform, holding on to floor-to-ceiling metal poles and standing on disks that rotate, so that the customers get a full view of each one in turn.

Most of them are slender; many are very pretty. Most men tend to like the women in the places where they find them, and the greater availability of sexual possibilities in the East than in the West has, in most cases, little to do with the physical attributes, desirable as they may be, of Asian women. But there are certainly plenty of men powerfully drawn to the slim, small-boned, black-haired women of Asia, more plumlike than melonlike of breast, spare rather than full of buttocks and hips, and for those men some of the women onstage at AngelWitch do come close to Larsen's notion of breathtaking beauty. Indeed, the relative smallness of many Asians, and the relative thinness of their facial and body hair, is what makes Thailand's transsexuals so difficult, on casual inspection, to distinguish from women, and so desirable to men captivated by what is often called the third sex.

Each of the onstage performers at AngelWitch has a number pinned to her very scanty uniform, and any customer can invite one of them to sit next to him. He'll then be obligated to buy her a little glass of what, during the Vietnam War, used to be called Saigon tea. Or he might be disappointed to learn that the one he wants has already been asked for by somebody else, in which case he might repeat a standard bit of earthy bar-girl lore—namely, you never lose your girlfriend in Thailand; you just have to wait your turn in line. If she does sit down next to the customer, she will seem very happy to have been asked for. After a short time, she will nestle up against the man who has chosen her, hold his hand in one of hers, rest her other hand on his thigh, allow the perfume on her neck to penetrate his sense of smell, and discreetly wait for him to offer to pay what is called the bar fine and take her out, the bar fine being a sum—about $20 at AngelWitch in 2007—to compensate the bar for the loss of her services for the one or two hours she will be gone.

The night I was there, the bar was crowded with men sitting on the bleacher-like seats that surround the stage, some of them well into middle age, paunchy and balding, though there were also younger men, husky and muscular, with close-cropped hair. I met Dave the Rave, a former social worker and martial arts competitor from England who manages AngelWitch for its owner, who, I was told, is German (though he would, under Thai law, have to have a local partner). Dave is a cornucopia of information about the bar-girl culture and the men who are drawn to it, a connoisseur of its charms and, like Larsen and Barrett, an expert on its hazards.

He told me that a popular bar girl can make well over 100,000 Thai baht a month, which would be about $3,000, a substantial salary in Thailand. At AngelWitch, Dave the Rave said, the girls receive a salary of 9,000 baht a month, about $300. They get a commission every time a customer buys them a drink. They get tips. And they make $50 to $70 every time a customer pays their bar fine and they provide him with sex. Some bar girls on a busy evening might be bar-fined two or three or even more times in a single night.

The scene is unavoidably mesmerizing. Like the Darling Massage Parlor, it is eerily reminiscent of that Thomas Rowlandson drawing alluded to earlier, of an aroused sultan looking at two tiers of naked women, each of them striving to get his attention. But AngelWitch is an improvement on Rowlandson's harem because the truth is that Rowlandson's women, aside from looking alike, are not very pretty. Naked, blatant, and a bit bovine as they are, there is little truly seductive about them. The Thai bar girls, however, are all young, and some of them are very seductive. I noted that their pose, in contrast to that of Rowlandson's women, is one of seeming indifference to the men looking at them. They don't make eye contact. There is no obvious come-hither. The pose is one of aloofness and unavailability struck by a young woman, who, by definition, is entirely available, but the effect is of a certain hard-to-get-ness. The women have silky hair, almond eyes, and light brown skin. I understand, in describing them so rhapsodically, that I seem to be losing sight of their situation in life, that these young women are prostitutes and that in the view that prevails in the West, they are being both humiliated and exploited, forced by their poverty to expose themselves as if they were dogs in a kennel and to have sex with any man who asks for her, no matter how unappealing he may be.

We'll return to an assessment of that view of things later, but for now let's dispense with judgment, except perhaps to note that that very judgment is one of the things that has always distinguished the Christian sin-and-guilt culture of the West from the harem culture of the East. The point here is this: what was for Rowlandson an ambiguous sort of satire on male dreams about the East has become, in places like Thailand, a nonsatirical, hypnotizing reality. As the long historic encounter between East and West is entering its current phase, it is in places like AngelWitch that the West's age-old dream of the East is coming true.

"In New York, I'd crawl over glass for any one of these girls," Barrett said to me over the beat of "Born to Be Wild," which was coming through AngelWitch's loudspeakers. "Here you have the luxury of holding out for your definition of perfection."

But Dave the Rave didn't skip the dangers. "You have to have some focus in your life when you live in Thailand," he said. We were sitting on one of the banquettes at AngelWitch, while in front of us about fifteen of the club's young women moved their bodies sinuously on the stage, the lights glowing and the music throbbing in my ears. All of that distracted me from my note-taking, though Dave hardly seemed to notice. He enumerated the special challenge that foreign men face to their well-being in Thailand. It's not the risks of heart disease or lung cancer or gastric discomfort from all that spicy Thai food. Nor is it the risk of sexually transmitted diseases, especially AIDS, because in Thailand these days the motto of most bar girls is "no condom, no sex." The danger is a kind of male erotomania, a sexual addiction leading to many hours night after night at bars like AngelWitch in a state of near-complete dissolution.

"It's easy to go crazy here," Dave said. "There are guys who never see daylight. You have to have something—playing golf, studying the Thai language, writing—to give you focus. I do a Web site" (although a check of his site a year or so after my visit with him indicates that he had added very little to it).

Dave has stories about men who go home to Munich or London and send monthly remittances, $100 perhaps, or more, to the bar girl they have fallen for in Bangkok in an effort to win her genuine affection. "They do that because they think in their minds that the girl will be more appreciative of him," he said.

Some girls, in addition to getting their salaries, commissions, and payments from customers, receive stipends from several men at the same time, Dave said, and when one of those men comes to Bangkok for a week or two of vacation, she spends the time with him—and has to hope that only one of her usually distant benefactors shows up at a time. It's like participating in a time-share for a ski chalet or beach house. The women can be seen at Internet cafés on Sukhumvit Road in Bangkok e-mailing their benefactors in an effort to keep the money rolling in, saying to each of them how much she misses him and wishes he would come to Bangkok because she has a lot of problems and needs somebody to take care of her.

"The men are sentimental," another long-term resident of Bangkok told me. "The women are running a business."

The Western men fall for these women. They want to be loved by them, or, seized by a sort of sexually driven missionary impulse, they want to save them from the lives that penury has driven them to.

"Americans are like that," Barrett added. "It's in the culture."

They think of that girl named Nana, or Noi, or Am when they have gone back home to their lonely apartments or to their unexciting wives of many decades, and the Thai women they meet at places like Angel-Witch are very good at seeming to have genuine affection for them. They behave so sweetly that it is impossible not to entertain the illusion—or could it actually be the reality?—that these poor young women with younger sisters and brothers to put through college, parents with medical bills to be taken care of, houses to be fixed, and motorbikes to be bought really care about them.

"My advice to guys is to pay as they play," Dave the Rave told me. "I ask them, 'What do you think you have in common with one of these girls? She's half your age, maybe one third your age; she comes from a different culture and speaks a different language. What do you have in common except she loves money and you love sex?' "

THERE IS EVIDENCE from the records left by European traders of yesteryear that Thailand has, for at least four hundred years, offered a warm sexual welcome to visiting men. "They are always approaching the men and urging them to go with them into their houses and have sex with them," one such merchant, Christoph Carl Fernberger von Egenberg, wrote of the women in the port of Ayutthaya, which he visited in 1624. Von Egenberg, whose diary was discovered in Austria in 1972, said that the Siamese women were "excessively lewd." (One wonders what is the moral distinction between lewd and excessively lewd.) Another Dutch merchant, Jacob van Neck, who visited Thailand (then Siam) in the early 1600s, described a system of temporary marriage similar to what existed in Nagasaki, by which foreign traders could enjoy the company of one of the country's supposedly lewd women for a specified length of time. "Once they agree about the money (which does not amount to much for so great a convenience), she comes to his house, and serves him by day as his maidservant and by night as his wedded wife," van Neck wrote.

It is remarkable in a way how little has changed in this sense, the visitors of the seventeenth century being not all that different from the visitors of the twenty-first. What has changed is the scale and the appearance of it, not the content. The two periods are similar in another way as well: the behavior of seventeenth-century prostitutes was no more a clue to the behavior of Siamese women in general than the behavior of twenty-first-century prostitutes is to that of all Thai women today. For von Egenberg to say that Thai women were "lewd," rather than to confine his remarks to portside prostitutes, was no doubt inaccurate. If the Siamese then were anything like the Thais now, they were notably prudish in matters of sex, although in Thailand then as now the culture of the harem prevailed. Certainly there is very little in the way of open displays of affection in Thailand now. The only people you see holding hands on the street are foreigners and their hired girl-friends. "Nice" Thai boys and girls, men and women, don't do that. Sex outside marriage for men is not seen as sinful in Thailand, as it is, at least formally, in the mostly Christian West, and there has never been much of an effort by the political authorities—or much pressure on them from the public—to "do something about" the local sex trade. But like other countries with harem cultures, Thailand is a male-dominated society, in which most women, and especially most young, unmarried women, are kept under tight control and supervision.

Just how male dominated is evident in the strict rules that Thai tradition imposed on women. "The woman sleeps on the left of the husband, the left being the lesser rank," William Klausner, an anthropologist who has lived in Thailand and has studied it since the 1950s, said in an interview in Bangkok in 2007. "The husband has to have eaten three mouthfuls before the woman can eat. The wife at year's end brings candles and joss sticks and the like and begs forgiveness of her husband for her mistakes. The husband doesn't beg forgiveness of the wife. Of course, these practices are fading, hardly practiced, but they were part of the Thai tradition." And even if they aren't expected anymore to beg forgiveness of their husbands, modern Thai women are nonetheless still expected to be obedient to their parents, modest in appearance, virgins until marriage, and faithful to their husband. For husbands, on the other hand, it is and always has been a different story.

What was offered to foreign men in the seventeenth century and what is offered to them today is a variation—adapted, like Chinese food in the American Midwest, to Western tastes—of what Thai men have always seen as their due, as long as nobody is getting his due with their daughter. The East, and especially Southeast Asia, has always offered sexual hospitality, the giving of women as an element of the interchange with a visitor. On Taiwan in the 1970s, as foreign trade and foreign investment were picking up steam, sexual hospitality was a standard element in the treatment of foreign business partners. In the early 1970s, when I was a Chinese-language student in Taipei, I knew a man, fresh out of the Peace Corps, who had a job as the Taiwan representative of a company that imported plastic Christmas trees to the United States. He frequently had business dinners with factory owners who had, or wanted to have, contracts to manufacture the trees. A standard event was for the dinner to be served by nude or nearly nude waitresses, and, when the meal was over, for the foreign guest to be offered his choice of waitress, or maybe two waitresses, and to retire to a private room for a dessert of sorts.

On Taiwan, it was a hardheaded calculation that led the authorities not to enforce the laws against prostitution. They wanted foreign investment, and one way to get it was to give the investors, mostly men, the sort of good time they couldn't have at home. In China in the mid-1980s, when economic reforms had led, as in Taiwan a decade earlier, to large-scale foreign investment, local officials debated whether to relax the country's hitherto strict rules against prostitution, with officials in some localities deciding that enforcing the ban on the sex trade put them at a competitive disadvantage, since investors, mostly men, would go to the places where they could have girls. Since then, while prostitution remains illegal in China, as I said earlier, almost anyone staying in almost any hotel can find without much difficulty a woman for the night.

What Thailand offers the visiting man is a sort of self-service sexual hospitality. The Thais, of course, didn't plan things that way. Indeed, there is a certain almost palpable national embarrassment that the country has become the world's sex-tourism capital, but it happened organically, as it were, not in accordance with some master design. The country, as is well-known, was a popular destination for soldiers on R&R during the Vietnam War, and in the 1960s and early 1970s, when thousands of American soldiers were stationed in Thailand itself, the sex trade simply expanded to accommodate their demand. Every one of the several towns in Thailand where U.S. air bases were situated had its strips of bars and short-time hotels. Strikingly, those towns still have them. They cater to tourists and other male travelers and to older Europeans and Americans who have come, often in retirement, to live in northeast Thailand, where they have married local women. Many of these men, as we will see, live in small villages outside the major towns, but some of them take the occasional trip to Udon Thani or Nakhon Ratchasima or Khon Kaen for a bit of easily available extramarital sex.

It's so easy in Thailand, and it's difficult to resist. "Great food, drinks, pool, girls" is the way one restaurant in Udon Thani advertised its offerings when I visited the town in 2007. The ad was printed on the official tourist map distributed by the town's hotels.

Bangkok and Pattaya were the main R&R destinations in Thailand. In Bangkok, the GIs, who didn't have much money, were concentrated on a newly developed street called New Petchburi Road, where everything was at hand, hotel rooms for $5 a night, bars, massage parlors, and restaurants. Thousands of GIs could descend on Bangkok for their seven days of respite from the war in Vietnam, and the rest of Bangkok would hardly know they were there.

Slowly in the late 1960s and early 1970s, it was Patpong Road, named for Udom Patpong, a British- and American-educated son of a rice merchant from China, that became the foreigners' choice destination—not the GIs but the more affluent civilian contractors, businessmen, CIA agents, Air America pilots, and journalists, many of whom had been stationed in Thailand during the Vietnam War. Udom's father, Poon Pat, had bought the land that the street now runs through, though at the time it was still a rural area of rice and vegetable farms. In the early 1930s, the Hongkong and Shanghai Banking Corporation (HSBC) built its headquarters there. As late as the early 1960s, photographs show it as a street more or less like any other in Bangkok, a stretch of 250 yards or so connecting two larger avenues, Silom (which means "Windmill," because there were Dutch-style windmills to irrigate the agricultural fields) and Suriwongse. It consisted mostly of two-story wooden frame buildings, among which were a few quiet and discreet drinking places with unpaid waitresses known as ghosts—officially, they didn't exist.

But in 1969, Rick Menard, an American helicopter mechanic who had seen duty in Vietnam, opened a place called the Grand Prix, and he had the brilliant idea of having young women dance on a stage above the bar—the first of the so-called go-go establishments of Patpong Road. The idea was actually an imitation of a fad that had recently started in San Francisco's North Beach, where Carol Doda, she of the famous silicone-enhanced breasts, was achieving renown for topless dancing, which was seen as extremely daring in its time. The Thai women did not dance topless; they wore bikinis—another American import and emblem of the sexual liberation of the 1960s. More go-go bars opened, and so did massage parlors, short-time places, and sex-show clubs, all lightly supervised by the Thai police. An almost identical development took place in Pattaya, which at the time was a quiet fishing village with a white-sand crescent beach two hours' drive from Bangkok on the Gulf of Thailand. Both places were reflections of the image of Tu Do Street in Saigon. The Vietnam War ended, but both Patpong Road and Pattaya stayed in business, offering their attractions to the international sex-tourism trade and the ever-growing resident foreign male community. And that's the way it is now. In Pattaya, the entertainment zone is to be found mostly on a portion of boardwalk along the beach and a maze of nearby streets, where car traffic is barred at night. It is a stunning carnival, phantasmagoric, a gorgeous, garish, heavily populated circus worthy of a painting by a modern-day Hieronymus Bosch—a garden of earthly pleasures, indeed. In Bangkok, a place like Nana Plaza is similarly fabulous, lubricious, and grotesque, a three-tiered pleasure dome, an Oriental bazaar of what the GIs used to call I&I—intercourse and inebriation.

And intercourse and inebriation, with a certain priority given to the former (or "gin and sin") are as applicable as ever to Pattaya and such places in Southeast Asia where the tradition of sexual adventuring continues to be followed by the descendants of eighteenth- and nineteenth-century colonialists. But there are all kinds of patrons of Thailand's retail sex industry. Some, like the guys sending monthly stipends to the women of AngelWitch, are seeking to live out a fantasy of perfect bliss; others, like the men at Eric Larsen's bar in Pattaya, are living a permanent alternative to what they see as the deadening routine of home. But in recent years, Thailand has offered an interesting variation on these themes. It's now a destination for a sort of European bohemian for whom the garishness of Pattaya would be anathema and whose dream is not to have thrice-monthly paid-for trysts with Thai bar girls but something permanent instead, a late-in-life chance for contentment with another person, after earlier, more conventional chances have failed. There's a touch of Kipling in this, evoked in the line in the poem "Mandalay" about "a neater, sweeter maiden in a cleaner, greener land." In fact, for men today who have settled in small Thai villages, living in a big house with a local wife, Kipling's line may be too romantic, since these are realistic persons who pride themselves on being devoid of illusions. Still, for them, too, living out in the sticks along the banks of the Mekong, the East offers, not a fantasy but a reality, with the sweeter maiden included, along with a place of quiet exoticism where the pressure is off and they can feel free.

The Yearning of the Wanderer's Heart

BAN CAO IS AN ORDINARY VILLAGE in the northeast region of Thailand known as Issan. It is a flat area with a population of 21 million people lying between the Mekong River to the north and east, on the other side of which is Laos and, to the south, Cambodia. The broad main road runs north from the district capital of Udon Thani, where one of the seven Vietnam War–era U.S. military bases was situated, to Nong Khai, diagonally across the Mekong from Vientiane, the capital of Laos.

On the main road are car dealers, nurseries, open-air restaurants, gas stations, and emporiums selling the small ornate shrines that the Thais use to shelter the house spirits. Rice is grown in the paddy fields here. But Issan is Thailand's poorest region, and that is why one of the main crops is the young women who populate the sex-entertainment districts of Bangkok and Pattaya and other places in Thailand. In recent years, many foreign men, thousands of them, in fact, have come to live here, generally bringing women they met in the big cities back to their home villages, where they have married them and now live with them, presumably till death do them part.

In Ban Cao alone, there are thirty Thai-foreign couples. "Normally in the northeast when you see a big house, you know that this house belongs to a foreigner who has married a Thai woman," Adul Khankeaw, Ban Cao's headman, explained to me. We talked at an out-door table at the Ban Cao post office, alongside the main paved road through town. Across the street was the Buddhist temple, which dou-bled as an elementary school. Most of the houses along the road were simple shacks with rusting corrugated-iron roofs sitting among clumps of banana trees and palms. Here and there water buffalo swung their heads in that mazy motion of theirs. Portraits of the king and queen in ceremonial dress decorated the post office. A few chickens poked around in the dirt of a small vegetable garden, in the middle of which was a small shrine to the house spirits. Khankeaw wore blue shorts, a printed shirt, plastic flip-flops, and a heavy gold pendant around his neck.

It worked this way, he said. A local woman who was divorced from her Thai husband went to work in Pattaya. There she met a German man who married her, built her a big house in the village (it loomed up, with porticoes, a fancy wrought-iron gate, and sloped orange-tiled roof, just a few steps from the post office) and provided nicely for her family. When other women saw how well she lived, they decided they also wanted to marry foreign men, and the wife of the German introduced some of them to friends of her husband's. But there weren't enough friends to go around, so other women went to Bangkok or Pattaya, and some of them found husbands there.

A study conducted by the Thai National Economic and Social Development Board found that 15 percent of all marriages in the province of Udon Thani are between Thai women and foreign men, with Germans, Austrians, and Swiss most numerous among the latter. In all, there were more than fifteen thousand Thai-foreign couples as of 2004. In one village in Roi Et Province with a total of two hundred families, two hundred local women have married foreign men, Thai newspapers have reported. Many, perhaps most, of the couples live in Europe at first, or at least the husband does, leaving the wife behind and joining her on vacations until he retires and moves to Thailand for good.

It's not a major global demographic phenomenon, this migration of European men who have found mates in northeast Thailand, though it is certainly, at first glance, a strange phenomenon. Would it be possible to find men and women more different in age, culture, language, religion, and educational background than these German, Swiss, French, English, and American men and their wives in Issan? But the very strangeness of the trend is what gives it its value as an illustration of the broader historical phenomenon by which Western men have gone to the East to find fulfillment. From the man's standpoint, clearly, some-

thing is very appealing in these Thai women, and vice versa. That study
by the Development Board found that 80 percent of the Thai women
had once been married to Thai men and were now divorced from
them. It also found many of the women saying that Western men are
"better" than Thai men—more faithful, more reliable, less prone to
gambling, whoring, and drinking (though, paradoxically, not a few of
the Western men were "whoring" when they met their Issan wives).
What the study called "the bad habits of Thai men" were among the
three main reasons cited by *mia farang,* wives of foreigners, for having
married Western men in the first place. One Thai newspaper quoted a
woman married to a German to the effect that not all Thai men are
bad, but a lot of them are. "Let's just say that without an order from
God, I would not marry a Thai man," she said.

As for the men, one letter writer to *The Nation,* an English-language
Thai newspaper that carried a series on the *mia farang,* called them "the
woe-begotten dregs of Western society, with fetishes for Asian women,"
who themselves are victims of the "blind worship of anything white/
Western." In fact, no studies seem to have been done on the foreign
men, so it is difficult to generalize about their circumstances and the
extent to which they are woe-begotten. My own tiny sample of them,
taken during my visit to Ban Cao in 2007, indicated nothing of the
kind. They seemed to be men who had had reasonable, sometimes very
successful careers, though, by definition, not very successful relationships with Western women. Like their Thai wives, many of them had
been in marriages that fell apart. It's not hard to find Western men in
Thailand who describe European women as emasculating, competitive, egotistic, mannish, and afflicted with what they regard as the ideological rot of feminism, though I interviewed four men married to
Thai women in Issan, and none of them gave voice to those views. But,
yes, they did find, as a Frenchman named Jean-Claude put it, that Thai
women have a rare gentleness about them; they are less demanding,
more willing to serve a traditional woman's role. Needless to say, there
are no known cases where a Western woman, perhaps escaping a bad
marriage with a coarse, selfish, and abusive Western husband, has come
to Issan to marry a Thai farmer. It is so difficult to imagine, say, a sixty-
year-old female German lawyer married to a Thai man half her age
with a grade-school education that it seems almost ridiculous to ask

why. The fact is that it has always been, and still is, a lot better to be a man in Asia than a woman.

This does not mean that there is never trouble for the Western men who seek happiness in Issan. Given the unabashedly pecuniary arrangement that is at the bottom of the Thai-foreign relationships, there is bound to be tragedy and deceit. One Austrian resident of Ban Cao, who gave his name as Christoph Killy, told the story of a compatriot, nearly eighty years old, who lost the house he built and a good deal of his savings to his much younger Thai wife. Houses and land by law have to be owned by Thais, and so there have been cases, like that of the Belgian I met in Pattaya, in which Thai wives have simply expropriated the property built for them by their foreign husbands and even have had their much-younger Thai boyfriends move in with them. That was the case with the luckless eighty-year-old Austrian.

"I told him, 'Look in the mirror,' " Killy told me. We were sitting in Killy's house, one of the large ones in Ban Cao, which he shares with his wife, whom we will call Lit. "I said, 'Do you really think this young Thai girl is in love with you?' " The capacity of men for self-delusion is infinite, Killy observed. "A Thai lady will never take a *farang* man for love," he said. "They only take him because they think he is rich. I can put it in one sentence. If you have a *farang,* you are out of the shit. Because we are different, we *farang* men, from the Thais. They think we are all stupid. She thinks I am stupid," he said, and he pointed to Lit.

"Yes, he is stupid," she said and smiled. She is petite, with a delicate oval face and closely cropped hair.

"*Farang* men go straight in Thailand," Killy continued, "but in Thailand, you have to go crooked," and he made a wavy motion with his hand. "The *farang* are stupid because they believe so much in love," he continued. "So she makes eyes and she says 'I love you,' and he believes her. The other thing is that he takes pity on her. She says, 'I have two babies. I have a sick mother,' and we stupid *farang* feel we have to protect someone who is weak. I don't know why. It comes from our religion.

"I've seen terrible things here," Killy said. "I've seen some women who are married to a Thai husband and they introduce him to the *farang* as her brother. So they sit together, and they eat together, and the *farang* spends money. He buys the 'brother' a motorbike, but he isn't a brother."

As for the elderly Austrian, he took mysteriously ill one day after eating, went back to Austria for medical treatment, and has never returned to Ban Cao. His total financial loss, according to Killy, was about 3 million baht, or a bit less than $300,000. In any case, according to Killy, a retired international lawyer who specialized in the oil business, the foolish Austrian has no legal claim on the house or the money he gave to his wife.

KILLY HIMSELF TURNED OUT to be a rather remarkable figure, an eccentric original. During World War II, he and his family had left their native Vienna and gone to live with relatives in Katowice, then part of German Silesia, now in southern Poland. When the Soviets liberated the area, the whole family was taken to a displaced persons camp, where they remained for two years. They were then sent to East Germany and spent another year in a camp near Dresden before they were finally repatriated. Killy remembered in particular a moment in the camps when newly arrived German internees were brought to a disinfecting room. They all assumed that it was a gas chamber built to look like a shower and that they were about to be killed—proof to Killy that despite their denials, the Germans knew about the gas chambers and what had been done to the Jews during the war.

Killy almost wept as he told this story. He stared out the window and into the distance to regain his composure. Then he took me into his office and played Yiddish songs that he had collected online, downloading them onto his computer. "There is a deep sadness in this song," he said of one of them.

Killy is a tall, craggily handsome man with graying hair, a slightly concave face, and silver-framed glasses that almost perfectly match his hair. On the day I met him, he wore a checked short-sleeved shirt, shorts, and sandals. He's a tough, gangly bird, a wiry seventy-three years old. After his experience of internment, he went to school in Vienna and eventually began his career doing legal work for oil companies in Nigeria and the Middle East. He was married, but the marriage soured. He had women all over the world. He met Lit in Vienna. She had a life story just as eventful as his. She was married at seventeen to a young Thai man who slept in his mother's room and came into Lit's room only to have sex with her. She had a child with her husband but left him for another man, a Chinese businessman, with whom she also had a child.

"I fought with him all the time," she said of her Chinese partner. Wanting to leave him, she agreed to take a job in a shoe factory on Phangnga Island in the south. Perhaps Lit believed that it really was a shoe factory and was genuinely surprised to learn that it was a brothel servicing Thai offshore tin-mine workers. She said that every woman was forced to read a statement into a tape recorder saying that she was working at the brothel of her own free will. She was, to put the correct name on her condition, a slave. She stayed for a year, and then, because the brothel owners wanted constant turnover, she was kicked out. She met a policeman with one leg and had a baby with him but left him when she found out that he was already married. She went to Phuket, a resort island in the Andaman Sea, where she knew somebody who ran a bar, and that's where she met her first Austrian husband.

He was a sex tourist. He fell for Lit and took her back to Vienna, thinking, it would seem from the story Lit told, that she would be docile and controllable. When she turned out to want to do things on her own—one of them was to visit the casino in Vienna—he beat her. When Killy met her, she had a broken nose and a bruised face. He bought her a ticket to Thailand, but she'd had a baby—the fourth she'd had, each with a different man—with her Austrian husband, so Killy got her a return ticket so that she could come back and look after her baby in Vienna. Eventually, however, that baby stayed with her father in Vienna, and Killy and Lit went to live in Ban Cao. That was in 1996, eleven years before I met them.

It's hard to tell in a single visit of an afternoon, but there seemed to be an honesty about Killy and Lit and their feelings for each other that made them solid and genuine. For Lit, Killy was a way out, and she liked him for that. "I'll leave her the house and some money," he said, "so she'll be a rich woman. Every Thai village girl wants to be a rich woman."

But what of Killy himself? Why did a man like that, an international lawyer, a prominent and successful citizen, end up in a house in the sad tropics, in Ban Cao, Thailand? He reminded me of a scene described by the explorer Richard Burton. In the region of Seroda near the west coast of India in 1845, he came across the tomb of a certain Major G, a man well-known to Burton, who had left England at an early age and had made India, where he fell in love with a dancing girl, his home and his passion. Major G, Burton said, "sold out of his regiment, . . . bought a house at Seroda, married his enchantress, and settled there for the remainder of his years." His tomb was just a pile of masonry marking the spot where his ashes had been deposited, and seeing it, Burton remarked: "It is always a melancholy spectacle, the last resting-place of a fellow-countryman in some remote nook of a foreign land, far from the dust of his forefathers—in a grave prepared by strangers, around which no mourners ever stood, and over which no friendly hand raised a tribute to the memory of the lamented dead. The wanderer's heart yearns at the sight."

Killy and most of the other European men who live in Ban Cao are different from Burton's Major G in that they came not in youth but in advanced middle age, though they did marry their enchantresses and they had wanderer's hearts. For Killy, the why is deeper than for many others because he feels endangered in Ban Cao. He has had run-ins with one of his brothers-in-law, whom he doesn't trust. And a while before I met him, the policeman with one leg had turned up and demanded that Killy give him a laptop computer for the daughter, now a teenager, he'd had with Lit. Everybody wants to cash in on the wealthy foreigners in their midst. Killy refused because, as he explained it, he didn't like the policeman's lack of manners. A few days later, somebody broke into the house and stole a computer and a video camera.

Since then Killy has had new locks put on the doors, but he knows that he is conspicuously rich and others in Ban Cao are poor and that he might be an inviting target. Thailand has one of the highest murder rates in the world. Killy has written a letter, put it in a sealed envelope, and left copies of it in several places, describing his run-ins with the one-legged policeman and his brother-in-law, so in case he is murdered, the police will know whom to question. And he swears that he will fight if he is attacked, and if he dies, so be it. Better to go down fighting than to die in a hospital with some machine attached to your heart.

"I don't believe in love," he said, "but love can have many faces. I never met a person like her," he said of Lit. "It's not for sex. I've had so many women over the years.

"When I first met her, I felt pity for her," he said. He associated her with the Jewish victims of Nazism for whom he has deep feelings. He couldn't save a Jew, but he could save Lit. And then, "the more I got to know her, the more I had a very great respect for her. She is an optimist. She sees something good in the most dismal situation. I feel she is a great person." In other words, he loves her.

Jean-Claude, when I asked him what was special about Thai women, repeated the standard Western male line: "They have a gentleness that you don't find elsewhere." Killy, in fact, doesn't attach particular importance to the alleged difference between Asian women and their Western counterparts. Both he and Jean-Claude, it must be remembered, have the companionship of women who are thirty years younger than they are, frankly prettier and more bewitching than any woman likely to accompany them in their old age back home, and where but in Asia would men of seventy or so, not especially glamorous and not extremely rich by Western standards, find women that much younger who are, as Jean-Claude said, "nice." Another Thai wife I spoke to, married to the German who built the big, showy house near the post office, put it simply and bluntly:

"Thai women are better than German women. They take care of their husbands before they take care of themselves. The butter is on the toast when they wake up. Coffee is on the table. Their clothes are hanging neatly in the closet. Their shoes are ready outside the door. Thai women tell their husbands not to drink too much. They're better at saving money, not like German women who are always out shopping. German women are also very argumentative, but Thai women try not to make their husbands upset. They try never to say anything that will hurt the feelings of their husbands. This is the difference."

These are stereotypes, of course, and they clash with Killy's portrayal of many Thai women as scheming and deceitful. For him, living in Thailand is to realize a sort of ultimate fantasy of escape.

"Marriage is good to raise children, but afterwards you are in handcuffs, so I left everything behind, two children and my wife in Europe," he said.

"In Vienna," he continued after a pause, "you have so many obligations, so much that you have to do, and so many things that you're not allowed to do. Here I have freedom. Here I have no obligations."

CHAPTER THIRTEEN

Judgments

THE STANDARD, MORALLY CORRECT VIEW of the Western exploitation of the East for sexual purposes is that it was mostly a form of prostitution and prostitution is always unjust and degrading. Concubines, *mia noi, xiao-nai, bibis, mi-tay,* Okichis of the modern era—whatever you want to call them and in whatever language—are unequal. For Western men to take advantage of what I have called the harem culture made them complicit in the treatment of women as commodities in an exchange in which the women were and are required to perform the very private and intimate act that is most shrouded in mystery and meaning, the act of sex. So, yes, from the morally correct point of view, the sexual exploitation of local women is a blot on the record, especially in those cases, past and present, where the women involved weren't and aren't free agents but have been forced by pimps, traffickers, or even governments into what amounts to sexual slavery.

But is it really so easy to make a sweeping judgment, so abstract, divorced from concrete reality? There is the world that lives up to a moral ideal and there is the world in which men and women succumb to their natures and their circumstances. For Gustave Flaubert and Richard Burton, the pursuit of pleasure in the Orient was the very pungency of the experience of traveling there; it was a savoring of the messy splendor of desire. They used no force; they abused no children; they did what they were invited to, and such is also the case with the many thousands of lesser-known men who have done likewise, whether, like David Ochterlony in the refined quarters of a Delhi reception room, or, like so many others, within the tawdry precincts of a whorehouse.

So how are we to think of all of this? Were the British and the French who took local mistresses in the time of empire guilty of colonizing the bodies of subjugated and humiliated women just as they colonized the land of their countries? Are the men who go to Thailand and the Philippines today contemptible? I remember the first time this issue came to my attention. It was in the early 1980s when I was the *Time* correspondent in China, and I was vacationing on the Philippine coast south of Manila. Seated at an open-air restaurant early in the evening, I saw a car pull up to the entrance and a heavy-set, gout-afflicted white man well beyond middle age get out, accompanied by a young, slender Filipina, who held his arm as she helped him hobble into the restaurant. I learned that the man had been an American government employee stationed in the Philippines, where he had retired, enjoying the company of a woman easily forty years younger than he. I felt a powerful repulsion for the man, for his being unwilling to grow old with more dignity, for his being an old lecher who clearly had bought the companionship of his Filipino girlfriend, setting himself up like a sort of Mr. Kurtz in Conrad's "Heart of Darkness," subjecting his attendant to what must surely have been disagreeable intimate relations.

Most men, of course, do not follow that man's example. Many men form lasting, exclusive relationships with their wives, and they find far deeper meaning in doing so than the chronically unfaithful or the subscribers to Angeles sex tours find in the way they manage their private lives. One naturally feels a good deal more respect for men who are loyal to one woman than for those who cheat on their wives or, even if they are not married, squander their time and money chasing after many women. And even among men who are lifelong bachelors, or who are divorced, or who are in marriages that have long been depleted of love and affection, most of them probably do not believe that going to Thailand or the Philippines will bring happiness. Better to live in dignified abstinence than to slobber over girls for hire.

In this sense, and with due, relativistic respect for other cultures, there is surely something to be said for Christian monogamy and for the heritage of chivalry to which it is related. It sets a higher standard. It holds certain values, like sexual fidelity, to be sacred, worth sacrificing a certain selfish pleasure to have. It holds women in far higher regard than the cultures of the harem, not expecting that an entire class of them will live lives whose main purpose is to provide pleasure to men who are not even under the obligation to love them and be faithful to them in return.

And yet is there less infidelity in Christendom than in the countries of the East? There are no statistics in this regard, although, as indicated earlier, the anecdotal evidence is strong that having sex outside of marriage is both more commonly practiced in the East than in the West and certainly more socially acceptable. Still, in the West, too, the rules of monogamy and fidelity are disregarded on a massive scale. Certainly, millions of Western men, sailors and aristocrats, bachelors and married men, soldiers and scholars, have gone East, engaged prostitutes, found mistresses, fathered children whom they left behind, engaged in sexual relations that would be criminal acts at home, and lived lives of dissolution and debauchery—a historical record that not only shows something about the nature of men but also indicates the reason the culture of the harem, historically speaking, was far more widespread across the globe than the culture of Christian monogamy. As an institution, the harem may represent lower expectations of men but it is also more realistic than the institution based on monogamy and guilt, more attuned to the true nature of human beings, or, at least, to the true nature of males, even as it attaches very little importance to the true nature of women. It recognizes the male impulse toward polygamy and finds a way to satisfy it without creating havoc with the institution of marriage, and, along the way, it opens up, again for men, not women, the possibility of renewed passion and sexual intensity, even as it accepts that passion and sexual intensity dim inside of marriage. The harem by definition is a sexist institution, but it leads also to less sanctimony and less hypocrisy than is commonly found where Western sexual values prevail. The evidence of the centuries is overwhelming that the flesh is weak, monogamy a difficult standard, loneliness and desire powerful inducements, so that when local women gladly and even charmingly offer themselves up to Western visitors, holding out the prospect of a moment or two of illicit paradise, not all that many men turn out to be saints.

Even that gout-ridden American in the Philippines who so aroused my contempt might be deserving of some understanding. The man bore no moral responsibility for the poverty that induced his companion to be his companion. Presumably she entered into her relationship with him because it was to her advantage. Maybe she even advertised herself, posted her picture and a note about herself in one of those magazines—since replaced by online matchmaking services—by which Asian women looked for Western men to take care of them. Very likely she yearned for a situation that would, as Killy put it in his Thai village, take her out of the shit. It is certainly probable that the money she earned from being his courtesan went to help her family, because it is the case in Asia that many, perhaps most of the women in the sex trade are attached to their families; they are not social vagabonds cut loose from all ties, and they can make a lot more money, for themselves and their relatives, serving the need for companionship and sex of Western men than they can working as maids or on assembly lines. And come to think of it, is the Filipino woman taking care of that gout-ridden American more pitiable than others forced by circumstance to perform unappealing labor—the bathroom attendant in the Manila Hotel for example, or the people, men and women, who live beside garbage heaps salvaging things from the refuse to sell. To those who would judge the American retiree or his Filipino mistress to be immoral or contemptible, it's fair to ask, what would you do if you were in the same situation?

IN THAILAND, where the encounter between East and West continues most actively and on the largest scale, the entire spectrum of views of the sex trade exists, and a discussion takes place about whether it is benign or disgraceful. Certainly it is not difficult to find people who believe that there are legitimate alternatives to Western ways and Western sexual morality, and others (sometimes the same people) who find the country's status as the world's most famous sex-tourism capital shameful.

"Thailand is a society of multiple sexual partners," Dr. Chulanee Thianthai, a social anthropologist at Chulalongkorn University in Bangkok, told me in August 2007. She was explaining, but not approving of, the Thai culture. "It's socially acceptable for a man to have more than one sexual partner. When you get old and ready to die, you might have another young wife—not for sex perhaps and certainly not for romantic reasons, but more as a guardian." She might have been talking here of that American in the Philippines—there are more than a few such American men in Thailand, as we have seen. "He gets a loyal person who is devoted to him, to cook, look after his finances, watch over other employees. So the rich man might have several wives, not all of them sexual partners."

Chulanee, in her identity as a disinterested scholar, declined to impose her values on the subject she studies. But when I asked how she felt about sex tourism in Thailand, she was very clear and emphatic: she didn't like it. "Of course I don't, being a Thai female," she said. "But I don't blame the Thai prostitutes," she continued. "People make their own choices."

I asked if she blamed the foreigners who hired the prostitutes.

"Yes, I do. They are using money to buy the bodies and souls of people, and that is dehumanizing." Chulanee had special feelings about patrons of go-go bars. "The women are being devalued to the point where men gaze at them like animals in a zoo," she said. "It eliminates the value of the woman as a human being. She's no longer a living soul."

But Thai men, I insisted, also widely hire prostitutes in Thailand, though Thais go not to go-go bars but to brothels or massage parlors that double as brothels. Is there a moral difference between dancing nearly naked on a bar and sitting in a fishbowl of tinted glass, in both instances waiting to be chosen to provide sexual pleasure?

"I think it's always dehumanizing," Chulanee said, "but in different ways. Selecting a woman from behind the glass also turns her into a sexual object, but in the go-go bars it's being turned into an animal."

Chulanee's point, powerfully made and echoed by other Thai women, is impossible to disregard. But even here there are moral wrinkles, indications that cultures are truly different. Chulanee herself allows that even female university students have been known to ply the sex trade, at least for an occasional night or two, their motive being able to buy, say, a chic handbag or expensive pair of shoes they've been coveting at the Emporium department store. So it isn't always abject poverty that leads women to prostitution. Moreover, even among the middle class in Thailand, old habits die hard, and a modern-day variation on the culture of multiple sexual partners has come into being in today's Thai youth culture.

"The teenage slang for this is *kik* [pronounced keek]," Chulanee told me. "You have your steady girlfriend and you also have romantic relations with another girl, your *kik*. It allows them to have multiple partners. Your *kik* is more than a friend but not quite a girlfriend. Boys are more likely to have a *kik* than girls," Chulanee added, but the term is genderless and can apply to the minor boyfriend of a girl as well as the minor girlfriend of a boy. And if young, unmarried people can have their *kik,* it would seem inscribed in the nature of things that married people, especially men, can have *mia noi* without suffering much social opprobrium.

Chulanee has even found that Thai women tend not to have strong negative feelings about prostitutes, even if their husbands or boyfriends visit one. "Because she knows that it doesn't mean that he doesn't love her—it's only to serve his sexual needs," she said. William Klausner, the anthropologist, who also teaches at Chulalongkorn University, has come to the same conclusion. "When I've asked my female law students how they'd view it if their husbands engaged in an extracurricular activity," he told me, "their first question would be: is it with the same woman? Because if it is, then it would be a rivalry, and she wouldn't like it. But if it's with Noi in Songkhla and Yum in Chiangmai, that doesn't bother them so much."

Of course, a discreet acceptance of multiple partners is not the same thing as an acceptance of a massive, globalized sex trade. The truth remains that very few Thai women with good alternatives would consent to being prostitutes even if they might look the other way if their husband visited one. Nor, of course, would any man you are likely to know, including the Thai and Western men who frequent Bangkok brothels, tolerate the thought of any daughter of theirs doing for other men what they are perfectly ready to do with other men's daughters. It is difficult in this sense not to view the scene in a place like Bangkok as the ultimate in tawdriness: all those foreign men roaming the streets and the bars, the global horde who pack their suitcases full of condoms, spend hours exchanging blunt and brutal misogynist views online, and jet off to Manila or Bangkok for a week or two of a kind of sexual cramming; all those women having sex with a different man every night, perhaps several men in one night. Surely this is not humankind at its most noble.

And yet, for what it's worth, the burgeoning of the sex trade occasions very little public outcry in Thailand, no local demands for change, much less prohibition. Many reasons can be cited to explain this indulgent attitude toward the foreign enjoyment of Thai women, among them: it brings in lots of foreign exchange; it involves mostly ethnic Lao women from Issan that Bangkok society doesn't much care about; it is restricted to a few streets in the cities where it flourishes and where most Thais don't go. But the absence of an outcry can't be separated entirely from the overall Thai attitude about sex, marriage, and monogamy, so different from the attitudes of the Christian West.

"In my grandfather's day, it was perfectly accepted to have major wives and minor wives, and often the major wife selected the minor wives," Mechai Viravaidya, a member of the Thai legislature and one of the country's most prominent social reformers, told me in Bangkok in 2007. Speaking of the major wife, Mechai said, "She was the managing director. If you visited a wealthy man, you'd see a compound with six houses—the major wife's was the biggest, and each of the others was for a minor wife.

"It's only in recent years that the kings have only one wife," Mechai continued, stressing that the polygamy of centuries past has not applied to the country's recent kings, who have been monogamous. But among those who are not royalty, it is fairly common for a major wife to discover a minor wife at her husband's funeral—and previously unheard of children as well. Legally in Thailand, a man can have only one wife, but if he has children with his *mia noi,* those children—known as *khao nok nah,* or "rice grown outside the paddy"—have the same rights to their inheritance and to the use of their father's name as the children of his legal wife.

"It is responsibility rather than fidelity," Mechai said, identifying the prevailing value. "If paternity is claimed, the father is responsible."

Klausner believes that Buddhism may play a role in the Thai attitude—in particular, Buddhism's notion of karma, the way in which a vast accumulation of past actions undertaken in many past lives creates present circumstances. In Klausner's view, the belief that each person's condition is a consequence of his or her karma produces both a sort of fatalism about others and a hesitancy to impose moral judgment.

"The attitude is 'there but for the grace of God go I,' " he said. "It's the habit of seeing someone who is disadvantaged, like a crippled person or a prostitute, and feeling, 'This is her misfortune; this is her karma.' "

And the fact that most prostitutes actually do use their earnings to help their families also lessens the degree of contempt one might feel for them if they were in the trade entirely for themselves. "From a Buddhist perspective, she takes on merit by helping her parents, and that helps her to a better rebirth," Klausner said. And her customer, if he is also a Buddhist, can feel that, even as he is having his pleasure, he is helping her to achieve this merit. "You are gentle to the prostitute," Klausner continued. "You give her money, you help her in gaining merit. Men do that by going into the monkhood and following the 227 rules of conduct. But this is not available to women, who can become nuns but for whom there is no monkhood. In Western terms, it all sounds like a rationalization, but in many conversations I've had over the years, with government ministers, eminent doctors, and scholars, they never think anything of going to a massage parlor."

It might still seem like a rationalization, and no doubt there is some rationalization in it. It is hard for most of us, at least most of us who come from the sexual culture of Christianity, to see sex as nothing more weighty or momentous than a game of tennis or a glass of wine. Certainly the fuss that we make whenever some prominent person, especially a politician, is caught with a woman not his wife is an indication of how different our expectations of eminent people are from those of the Thais. Does that mean that the Western vision of prostitution as a special category of injustice—a unique misfortune, the worst imaginable form of degradation—always applies or that it applies in the case of Thailand? Or is it the case that even raising the question of how we are to feel about this is a sort of enactment of the historical encounter of the sexual cultures of East and West?

My own feeling is a pragmatic one—namely, that the moral deliberation can't take place on an abstract or absolutist level, divorced from the conditions of the Thai women who play host to foreign sexual desire. Given the real alternatives for many poor Thai women, the choice that they make to be prostitutes is a rational one, and one that is, in practical terms, no worse than the alternatives they face. This point of view is stated colorfully by John Burdett, author of the novel *Bangkok Tattoo,* whose main character warns against "those childish notions" that foreigners are likely to harbor "about our working girls being downtrodden sex-slave victims of a chauvinistic male-dominated culture." In fact, the character, a policeman who is also a living Buddhist saint, declares, "These are all country girls, tough as water buffalo, wild as swans, who can't believe how much they can make by providing to polite, benevolent, guilt-ridden, rich, condom-conscious *farang* exactly the same service they would otherwise have to provide for free without protection to rough drunken whoremongering husbands in their home villages."

This view is echoed by Mechai, whose network of restaurants, hotels, and other businesses raises money for rural development in the very poor areas of Thailand, whence the bar girls emerge. "Why is selling sex bad anyway?" he asked, making the case that the vision of the Christian West, which makes nonmarital sex an especially mortal form of sin, is an arbitrary imposition of foreign values, and an imposition, moreover, that doesn't improve the lot of a single Thai. Many women, if they had the choice, would be doing something other than what they do, whether they are working as waitresses or bending over the muck of a tropical rice paddy or serving as dancer-prostitutes at AngelWitch. Most women would rather be university professors or the wives of rich men, but few prostitutes have that option.

"Isn't selling arms worse?" Mechai said, defending the morality and the integrity of a young woman's decision to exchange sexual favors for money. "They're not shooting at anyone," he said. "They're using their own assets because they're poor."

Mechai, it should be noted, initially became famous in Thailand by standing outside bars and handing out condoms to encourage safe sex. His restaurants and hotels, very popular among foreign visitors, are called Cabbages and Condoms. At the restaurants, condoms are handed out to diners on the off chance that some guests will move on from dinner to sex.

"It's very much a Western thing to see selling sex as bad," he said. He allowed, as he put it, that Thailand itself is "a very hypocritical society." Thais, he acknowledged, are embarrassed by their country's prominence as a destination for sexual tourism in part because, in spite of themselves, they see themselves through the prism of Western standards, and they worry about their country's reputation. At the same time, aside from policing certain aspects of the sex trade, notably by prosecuting pedophiles and the gangs that force underage children into the sex trade, they allow it to go on largely unregulated. And, of course, it brings in money.

"Which is better as foreign assistance," Mechai asked, "foreign assistance through sex, or foreign assistance through the government that never gets to the people anyway?"

In any event, as we've seen, it's a very long story, going back at least as far as that Portuguese sailor who arrived on the island of Tanegashima in 1543 and was given the daughter of the local sword smith in exchange for the secret of the harquebus. It's the world as it was and is. At the very least, it is testimony to the raw power of the urge that has populated the globe, that drives some men crazy and makes other men wise, the urge for a moment of delirious, primal, sublime contact with an exquisite perfumed creature free from the judgment of an unsympathetic God and far from the domain of restriction and repression that is home.

ACKNOWLEDGMENTS

I WANT TO THANK, in no particular order, Seth Mydans of *The New York Times* bureau in Bangkok and Francis Deron of *Le monde* in the same city; Qin Liwen and Huang Yuanxi in Beijing; Dave Smith at the New York Public Library; Christine Schwartz, Richard C. Holbrooke, Ben Skinner, Cho Yangsook in New York, and Michael George, who came to me through the generosity of the Hertog Research Assistantship Program at Columbia University; Souad Mekhennet in Frankfurt; Daphne Angles and Maia de la Baume in Paris; Jim Maguire in Wilton, Connecticut; Christian Appy at the University of Massachusetts, Amherst; Pascal "Ron" Politano in Boonville, New York; and Nguyen Ngoc Luong in Ho Chi Minh City. In Thailand, also, Nikki Assavathorn, Dean Barrett, Hannah Beech, Alan Dawson, Denis Gray, William Klausner, Eric Larsen, Jim Oden, Les Strouse, Chulanee Thianthai, Voranai Vanijaka, Mechai Viravaidya, and Jane Wongakanit. My thanks also to Jim Reckner at the indispensable Vietnam Center and Archive at Texas Tech University in Lubbock, Texas, and to Steve Maxner of the same institution.

As always, there are two people to whom my debt of gratitude is immeasurable: Jonathan Segal, my editor at Knopf, for his steadfast support, encouragement, critical discernment, and friendship, and my agent, Kathy Robbins, who has prodded me through four books so far. Keep on prodding! My thanks also to Sonny Mehta, the editor in chief of Knopf, whose interest in this project never flagged even as my day job forced me into a four-year delay, to Joey McGarvey, also at Knopf, and to Abigail Winograd, a great copy editor.

I have consulted many books and articles in the preparation of this project and am deeply grateful to the scholars and writers whose research guided and informed my own. Several books should be mentioned as of particular value: *Empire and Sexuality: The British Experience* by Ronald Hyam; *Harems of the Mind: Passages of Western Art and Literature* by Ruth Bernard Yeazell; *Flaubert in Egypt: A Sensibility on*

Tour, edited by Francis Steegmuller; *Captain Sir Richard Francis Burton: A Biography* by Edward Rice; *The Devil Drives: A Life of Sir Richard Francis Burton* by Fawn M. Brodie; *Sexual Life in Ancient China: A Preliminary Survey of Sex and Society from ca. 1500 B.C. till 1644 A.D.* by Robert Hans van Gulik; *Interracial Intimacy in Japan: Western Men and Japanese Women, 1543–1900* by Gary P. Leupp; *Embracing Defeat: Japan in the Wake of World War II* by John Dower; and several essays by William Dalrymple. Also very important in my research was the unique collection of oral interviews of American veterans done by the Vietnam Archive.

And then there is Zhongmei Li, my vision of the East, whose insights, support, and patience were precious and whose presence by my side is what makes it all worthwhile.

NOTES

Chapter One / Bohemians at Home and Abroad

10 *"China's nouveau riche":* Craig S. Smith, "Design Dispatch: Shanghai Discovers Its Inner Paris," *New York Times,* November 14, 2002.

14 *Professor Zhang wrote a scholarly paper:* Zhang Jiehai, "White Paper on the Psychological Problems of Chinese Men": In Chinese on NetEase, www.talk.163.com/06/0805/12/2Q8VA0030/JH.html.

21 *"relationships with Chinese nationals of the opposite sex":* Jerome A. Cohen, "Sex, Chinese Law, and the Foreigner," *Hong Kong Law Journal* 18, no. 1 (1988): 102.

22 *every schoolchild knows of it:* Frederic Wakeman Jr., *Strangers at the Gate: Social Disorder in South China, 1839–1861* (Berkeley: University of California Press, 1966), 21.

22 *"two very pretty girls":* William Hickey, quoted in Rupert Faulkner, "Personal Encounters: Europeans in East Asia," in *Encounters: The Meeting of Asia and Europe, 1500–1800,* ed. Anna Jackson and Amin Jaffer (London: Victoria & Albert Museum, 2004), 179.

22 *"xenophobia and sexual hysteria":* Wakeman, *Strangers at the Gate,* 56.

22 *impeded the increase of military strength:* Frank Dikötter, *Sex, Culture and Modernity in China: Medical Science and the Construction of Sexual Identities in the Early Republican Period* (Honolulu: University of Hawaii Press, 1995), 18.

22 *Some Chinese social reformers:* Gail Hershatter, *Dangerous Pleasures: Prostitution and Modernity in Twentieth-Century Shanghai* (Berkeley: University of California Press, 1997), 245.

23 *"Only a display of gentleness":* Dikötter, *Sex, Culture and Modernity,* 53.

23 *Some radical reformers talked of the need:* Ibid., 109–11.

23 *"the poison of the plum":* Ibid., 126.

23 *had a syphilis-infection rate three times that of the United States:* Ibid., 129.

23 *"allowed the ultimate blame":* Ibid., 130.

24 *the title of one book:* Ernest O. Hauser, *Shanghai: City for Sale* (New York: Harcourt, Brace, 1940).

24 *most notably a newspaper called* Jingbao: Hershatter, *Dangerous Pleasures,* 17.

24 *Surveys conducted around 1935:* Ibid., 39.

24 *one in three of them:* Frederic Wakeman Jr., *Policing Shanghai, 1927–1937* (Berkeley: University of California Press, 1995), 109.

24 *At the very lowest level:* Hershatter, *Dangerous Pleasures,* 49–50.

26 *Mao was provided with sexual partners:* Li Zhisui, *The Private Life of Chairman Mao* (New York: Random House, 1994), 295.

26 *"Asceticism was the public watchword":* Ibid., 517.

26 *"some of the young female attendants":* Ibid., 345–46.

27 *party leaders depended on the unique lip-reading skills:* Liu Heung Shing, ed., *China: Portrait of a Country* (Tokyo: Taschen, 2008), 236.

27 *he used to give a Daoist sex manual:* Li Zhisui, *The Private Life of Chairman Mao.* 358.

29 *those "whose acts are more serious":* Web site of China News Agency, April 29, 2007.

30 *attracted both missionaries and libertines:* Ian Buruma, *Missionaries and Libertines: Love and War in East and West* (New York: Random House, 2000).

Chapter Two / The Whole World as the White Man's Brothel

32 *a great many of this cohort:* Quoted in Ronald Hyam, *Empire and Sexuality: The British Experience* (Manchester, U.K.: Manchester University Press, 1990), 91.

33 *this in turn diminished the glory and prestige of the empire:* Ibid., 71.

33 *"turning the whole world into the white man's brothel":* Ibid., 148.

38 *"The western knight":* Paul Rycaut, *The Present State of the Ottoman Empire* (London: John Starkey and Henry Brome, 1668), 104.

39 *"Civilization always needs":* Johan Huizinga, *The Waning of the Middle Ages,* trans. F. Hopman (London: Folio Society, 1998), 115.

39 *"an attempt to substitute for reality":* Ibid., 100.

40 *"The spontaneous ardor":* Denis de Rougemont, *Love in the Western World,* trans. Montgomery Belgion (New York: Harcourt, Brace, 1940), 37.

40 *"the kiss and the embrace":* Andreas Capellanus, *The Art of Courtly Love,* trans. John Jay Parry (New York: Columbia University Press, 1990), 122.

42 *The coins show a Roman soldier:* George C. Brauer Jr., preface to *Judea Weeping: The Jewish Struggle against Rome from Pompey to Masada, 63 B.C. to A.D. 73* (New York: Thomas Y. Crowell, 1970).

45 *"And when he hath several wives":* William of Rubruck, *The Journey of William of Rubruck to the Eastern Parts of the World, 1253–55, as Narrated by Himself,* trans. and ed. William Woodville Rockhill (London: Hakluyt Society, 1900; New Delhi, India: Asian Educational Services, 1998), 61. Citations are to the Asian Educational Services edition.

45 *"They punish homicide":* Ibid., 80.

45 *"For they are inhuman":* Ibid., xv.

46 *"the women of all India":* François Pyrard quoted in Owen Lattimore and Eleanor Lattimore, eds., *Silk, Spices, and Empire: Asia Seen through the Eyes of Its Discoverers* (New York: Delacorte Press, 1968), 154.

47 *a man named Mandeville:* John Mandeville, *The Travels of Sir John Mandeville,* trans. and ed. C.W.R.D. Moseley (New York: Penguin Classics, 1983), 10.

47 *Christopher Columbus read it; Rabelais read Mandeville:* Ibid., 9.

47 *"The men of that country":* Ibid., 157.

48 *"There is another fair and good isle":* Ibid., 175.

48 *"It is their opinion there":* Ibid., 176.

49 *"The lord leads a marvelous life":* Ibid., 187.

49 *"He has four wives":* Marco Polo, *The Travels of Marco Polo, the Venetian,* ed. Manuel Komroff (Garden City, N.Y.: Garden City, 1926), 125.

50 *"qualified persons to inspect them":* Ibid., 125–26.

51 *"The procuresses were the antimothers":* Simon Schama, *The Embarrassment of Riches: An Interpretation of Dutch Culture in the Golden Age* (New York: Alfred A. Knopf, 1987), 467.

Interlude 1 / Yangsook

56 *a famous soap opera actress:* Choe Sang-hun, "Koreans Agog as Off-Screen Soap Becomes Courtroom Drama," *New York Times,* May 19, 2008.

Chapter Three / That Cad Ludovico

59 *"The knight and his lady":* Johan Huizinga, *The Waning of the Middle Ages,* trans. F. Hopman (London: Folio Society, 1998), 67.

59 *"defending imperiled virginity":* Ibid., 68.

61 *"the foremost rank of the old Oriental travelers":* Richard F. Burton, *Personal Narrative of a Pilgrimage to al-Madinah and Mecca* (London: George Bell & Sons, 1906), 2:337.

61 *"subject to a Moorish lord":* Ludovico de Varthema, *The Itinerary of Ludovico di Varthema of Bologna,* trans. John Winter Jones (1863; repr., New Delhi, India: Asian Educational Services, 1997), 25.

61 *a "Christian dog":* Ibid., 60.

61 *was now "a good Moor":* Ibid., 62.

62 *"one of the three wives":* Ibid., 65.

62 *"should pretend to be mad":* Ibid.

63 *"She, being a clever woman":* Ibid., 31.

63 *"as though I had been a nymph":* Ibid.

63 *"for I will stake my own head":* Ibid., 70.

63 *"I should never have been able":* Ibid.

64 *"If thou wilt be good":* Ibid., 72.

64 *"eggs, hens, pigeons":* Ibid.

64 *"a promise to God and to Mahomet":* Ibid., 33.

67 *"the partiality of the women of Arabia":* Ibid., 65.

67 *"gold and silver, horses and slaves":* Ibid., 70.

Chapter Four / The Harem in the Mind of the West

74 *"The Grand Signior himself":* Paul Rycaut, *The Present State of the Ottoman Empire* (London: Cleave, 1701), 4.

75 *"Whenever the Grand Signior has an Inclination":* Ibid., 18.

76 *"of which are chosen the most beautiful":* Ibid.

76 *The eunichs were needed:* Ibid.

76 *"illicit sexual practices":* Martin Luther, quoted in Silke R. Falkner, " 'Having It Off' with Fish, Camels, and Lads: Sodomitic Pleasures in German-Language Turcica," *Journal of the History of Sexuality* 13, no. 4 (October 2004): 408.

76 *"so not the slightest hint":* Martin Luther, quoted ibid., 406.

77 *"the embodiment of depraved tyranny":* Leslie P. Peirce, *The Imperial Harem: Women and Sovereignty in the Ottoman Empire* (New York: Oxford University Press, 1993), 114.

78 *the harem was an important theme:* See Ruth Bernard Yeazell's *Harems of the Mind: Passages of Western Art and Literature* (New Haven, Conn.: Yale University Press,

2000), both for reproductions of European artworks inspired by the Turkish harem and for a full scholarly analysis of them.

79   *"cloistered sensuality"*: Ibid., 228.

79   *"neither did what he made"*: Marquis de Custine, quoted ibid., 91.

79   *"Each Turk is allowed four wives"*: Rycaut, *The Present State of the Ottoman Empire*, 59.

80   *"The word* harem*"*: Peirce, *The Imperial Harem*, 5.

80   *more nunnery than bordello:* Ibid., 6.

80   *a "site of Muslim promiscuity"*: Ibid., 7.

80   *an Italian visitor:* Ibid., 120.

81   *it would be dangerous for the security of the ruler:* Ibid., 87.

81   *widely deemed to have been a sorceress:* Ibid., 63.

82   *by elevating slaves:* Ibid., 41.

82   *"I will not only trace"*: Aaron Hill, *A Full and Just Account of the Present State of the Ottoman Empire* (London: John Mayo, 1710), 149.

83   *Rycaut's story of the handkerchief:* Ibid., 171.

83   *was deemed literarily important enough:* William W. Appleton and Kalman A. Burnim, eds., *The Prompter: A Theatrical Paper by Aaron Hill and William Popple* (New York: Benjamin Blom, 1966), vii.

84   *they helped to inspire masterpieces:* Yeazell, *Harems of the Mind,* 36.

84   *"When a husband happens to be inconstant"*: Lady Mary Wortley Montagu, quoted ibid., 16.

84   *Montagu called that business:* Ibid., 18.

84   *"a Beautifull Maid"*: Lady Mary Wortley Montagu, quoted ibid., 37–38.

84   *the "extreme Stupidity" of previous writers:* Ibid., 84.

85   *"the only Women in the world"*: Ibid.

85   *the "perpetual Masquerade" allowed women to "go abroad"*: Ibid., 85.

85   *"peculiar ceremony"*: Julia Pardoe, quoted ibid., 19.

86   *"gave her access to those forbidden 'Abodes' "*: Emmeline Lott, quoted ibid., 20.

86   *"perfectly safe from an idle, curious, impertinent public"*: Elizabeth Craven, quoted in ibid., 89.

86   *"associate them not with sexual freedom"*: Ibid., 89.

88   *"a country of enigma and mysteries"*: Gérard de Nerval, quoted in Ali Behdad, *Belated Travelers: Orientalism in the Age of Colonial Dissolution* (Durham, N.C.: Duke University Press, 1994), 24.

88   *"Beautiful hands ornamented with talismanic rings"*: Gérard de Nerval, quoted ibid., 28.

88   *"an erotic urge to see the imaginary nakedness"*: Ibid., 24.

Interlude 3 / The Fantasy Comes True

89   *"the dream of infinite possibility"*: Ruth Bernard Yeazell, *Harems of the Mind: Passages of Western Art and Literature* (New Haven, Conn.: Yale University Press, 2000), 99.

89   *"As if the alternative to monogamy"*: Ibid.

Chapter Five / The Eternal Dream of Cleopatra

92   *"take ship for Jidda"*: Gustave Flaubert, *Flaubert in Egypt: A Sensibility on Tour; A Narrative Drawn from Gustave Flaubert's Travel Notes & Letters,* ed. and trans. Francis Steegmuller (Boston: Little, Brown, 1972), 201.

92   *"a whole veiled harem"; "it was one of the most voluptuous pleasures"*: Ibid., 201, 202.

93   *"made between the Orient and the freedom of licentious sex"*: Edward W. Said, *Orientalism* (New York: Pantheon Books, 1978), 190.

94   *"It may be a perverted taste"*: Flaubert, *Flaubert in Egypt,* 9–10.

94   *"The next two days I lived lavishly"*: Ibid., 21.

95   *"almost six feet tall"*: Ibid., 9.

95   *"Oh, how willingly"; "youthful 'oriental' effusions"*: Ibid., 11.

95   *"I am afraid of becoming giddy"; "We don't have emotions"*: Ibid., 50, 51.

96   *"were especially inclined"*: Ruth Bernard Yeazell, *Harems of the Mind: Passages of Western Art and Literature* (New Haven, Conn.: Yale University Press, 2000) 236.

96   *"gnaw[ing] at the end"; "eleven days of rolling and pitching"*: Flaubert, *Flaubert in Egypt,* 26.

96   *"The psychological, human, comic aspects"*: Ibid., 16.

96   *"febrile and intoxicating"*: Ibid., 216.

97   *"It is unbelievable how well"*: Ibid., 43.

97   *"the respect, or rather the terror"*: Ibid., 29.

97   *"with a boy of six or seven"*: Ibid., 38.

97   *"It's at the baths that such things take place"*: Ibid., 84.

98   *"rolling and stony"; "large plaques of yellow"; "the Arab boats"; "bare-headed, wavy hair"; little red-haired girl"; "one to row"; "walk[ing] in groups"; "white birdshit"; "Inscriptions and bird-droppings"*: Ibid., 165, 180, 181, 187, 189, 200, 202, 209.

98   *"bore me profoundly"*: Flaubert, p. 142.

98   *"When a man is to be killed"*: Ibid., 145–46.

99   *"a pockmarked young rascal"*: Ibid., 203.

99   *"nauseating odor"*: Ibid., 220.

99   *"fat and lubricious"*: Ibid., 201.

99   *"I suspect a Maronite"*: Ibid., 215.

99   *a place called la Triestine*: Ibid., 39–40.

100 *"a strange coitus"*: Ibid., 44.

100 *her dance "is brutal"*: Ibid., 115, 117.

100 *"My night was one long, infinitely intense reverie"*: Ibid., 130.

100 *"I have lain with Nubian girls"*: Ibid., 126.

100 *"infinite sadness"*: Ibid., 159.

100 *"had a beautiful whore"*: Ibid., 201.

100 *"The boat left"*: Ibid., 213.

101 *"the longing to see a palm-tree"*: Ibid., 222.

Chapter Six / Enlightenment from India

102 *"under the roof of a bigoted prince"*: Richard Francis Burton, *First Footsteps in East Africa* (1856; repr., Whitefish, Mont.: Kessinger Publishing, 2004), 126.

102 *"to see the light"*: Ibid., 125.

103 *"Stars are tattooed upon the bosom"*: Ibid., 133.

103 *"the use of the constrictor vaginae muscles"*: Richard Francis Burton, *A Thousand Nights and a Night* (The Burton Club for Private Subscribers only, 1885), 4:227.

104 *"The Hig is called 'Salab' "*: Burton, *First Footsteps in East Africa*, 100.

104 *" 'Conscience,' I may observe"*: Ibid., 74.

104 *the Yemenis derided the Somali women:* Ibid., 57.

104 *"Who but Burton"*: Edward Rice, *Captain, Sir Richard Francis Burton: A Biography* (New York: Charles Scribner's Sons, 1990), 236.

105 *"the Somalis have only one method"*: Richard Francis Burton, quoted ibid., 236.

105 *"this barbarous guarantee"*: Richard Francis Burton, quoted ibid., 237.

105 *"Those who suspect"*: Richard Francis Burton, quoted ibid., 238.

105 *"The fair sex lasts longer"*: Burton, *First Footsteps in East Africa*, 57.

105 *"I have forgotten as much"*: Richard Francis Burton, *Love, War, and Fancy: The Customs and Manners of the East, from Writings on the Arabian Nights,* ed. Kenneth Walker (New York: Ballantine Books, 1964), 15.

105 *"the savoring of animal existence"*: Richard Francis Burton, *Personal Narrative of a Pilgrimage to Al-Madinah and Meccah* (London: George Bell & Sons, 1906), 1:9.

106 *the local men who had agreed to be executed:* Fawn M. Brodie, *The Devil Drives: A Life of Sir Richard Burton* (New York: W. W. Norton, 1984), 63.

106 *He knew about the fathers and brothers:* Ibid., 64.

106 *"The scrotum of the unmutilated boy"*: Richard Francis Burton, "Terminal Essay," from *A Thousand Nights and a Night*, 10:205.

106 *"a compulsory rest"*: Gustave Flaubert, *Flaubert in Egypt: A Sensibility on Tour; A Narrative Drawn from Gustave Flaubert's Notes & Letters,* ed. and trans. Francis Steegmuller (Boston: Little, Brown, 1972), 109.

106 *"The parts are swept off"*: Richard Francis Burton, quoted in Brodie, *The Devil Drives*, 126.

107 *"rich nut-brown" skin and "perfect symmetry"*: Burton, *First Footsteps in East Africa*, 86.

107 *"A conviction was born in him"*: Brodie, *The Devil Drives*, 77.

109 *"an opportunity of seeing 'Al-nahl' "*: Burton, *Pilgrimage to al-Madinah and Mecca*, 11.

109 *The assumption drawn:* Rice, *Captain Sir Richard Burton*, 182.

109 *"arch-seductresses"*: Richard Francis Burton, quoted ibid., 235.

110 *"It was precisely because most of them"*: Peter Gay, *The Bourgeois Experience: Victoria to Freud,* vol. 5, *The Pleasure Wars* (New York: W. W. Norton, 1999), 7.

110 *"purposeful propriety"*: Peter Gay, *The Bourgeois Experience: Victoria to Freud,* vol. 2, *The Tender Passion* (London: Oxford University Press, 1986), 4.

110 *"Sexual intercourse was"*: Ronald Pearsall, *The Worm in the Bud: The World of Victorian Sexuality* (London: Pimlico, 1969), xi.

110 *Masturbation, he wrote:* William Acton, quoted in Steven Marcus, *The Other Victorians: A Study of Sexuality and Pornography in Mid-Nineteenth-Century England* (New York: Basic Books, 1964), 19.

110 *fulfilling sexual desire:* Ibid., 18.

111 *"the best mothers"*: William Acton, *The Functions and Disorders of the Reproductive Organs in Childhood, Youth, Adult Age, and Advanced Life* (Philadelphia: P. Blakeston, Son, & Co., 1894), 209–10.

III   *"there were almost certainly more brothels in London":* Ronald Hyam, *Empire and Sexuality: The British Experience* (Manchester, U.K.: Manchester University Press, 1990), 60.

III   *A mid-century attorney general:* Pearsall, *The Worm in the Bud,* 384.

III   *one well-known publisher:* Ibid.

112   *"It would be a gross misreading":* Gay, *The Tender Passion,* 4.

112   *if infected, forced to stay:* Marcus, *The Other Victorians,* 3.

112   *"the dull stupidity":* William Acton, quoted ibid., 4–5.

113   *"The prospect of a book":* Richard Francis Burton, quoted in Pearsall, *The Worm in the Bud,* 372.

113   *the Anglican bishop of Calcutta:* M. J. Akbar, "Open to All Interests, Subject to None," *Hindu* (Chennai, India), January 29, 2005.

113   *"all the purposes of a wife":* Viscount Wolseley, quoted in Hyam, *Empire and Sexuality,* 118.

114   *Both were guests of an Italian:* Rice, *Captain Sir Richard Francis Burton,* 219.

114   *an avid collector of erotica:* Marcus, *The Other Victorians,* 37.

115   *My Secret Life:* Brodie, *The Devil Drives,* 295.

115   *"a second de Sade":* Henry Ashbee, quoted in Marcus, *The Other Victorians,* 37.

115   *"Our ignorance of aphrodisiacs":* Richard F. Burton, *Sindh and the Valley of the Indus* (Oxford: Oxford University Press, 1973), 146.

115   *"are contemptuously compared":* Richard F. Burton, *Ananga Ranga, or the Hindu Art of Love* (Benares, The Kama Shastra Society, 1885), 404.

116   *"Among savages and barbarians":* Richard F. Burton, *Supplemental Nights to the Book of a Thousand and One Nights* (Benares: The Kama Shastra Society, 1887), 4:404.

116   *"Moslems who do their best":* Richard F. Burton, quoted in Brodie, *The Devil Drives,* 186.

116   *some mothers are idiots:* Richard F. Burton, *A Thousand Nights and a Night,* 10:42.

118   *"swamped with returns":* Rice, *Captain Sir Richard Francis Burton,* 456.

118   *"Debauched women prefer negroes":* Richard Francis Burton, *A Thousand Nights and a Night,* 1:6.

118   *Ali Shar and the slave girl:* Richard Francis Burton, *A Thousand Nights and a Night,* 4:27.

119   *"I struggled for forty-seven years":* Richard Francis Burton, quoted in Brodie, *The Devil Drives,* 309.

Chapter Seven / Colonialism and Sex

121   *the joyful life of a Portuguese settler:* William Dalrymple, "Personal Encounters: Europeans in South Asia," in *Encounters: The Meeting of Asia and Europe, 1500–1800,* ed. Anna Jackson and Amin Jaffer (London: Victoria & Albert Museum, 2004), 158.

121   *"the delights of a society":* Ibid.

122   *the Portuguese were becoming Goan:* Ibid.

122   *a certain John Leachland:* Ibid., 369.

122   *because of what Burke termed his promotion:* Nancy L. Paxton, *Writing under the Raj: Gender, Race, and Rape in the British Colonial Imagination, 1830–1947* (New Brunswick, N.J.: Rutgers University Press, 1999), 1–2, 37–38.

123 *"Virgins who had never seen the sun"*: Edmund Burke, quoted in ibid., 2.

123 *a letter to Clive*: Ronald Hyam, *Empire and Sexuality: The British Experience* (Manchester, U.K.: Manchester University Press, 1990), 28.

123 *near his Indian mistress's home*: M. J. Akbar, "Open to All Interests, Subject to None," *Hindu* (Chennai, India), January 29, 2005.

123 *he wished he could be castrated*: Hyam, *Empire and Sexuality*, 28.

123 *but Clive certainly was*: Lawrence James, *Raj: The Making and Unmaking of British India* (New York: St. Martin's Press, 1997), 45–49.

124 *"Those responsible for India"*: Lawrence James, *The Rise and Fall of the British Empire* (New York: St. Martin's Press, 1994), 135.

125 *"the greatest entertainment imaginable"*: Dalrymple, "Personal Encounters," 160.

125 *thirteen wives*: Ibid., 168.

126 *"Of course, the lascivious-minded man"*: Hyam, *Empire and Sexuality*, 88.

127 *"promiscuous and hazardous"*: James, *Raj*, 139.

127 *The British surgeon general of Bombay*: Kenneth Ballhatchet, *Race, Sex, and Class under the Raj: Imperial Attitudes and Policies and Their Critics, 1793–1905* (London, Weidenfeld and Nicolson, 1980), 10.

127 *"an attempt to make sinning safe"*: Ibid., 19.

127 *One scholar has counted*: Hyam, *Empire and Sexuality*, 123.

128 *"The empire was a Moloch"*: Quoted ibid., 91.

129 *The better prostitutes*: Edward Sellon, *The Ups and Downs of Life* (London: William Dugdale, 1867; Ware, U.K.: Wordsworth Classics, 1987), 55–56.

129 *"understand in perfection"*: Ibid., 56.

130 *"S'pose the Colonel Sahib"*: Ibid., 48.

131 *"I now commenced a regular course"*: Ibid., 55.

132 *"By 1936, there were"*: Frederic Wakeman Jr., *Policing Shanghai, 1927–1937* (Berkeley: University of California Press, 1995), 108.

132 *"even provided its big-stake customers"*: Ibid., 98.

133 *"announced reasons"*: *China Weekly Review*, January 5, 1929, quoted ibid., 110.

133 *a League of Nations report*: Ibid., 113.

133 *"The tendency at the present time"*: *China Weekly Review*, January, 23, 1932, quoted ibid., 13–14.

133 *"Shanghai was the place"*: Ernest O. Hauser, *Shanghai: City for Sale* (New York: Harcourt, Brace, 1940), 261.

134 *"crucially underpinned the whole operation"*: Hyam, *Empire and Sexuality*, 1.

134 *"The expansion of Europe"*: Ibid., 2.

134 *"the vice capital of the world"*: Frederic Wakeman Jr., *Policing Shanghai*, 115.

134 *"Many are the men"*: Edward Long, quoted in Hyam, *Empire and Sexuality*, 92.

135 *"There is no slavery"*: Gilberto de Mello Freyre, quoted in ibid., 93.

135 *In the Dutch Cape Town colony*: Ibid.

135 *"If you get into trouble"*: Alexander Barton Woodside, *Community and Revolution in Modern Vietnam* (Boston: Houghton Mifflin, 1976), 10.

135 *formally encouraged marriages*: Hyam, *Empire and Sexuality*, 116.

136 *"the traditional Muslim slave market"*: Christelle Taraud, "Prostitution and Colonization in the Maghreb," unpublished paper provided to the author.

136 *the pre-French sexual practices of Algeria*: Ibid.

136 *They banned slavery*: Ibid.

136 *a "condition of inferior civilization"*: Ibid.

137 *"The French arrived in Algiers"*: Ernest Feydeau, quoted ibid.

138 *"the sweet dream"*: Malek Alloula, *The Colonial Harem,* trans. Myrna Godzich and Wlad Godzich (Minneapolis: University of Minnesota Press, 1986), 3.

138 *"degraded, and degrading"*: Ibid., 4.

Interlude 4 / A Secret Life in Algiers and Paris

141 *"At a certain time, everything was permitted"*: Alain Ruscio, "Amours, relations, mariages dans le Maghreb colonisé: de la littérature à la réalité," contribution à la Journée d'études de la Société des amis d'Ismaÿl Urbain et d'Études Saint-Simoniennes, 25 janvier 2003, Houilles, Public, SAIU-SESS, 2004.

143 *"aesthetic facism"*: Mary Ann Frese Witt, *The Search for Modern Tragedy: Aesthetic Fascism in Italy and France* (Ithaca, N.Y.: Cornell University Press, 2001), 17–18, 195–201.

144 *Montherlant was accused and convicted:* Ibid., 204.

144 *W. H. Auden coined the term:* Jonathan Fryer, *André & Oscar: Gide, Wilde and the Gay Art of Living* (London: Constable, 1997), 106–7.

145 *an episode of life-transforming delirium:* Ibid., 117–20.

145 *Kenneth Searight, a captain in the British army:* Ronald Hyam, *Empire and Sexuality: The British Experience* (Manchester, U.K.: Manchester University Press, 1990), 131.

147 *"never did pederasty play"*: Roger Peyrefitte, *Propos secrets* (Paris: Albin Michel, 1977), 56 (my translations).

147 *Montherlant called the police:* Ibid., 53–58.

147 *According to Peyrefitte:* Ibid., 53.

148 *"Every day he takes a little more risk"*: Pierre Sipriot, *Montherlant sans masque,* vol. 1, *L'enfant prodigue* (Paris: Robert Laffont, 1982), 290 (all translations by Christine Schwartz Hartley).

148 *"all you needed to do is smile"*: Ibid., 389.

148 *"a great greed for the flesh"*: Ibid., 290.

149 *"In Paris Montherlant didn't dare"*: Ibid.

149 *Montherlant wrote at one point:* Ibid., 390.

149 *Montherlant wrote an essay:* Ibid., 383.

149 *"Montherlant distrusts and willfully ignores"*: Ibid.

149 *"the fantastic adventure"*: Ibid. 389.

150 *One scholar has counted fifty-seven titles:* Ruscio, "Amours, relations, mariages dans le Maghreb colonisé."

150 *"tired of the rough life"*: Ibid.

150 *a military doctor becomes attached to little Zohira:* Ibid.

152 *"Montherlant's suicide"*: Peyrefitte, *Propos secrets,* 78.

Chapter Eight / The Eastern Paradox

160 *The education minister of Rajasthan:* Amelia Gentlemen, "Sex Education Curriculum Angers Indian Conservatives," *International Herald Tribune,* May 24, 2007.

162 *"the devotional, the metaphysical"*: William Dalrymple, "India: The Place of Sex," *New York Review of Books,* June 26, 2008.

163 *"and desire was with God"*: Ibid.

163 *"The missionaries," Ian Buruma has written:* Ian Buruma, *Missionaries and Libertines: Love and War in East and West* (New York: Random House, 2000).

166 *"freedom of intercourse":* Edward William Lane, quoted in Edward W. Said, *Orientalism* (New York: Pantheon Books, 1978), 167.

166 *"suggestive ruins":* Ibid., 170.

166 *"So the Orient was a place":* Ibid., 190.

167 *"Why the Orient seems":* Ibid., 188.

167 *"a web of legal, moral, even political"; "where one could look for sexual experience"; "a different type of sexuality":* Ibid., 190.

168 *"you should insert it slowly":* Quoted in Fang Fu Ruan, *Sex in China: Studies in Sexology in Chinese Culture* (New York: Plenum Press, 1991), 30.

169 *"so that we can practice":* Quoted ibid., 33.

169 *"Their bodies are beautiful":* Quoted ibid., 34.

170 *Incest, pedophilia, and orgies:* Ibid., 90–91.

171 *"Changing partners":* Quoted ibid., 38.

171 *"his urine will become putrid":* Quoted ibid., 43.

173 Records of the Green Bowers: Robert Hans van Gulik, *Sexual Life in Ancient China: A Preliminary Survey of Sex and Society from ca. 1500 B.C. till 1644 A.D.* (Leiden, Netherlands: E. J. Brill, 1961), 252.

173 *"your job is to satisfy":* Quoted in Ruan, *Sex in China,* 73.

173 *registered brothels:* Ibid., 72.

174 *a woman with bound feet was forced to sway:* Howard S. Levy, *Chinese Footbinding: The History of a Curious Erotic Custom* (London: Neville Spearman, no date), 32.

174 *"both pity and lust":* Ibid., 34.

175 *"the ancestors would diminish":* Van Gulik, *Sexual Life in Ancient China,* 13.

176 *According to Matignon:* Ibid., 255.

177 *a Sri Lankan–born scholar:* Gananath Obeyesekere, *The Apotheosis of Captain Cook: European Mythmaking in the Pacific* (Princeton, N.J.: Princeton University Press, 1992), 19.

177 *"without taking the trouble of an ethnographic investigation":* Marshall Sahlins, *How "Natives" Think: About Captain Cook, for Example* (Chicago: University of Chicago, 1995), 148, 163.

Chapter Nine / What Happened to the Harem?

180 *All the old mosques and monasteries:* Jadunath Sarkar, *History of Aurangzib* (Calcutta, India: M. C. Sarkar & Sons, 1912–16), 3:92–103.

180 *"the innovators, atheists, heretics":* Ibid., 3:93.

181 *Akbar celebrated Hindu festivals:* John Keay, *India: A History* (New York: Atlantic Monthly Press, 2000), 313.

182 *"our religion is sublime":* William Wilberforce, quoted in James, *Raj,* 224.

182 *"Am I the keeper":* Samuel Wilberforce, quoted ibid., 229.

182 *"the crassest propaganda":* Ibid., 228.

184 *what he called "invisible persons":* Marthal Nalini, "Gender Dynamics of Missionary Work in India and Its Impact on Women's Education: Isabella Thoburn (1840–1901)—A Case Study," *Journal of International Women's Studies* 7, no. 4 (May 2006): 286.

184 *"cut off from the demoralization"*: Quoted in ibid., 273.

184 *"come up and out"*: Isabella Thoburn, quoted in ibid., 278.

185 *It is said to be especially patronized:* Ibid., 285–86.

185 *"If I had given a million dollars"*: Benjamin Harrison, quoted ibid.

185 *"No one, I say"*: Lilivati Singh, quoted in Sherwood Eddy, *Pathfinders of the World Missionary Crusade* (Manchester, N.H.: Ayer Publishing, 1945), 95.

185 *"the last example"*: Quoted in Rosie Llewellyn-Jones, *A Fatal Friendship: The Nawabs, the British, and the City of Lucknow* (New Delhi, India: Oxford University Press, 1985), 5.

186 *"had come to combine"*: Keay, *India*, 433.

186 *"a vision of palaces"*: Quoted in Veena Talwar Oldenburg, *The Making of Colonial Lucknow, 1856–1877* (Princeton, N.J.: Princeton University Press, 1984), 11.

186 *"a swarm of eunuchs"*: Keay, *India*, 435.

187 *Felix Rotton:* Llewellyn-Jones, *A Fatal Friendship*, 31.

187 *"was by nature attracted"*: Abdul Halim Sharar, *Lucknow: The Last Phase of an Oriental Culture*, trans. and ed. E. S. Harcourt and Fakhir Hussain (London: Paul Elek, 1975), 34–35.

187 *When the nawab traveled:* Ibid.

188 *Among Asaf's pleasures:* Ibid., 45.

188 *"a small army of beautiful girls"*: Ibid., 62.

188 *"beautiful and dissolute women"*: Ibid., 62–63.

188 *"few ministers and nobles"*: Ibid., 64.

188 *there was hardly a rich man in Lucknow:* Ibid., 91.

188 *that Sharar called* vasokht: Ibid., 85.

189 *included houses, orchards, factories:* Veena Talwar Oldenburg, "Lifestyle as Resistance: The Case of the Courtesans of Lucknow, India," *Feminist Studies* 16, no. 2 (Summer 1990): 159–60.

189 *"Association with courtesans"*: Sharar, *Lucknow*, 192.

190 *"The imposition of the contagious diseases regulations"*: Oldenburg, *The Making of Colonial Lucknow*, 260.

191 *She found Lucknow dazzling:* J. M. Thoburn, *Life of Isabella Thoburn* (New York: Eaton and Mains, 1903), 85–86.

191 *"which few women seem able to resist"*: Ibid., 81.

191 *"jewel-bedecked idleness"*: Ibid., 190.

191 *"The system is thoroughly bad"*: Ibid., 81.

192 *"the long night of Victorian morality"*: Llewellyn-Jones, *A Fatal Friendship*, 36.

193 *"Lal Bagh became a place"*: Quoted in Nalini, "Gender Dynamics of Missionary Work in India," 235.

193 *Among the graduates:* Ibid., 283.

193 *"Lihaf" is about a young bride:* Priyamvada Gopal, *Literary Radicalism in India: Gender, Nation and the Transition to Independence* (New York: Routledge, 2005), 66.

194 *"The women's colleges"*: Susan Seymour, "College Women's Aspirations: A Challenge to the Patrifocal Family System," in *Women, Education, and Family Structure in India*, ed. Carol Chapnick Mukhopadhyay and Susan Seymour (Boulder, Colo.: Westview Press, 1994), 214.

194 *"Education is looked on"*: Ibid.

194 *"What was left of the old Lucknow"*: William Dalrymple, "A City Lost to the Forces of Darkness," *New Statesman*, December 18, 1998, 32.

Chapter Ten / The Inescapable Courtesy of Japan

197 *"a menacing, masculine threat"*: John W. Dower, *Embracing Defeat: Japan in the Wake of World War II* (New York: W. W. Norton, 1999), 130.

197 *The cost on an individual basis:* Ibid.

198 *In his lacerating memoir:* Philip Caputo, *A Rumor of War* (New York: Holt, Rinehart and Winston, 1977), 47–48.

199 *"The sexual implications"*: Dower, *Embracing Defeat*, 124–25.

200 *"the lubricity of these people"*: Townsend Harris, quoted in Gary P. Leupp, *Interracial Intimacy in Japan: Western Men and Japanese Women, 1543–1900* (New York: Continuum International, 2003), 147.

201 *"the Okichis of the present era"*: Dower, *Embracing Defeat*, 126.

201 *"We are not compromising our integrity"*: Ibid.

201 *One nineteen-year-old woman:* Ibid., 129.

201 *"The panpan arm in arm"*: Ibid., 135.

201 *speaking to a reporter:* Seth Mydans, "An Ageless Saigon Basks in Peace," *New York Times,* May 1, 2000.

203 *the first known act:* Leupp, *Interracial Intimacy in Japan*, 1–2.

204 *"As soon as ever these Portuguese arrive"*: Francesco Carletti, quoted ibid., 49.

204 *In the early decades of the seventeenth century:* Andrew Gordon, *A Modern History of Japan: From Tokugawa Times to the Present* (New York: Oxford University Press, 2003), 17.

205 *"[We] Japanese desire"*: Quoted ibid., 64.

205 *"Whores only"*: Rupert Faulkner, "Personal Encounters: Europeans in East Asia," in *Encounters: The Meeting of Asia and Europe, 1500–1800,* ed. Anna Jackson and Amin Jaffer (London: Victoria & Albert Museum, 2004), 180.

206 *largely through the influence of a kimono-clad troupe:* Lesley Downer, *Women of the Pleasure Quarters: The Secret History of the Geisha* (New York: Broadway Books, 2001), 38.

207 *"Do you like that girl?":* Quoted in Faulkner, "Personal Encounters," 183.

207 *A print from the 1790s:* Ibid.

208 *said the Italian trader Carletti:* Ibid.

209 *Buddhist monks, forbidden sexual relations:* Downer, *Women of the Pleasure Quarters*, 39.

209 *Alessandro Valignano, a Jesuit missionary:* Faulker, "Personal Encounters," 181.

209 *The women of the pleasure quarters:* Downer, *Women of the Pleasure Quarters*, 46.

210 *the ultimate expressions of Japanese artifice:* Ibid., 2.

210 *"By the mid-nineteenth century"*: Leupp, *Interracial Intimacy in Japan*, 81–82.

211 *Lieutenant George Henry Preble:* Ibid., 145.

211 *"There was a fair sprinkling of men"*: Ernest Mason Satow, quoted ibid., 146.

211 *"Anyone, married or single"*: Ibid., 154.

Interlude 6 / The Butterfly Complex

217 *"the childish confiding, sweet Japanese girl"*: Lafcadio Hearn, quoted in Gary P. Leupp, *Interracial Intimacy in Japan: Western Men and Japanese Women, 1543–1900* (New York: Continuum International, 2003), 179.

217 *"gracious sweetness and bright serenity":* Sir Edwin Arnold, quoted in ibid., 164.

217 *"unselfish devotion":* Alice Mabel Bacon, quoted ibid., 179.

219 *"Nobody is, indeed, ever brutal":* Sir Edwin Arnold, quoted ibid., 164.

219 *"saw philandering as their God-given right":* Lesley Downer, *Madame Sadayakko: The Geisha Who Bewitched the West* (New York: Gotham Books, 2003), 68.

220 *the "flowery beauty" of Japan:* Yoko Chiba, "Japonisme: East-West Renaissance in the Late 19th Century," *Mosaic* (Winnipeg, Canada) 31, no. 2 (June 1998).

221 *the art critic and painter Zacharie Astruc:* Ibid.

221 *One critic wrote:* Downer, *Madame Sadayakko,* 200.

222 *Sadayakko, her biographer has written:* Ibid., 201.

222 *Siebold's story contains some of the elements:* Jan van Rij, *Madame Butterfly: Japonisme, Puccini, and the Search for the Real Cho-Cho-San* (Berkeley, Calif.: Stone Bridge Press, 2001), 24.

222 *Loti wrote a novel:* Ibid., 25–31.

223 *One close student of the origins:* Ibid., 119–122.

Chapter Eleven / "I Souvenir. You Boom-Boom."

226 *"exterminating our compatriots in a very cruel way":* Liberation Radio, November 8, 1965, monitored by the Foreign Broadcast Information Service, the Vietnam Archive, Texas Tech University.

226 *"The depraved, obscene U.S. cowboy culture":* Ibid.

226 *"It was the U.S. puppet clique's joint policy":* "Social Evils: U.S. Neocolonialism's Residue in South Vietnam," Hanoi International Service, July 14, 1975, the Vietnam Archive, Texas Tech University.

227 *"American men in South Vietnam":* Neil Sheehan, *A Bright Shining Lie: John Paul Vann and America in Vietnam* (New York: Random House, 1988), 598.

227 *"a chance for protracted debauchery":* James F. Dunnigan and Albert A. Nofi, *Dirty Little Secrets of the Vietnam War: Military Information You're Not Supposed to Know* (New York, St. Martin's Press, 1999), 166.

228 *"There's a lot of plain and fancy screwing":* Sheehan, *A Bright Shining Lie,* 598.

228 *"Strumpets trailed the trumpets":* "Disneyland East," *Time,* May 6, 1966.

228 *one third of the American forces:* Dunnigan and Nofi, *Dirty Little Secrets,* 166.

230 *out of deference to Diem's sensibilities:* William Prochnau, *Once upon a Distant War: David Halberstam, Neil Sheehan, Peter Arnett—Young War Correspondents and Their Early Vietnam Battles* (New York: Times Books, 1995), 23.

232 *"All the Young Turks":* Ibid., 270.

232 *"a stunning* Saigonnaisse*":* Ibid., 130.

232 *"You vill love zis place":* Ibid., 131.

233 *According to Sheehan:* Sheehan, *A Bright Shining Lie,* 599.

233 *He told Halberstam:* Ibid., 323.

234 *"We're going to lose":* Ibid., 512.

234 *Vann learned of one American aid official:* Ibid., 516.

234 *"It was a very sad experience":* Frank Maguire, "The Whole Attitude Was, Stand Back Little Brother, I'll Take Care of It," in *Patriots: The Vietnam War Remembered from All Sides,* comp. Christian G. Appy (New York: Penguin Books, 2003), 441.

235 *"Over at China Beach":* Eliseo Perez-Montalvo, interview by Richard Burks Verrone,

August 5, 2003, Vietnam Archive Oral History Project, Texas Tech University, Lubbock, Tex.

236   Time *reported on Sin City:* "Disneyland East."

238   *"Sin Cities were whorehouses":* Jim Cain, "Dazed and Confused: Vietnam, January 5th through December 8th 1970," http://evationonline.com/dazed/dazed andconfused.htm.

240   *"I don't think many of the girls became prostitutes":* Nguyen Ngoc Luong, "To Get Their ID Cards, the Girls Had to Go to Bed with the Police," in *Patriots,* comp. Appy, 375.

241   *"Both literally and figuratively":* E. W. Kenworthy, "Fulbright Issues a Warning to U.S.: Says Nation Is in Danger of Losing Its Perspective," *New York Times,* May 6, 1966.

242   *"I have not been to Saigon":* "Back to the Brothel," *Time,* May 20, 1966.

242   *she forthrightly declared:* "Saigon No Brothel, Mrs. Lord Asserts," *New York Times,* May 7, 1966.

242   *"Not everyone in Fulbright's own Arkansas":* "Back to the Brothel."

243   *"It's like a kid in a candy shop":* Michael Harris, interview by Stephen Maxner, August 22, 2000, Vietnam Archive Oral History Project.

243   *"Her name was Kim":* Phil Price, interview by Stephen Maxner, August 1, 1999, Vietnam Archive Oral History Project.

244   *"Viet Nam carwash girl":* William Foulke Collection, Department of the Army Special Photographic Office, item VAS031861, September 1967, Vietnam Center and Archive, Texas Tech University.

244   *Wayne Smith, a combat medic:* Wayne Smith, "I Was Thanking God They Didn't Have Air Support," in *Patriot,* comp. Appy, 365.

244   *"You'd walk around in Saigon":* Don Halsey, interview by Edwin Whiting, April 9, 1990, Vietnam Archive Oral History Project.

245   *"It was a whorehouse":* Smith, "I Was Thanking God They Didn't Have Air Support," 365–66.

246   *a generally upbeat cable:* Telegram from the American Embassy in Saigon to the Secretary of State: Vietnamese Reactions to the Presence of U.S. Forces, Larry Berman Collection (Presidential Archives Research), July 1, 1965, Vietnam Center and Archive.

246   *Brigadier General Nguyen Chanh Thi: Saigon Post,* January 10, 1964.

Chapter Twelve / Thinking of Nana, or Noi, or Am

265   *"Recreational sex is the sport of choice":* Hannah Beech, "The Forgotten Angels," *Time,* April 16, 2001.

267   *"All of a sudden":* John Burdett, *Bangkok 8* (New York: Vintage Books, 2004), 76.

272   *"They are always approaching the men":* Christoph Carl Fernberger von Egenberg, quoted in Subhatra Bhumiprabhas, "History's Wanton Women: The Journal of a 17th-Century Austrian Merchant Offers a Lopsided View of Siam's Lewd Ladies," *Nation* (Bangkok), July 23, 2007.

272   *"Once they agree about the money":* Van Neck, quoted ibid.

275   *In Bangkok, the GIs, who didn't have much money:* Alan Dawson, *Patpong: Bangkok's Big Little Street* (Bangkok: Thai Watana Panich Press, 1988), 47.

275 *Slowly in the late 1960s and early 1970s:* Ibid., 18–21.
275 *Rick Menard, an American helicopter mechanic:* Ibid., 48.

Interlude 8 / The Yearning of the Wanderer's Heart

279 *Thai National Economic and Social Development Board:* "Udon Thani Leads Nation in Foreign Husbands," *Nation* (Bangkok), November 23, 2003.
280 *One Thai newspaper:* "The *Mia Farang* Club: It's Not Just about the Money," *Nation* (Bangkok), June 14, 2004.
280 *one letter writer:* "Not Only Does the Govt Do Nothing for Mixed Couples, It Also Insults Them," *Nation* (Bangkok), June 16, 2004.
284 *"sold out of his regiment":* Richard Francis Burton, *Goa, and the Blue Mountains; or, Six Months of Sick Leave* (London: Richard Bentley, 1851), 130.

Chapter Thirteen / Judgments

295 *"those childish notions":* John Burdett, *Bangkok Tattoo* (New York: Alfred A. Knopf, 2005), 31.

INDEX

(Page numbers in *italic* refer to illustrations.)

A NOTE ABOUT THE AUTHOR

RICHARD BERNSTEIN, a journalist for more than thirty years, opened *Time* magazine's bureau in Beijing in 1980 and is the author of *From the Center of the Earth: The Search for the Truth About China.* He was head of the *New York Times* bureaus in both Paris and Berlin, and is the author of *Ultimate Journey: Retracing the Path of an Ancient Buddhist Monk Who Crossed Asia in Search of Enlightenment.* He lives in New York with his wife and son.

A NOTE ON THE TYPE

THIS BOOK was set in Adobe Garamond. Designed for the Adobe Corporation by Robert Slimbach, the fonts are based on types first cut by Claude Garamond (ca. 1480–1561). Garamond was a pupil of Geoffroy Tory and is believed to have followed the Venetian models, although he introduced a number of important differences, and it is to him that we owe the letter we now know as "old style." He gave to his letters a certain elegance and feeling of movement that won their creator an immediate reputation and the patronage of Francis I of France.

Composed by North Market Street Graphics,
Lancaster, Pennsylvania
Printed and bound by Berryville Graphics,
Berryville, Virginia
Designed by Virginia Tan